Mind Stimulation Therapy

This book presents a psychotherapy intervention model called Multimodal Integrative Cognitive Stimulation Therapy (MICST). It is grounded in information processing and cognitive stimulation techniques and operates out of a positive psychology framework. This model, designed for group work with clients with schizophrenia, can be easily tailored to working with clients in individual therapy sessions, as well as with other clinical populations, such as substance abuse clients and psychiatrically compromised geriatric clients. The three core MICST group activities comprise:

1. body movement–mindfulness–relaxation (BMR);
2. mind stimulation using group discussions; and
3. mind stimulation using paper–pencil cognitive exercises and self-reflection exercises.

A chapter is devoted to each of these core areas with actual case vignettes to illustrate ways in which these activities can be implemented in clinical practice. Homework recommendations included at the end of each chapter, each devoted to a core MICST group activity, provide suggestions on ways to practice various skills and exercises in between group sessions. Also provided are several handouts and worksheets which can be used with clients.

Mohiuddin Ahmed, PhD, is a consulting psychologist in Rhode Island and Massachusetts. He has nearly 40 years of clinical experience working with varied clinical populations of all ages.

Charles M. Boisvert, PhD, is a professor in the Department of Counseling, Educational Leadership, and School Psychology at Rhode Island College, and a practicing clinical psychologist at RICBT, a cognitive-behavioral therapy and coaching practice in North Kingstown, Rhode Island.

Mind Stimulation Therapy

Cognitive Interventions for Persons with Schizophrenia

MOHIUDDIN AHMED
and
CHARLES M. BOISVERT

Routledge
Taylor & Francis Group
New York London

First published 2013
by Routledge
605 Third Avenue, New York, NY 10017

Simultaneously published in the UK
by Routledge
2 Park Square, Milton Park, Abingdon, Oxon OX14 4RN

Routledge is an imprint of the Taylor & Francis Group, an informa business

Library of Congress Cataloging in Publication Data
Ahmed, Mohiuddin (Psychologist)
Mind stimulation therapy : cognitive interventions for persons with schizophrenia / Mohiuddin Ahmed & Charles M. Boisvert.
pages cm
Includes bibliographical references and index.
1. Schizophrenia–Treatment. 2. Mindfulness-based cognitive therapy. 3. Cognitive therapy. I. Boisvert, Charles M. II. Title.
RC514.A36 2013
616.89'8–dc23 2012048564

ISBN 13: 978–0–415–83740–8 (hbk)
ISBN 13: 978–0–415–63215–7 (pbk)
ISBN 13: 978–0–203–09592–8 (ebk)

Typeset in Caslon and Frutiger
by Keystroke, Station Road, Codsall, Wolverhampton

We dedicate this book to our respective wives, Josefina and Rachel,
and our loving children (and for Mohiuddin Ahmed, his grandchildren as well)
as they are always in our thoughts:
for Mohiuddin Ahmed, his son Rizal and daughter-in-law Sheila,
and their four children Lindsay, Tyler, Joseph, and Ryan;
and for Charles Boisvert, his son Gregory and daughter Kimberly.

Contents

Foreword

Psychosis, a global detachment from consensually agreed reality, is complex and still, at this date, poorly understood. Even from a purely neurological vantage point, it is impossible to define precisely, but it is the sort of thing that we generally know when we see it. People who suffer from psychosis cannot survive in the world without help, and responsibility for their care and treatment has generally fallen upon governmental authorities.

There is controversy as to whether this care should be primarily supportive and custodial as it was for many decades, or whether this care should be treatment-oriented with the expectation of recovery. Advances in psychopharmacology since the early 1970s have resulted in symptom alleviation and improvement in adaptive functioning to the point where most people who suffer from psychosis can be treated in the community in addition to hospital inpatient settings. Use of anti-psychotic medications is, however, also fraught with controversy, because these medications, which most patients receive, generally come with a significant side-effect burden, which worsens with long-term use. In mainstream psychiatry, the use of anti-psychotic agents is often the only significant treatment, and other interpersonal treatments are generally regarded as educational and supportive. The aim is to teach people how to live with their psychotic illness.

Yet significant evidence is accumulating that the majority of people who have psychotic conditions recover substantially over the course of several years or decades. There is also evidence that interpersonal treatments can do better than simply promoting adjustment to psychotic illness. Interpersonal treatments can promote recovery and, over the years, a reduction in the need for anti-psychotic medication with consequent improvement in quality of life. The types of interpersonal treatment that have been reported to be effective, at least anecdotally, have been primarily psychoanalytic, and more recently, cognitive and behavioral. There is a growing professional literature meeting scientific standards supporting the effectiveness of cognitive-behavioral therapy for psychoses. A major difficulty is that there are never enough therapists who are sufficiently skilled in these interpersonal methods to meet the need.

In this context, Drs. Ahmed and Boisvert have developed a model of treatment called Multimodal Integrative Cognitive Stimulation Therapy (MICST). Their starting point is that sufferers of schizophrenia, the quintessential disorder associated with psychosis, generally have cognitive defects which contribute a great deal to their inability to function in consensually agreed reality. Their idea is to stimulate cognitive and memory functioning in a positive way to enable patients to function better in their interpersonal environments. These patients have been traumatized by highly negative experiences in their environments—including their treatment environments—in part because of their cognitive inability to "catch on" to meaningful events. The positive thrust of the MICST approach presents them with the ability to acquire skills in a way that enhances their self-esteem and improves their adaptation skills. I first heard Drs. Ahmed and Boisvert present their MICST approach at a meeting on substance abuse, and it was clear that they had devised an approach that made a great deal of sense for that population of patients. I was even more delighted to hear that they had originally devised and refined the MICST system for the population of people who had psychosis due to schizophrenia.

Unlike more traditional psychotherapy approaches, which often focus on negative behaviors and thoughts to help promote insight and understanding, the MICST model emphasizes accessing and stimulating patients' intact cognitive and memory functioning to promote adaptive thinking and behavior. The authors contend that the traditional approach of focusing on "deficit symptoms" may have possible iatrogenic effects, by stimulating and reinforcing the underlying neural networks that support the patient's maladaptive thinking and behavior. The authors conceptualize this as following the same principle as the "law of exercise," whereby repeated practice and reinforcement of a certain movement or action serves to strengthen the underlying biological mechanisms responsible for that action.

While acknowledging the benefits of medication treatment for schizophrenia in reducing the core symptoms of the condition, the authors point out the limitations of current medication treatments and consider that for some patients, the active psychotic symptoms, such as hallucinations and delusions, may be expressions of long-standing behavioral habits, which may not be altered appreciably by medication treatment. Rather, the authors emphasize the need to use strategies that do not aim for psychopathology reduction *per se*, but which aim to enhance strengths in reality-based communication and promote more focused engagement in the present. Such strategies include, for example, active redirection to help patients stay focused on the present. These strategies can be incorporated routinely into patients' therapeutic milieu in conjunction with medication and other psychosocial treatments and supports. The authors further contend that persons with severe and persistent mental illness may have an impaired capacity to internalize and then generalize the insight and understanding gained from therapy sessions, unless some provision is made and built into the patient's therapeutic milieu to support the continued practice and reinforcement of these coping strategies.

In their book, Drs. Ahmed and Boisvert present data from their group and individual work with persons with schizophrenia in clinical practice settings, numerous case studies, and clients' recorded statements to highlight the process and effectiveness of the MICST model. In addition to presenting client self-assessment and staff evaluation questionnaire data, they present some "naturalistic event data" to support the effectiveness of the MICST model. These varied data collection methods are worth considering when evaluating clinical intervention models, especially when one does not have access to external research support. In Chapters 8 and 9, they present evidence of and guides for using the MICST model with other challenging populations such as substance abuse patients, and geriatric and physically compromised patients in nursing home settings.

The MICST techniques not only have a thorough theoretical grounding, but also have immense practicality. Their use can probably be generalized to many other types of clinical problems, as I learned from hearing the authors first speak about the MICST model's use in the treatment of addiction problems at the 23rd Cape Cod Symposium on Addictive Disorders (2010), and subsequently hearing the senior author (Mohiuddin Ahmed) speak at meetings of the Boston Area chapter of the International Society for Psychological and Social Approaches to Psychosis (ISPS) where he presented on the development and use of the MICST model in individual and group work with persons with schizophrenia.

In my view, as a practicing psychiatrist for 40 years, working with many patients with schizophrenia and other psychiatric disorders, the development of MICST adds to our array of tools to use with individuals who have schizophrenia and other psychotic problems. I strongly believe that clinicians working with challenging populations—such as people who have schizophrenia or long-term substance abuse, or elderly people with disabilities in nursing home settings—will find the model user-friendly and easy to adopt in their clinical practice.

I urge the reader to learn more about this promising approach.

Ronald Abramson, MD
Associate Clinical Professor of Psychiatry,
Tufts University School of Medicine
Chairperson of the New England Branch of the
International Society for Psychological and
Social Approaches to Psychosis (ISPS)

About the Authors

Mohiuddin Ahmed, PhD

Mohiuddin Ahmed did his undergraduate and graduate studies in philosophy in Bangladesh at Dhaka University (BA [Honors], and MA), and was awarded a Fulbright Scholarship to study in the United States. He completed his MSc in clinical psychology at Long Island University in Brooklyn, his PhD in clinical psychology at the University of Pittsburgh, and his clinical psychology doctoral internship at the Winnebago Mental Health Institute in Wisconsin. He has had nearly 40 years of clinical experience working with varied clinical populations of all ages in the Philippines, Bangladesh, and the United States. He has worked in psychiatric inpatient and outpatient facilities, institutions for people with developmental disabilities, and nursing homes; and has provided consultation to mental health agencies, residential programs for adults with behavior disabilities, and special education programs. He has supervised many pre- and post-doctoral-level psychology graduate students. Dr. Ahmed has pioneered innovative models of clinical services for children, adolescents, and adults, and has many publications in peer-reviewed journals that describe some of his innovative clinical practice work. For his full biography and publication list, please see his web site at www.psychologymentalhealth.com.

Charles M. Boisvert, PhD

Charles Boisvert received a BS degree in psychology from Le Moyne College, an MA in counseling from Rhode Island College, and a PhD in clinical psychology from the University of Rhode Island. He completed an internship in clinical psychology at the Edith Nourse Rogers Memorial VA Medical Center in Bedford, Massachusetts, and a two-year post-doctoral fellowship in clinical psychology in the Department of Psychiatry and Behavioral Medicine at the Lahey Clinic Medical Center in Burlington, Massachusetts. Dr. Boisvert has worked in a variety of clinical settings, including working for 12 years in community mental health centers, providing services to clients with schizophrenia. He serves as a member of the Quality and Planning Committee and Evidence-based Task Force for Gateway Healthcare, Inc., the largest community mental health center in Rhode Island. Dr. Boisvert is Professor in the Department of Counseling, Educational Leadership, and School Psychology at Rhode Island College and serves as Director of the graduate programs in Counseling. In addition, Dr. Boisvert is a practicing clinical psychologist at the Rhode Island Center for Cognitive Behavioral Therapy in North Kingstown, Rhode Island. His research and clinical interests include: science–practice relations in psychotherapy; specialized treatments for schizophrenia; the biopsychology of stress; psychiatric care in primary care; and predictors of psychotherapy outcomes. He has several publications in peer-reviewed journals and serves as an ad hoc reviewer for the journals *Professional Psychology: Research and Practice* and *Family Practice*. He also served as an ad hoc reviewer for *Schizophrenia Bulletin*.

Acknowledgments

We wish first to acknowledge all the pre-doctoral and post-doctoral psychology trainees, interns, and externs, as well as many other students in various mental health disciplines such as psychology, mental health counseling, nursing, and social work who were involved either in conducting or providing support to MICST groups or provided assistance in developing the paper–pencil cognitive exercises used in the groups. The enthusiasm which these trainees showed us—along with the clients who participated in MICST, and the clinical and administrative staff who readily accepted the model—demonstrated that the model was user-friendly, and made "intuitive clinical sense." Their acceptance and feedback helped to reinforce the "practice-based validity" of the model, and greatly inspired us to refine and further develop the model in clinical practice.

We present the names of those who assisted in conducting MICST groups in either inpatient or outpatient settings, developing paper–pencil cognitive exercises, or developing individual client workbooks. Since the list of those who contributed to the model is quite large and involves a time span of more than 20 years, we may have inadvertently left out some names, for which we sincerely apologize. The names are presented alphabetically: Susan Almeida, Robert Boucher, Erica Conners, Barbara Crowell, Jennifer Doucet, Susan Fusco, Judith Goldman, Trisha Gouin, Colleen Gregory, Benjamin Kerman, the late Marie King, Faith LaBrie, Timothy Le Jacq-Smith, Henry Lesieur, Susan Levin, Bradley McMillan, Neil Mendonca, Charles Moore, Aviva Moster, Jessica Nargisso, Amelia Pecora-Jewett, Jocelyn Rocha, Luz Teixeira, Manivone Thieko, Stephanie Toolin, Marjorie Walsh, Ryan Watson, and Christopher Willard.

Our special thanks go also to those administrators who provided support for the practice of the MICST model at their respective facilities: Judy Bolzani, Elizabeth Bronwell-Raffety, Mary Dwyer, Laura Etre, Colleen Gregory, the late Marie King, Peter La Confera, Richard LeClerc, Benedict Lessing, Anna Mitchell, Chris Stephens, Virginia Stiepock, and Laura Vear. We also thank Mary Dwyer, Jennifer Hawley, Joseph Langlois, Bradley McMillan, and Manivone Thieko for assistance with data collection and analysis. Additionally, a special thanks to Nikolai Blinow for assistance with references and paper–pencil exercises, and Corey Blais for assistance and guidance in helping us prepare the art work and figures for the book. We also thank Chris Tominich and George Zimmar from Routledge, as well as Helen Lund for her editorial expertise, and the staff at Keystroke for their editorial assistance.

We thank all the clients who over the years participated in different aspects of the MICST program. These clients' active participation in the various MICST activities, as captured through the case studies we present, along with sharing their individual and collective knowledge and insight has been a very inspiring force to us. In addition to their active involvement, their responses on various assessment questionnaires motivated us to explore using the MICST model with various other clinical populations.

In the development of the theoretical underpinnings of the MICST model, both of us were influenced by our mentors and teachers going back to our graduate school years and by others in our professional life whom we both want to acknowledge:

For the senior author, Mohiuddin Ahmed, many of his positive influences came from the following sources:

- the enunciation by Professor Kazimuddin (Dhaka University Philosophy Department) of Immanuel Kant's philosophy that the ultimate reality is unknowable (the world of noumena) because of the categories of the mind, which limit human perception of reality to the world of phenomena, and that as human beings all of us have to deal with the existential reality of the unknown;
- the inspiring lecture by G. C. Dev (who was brutally murdered by the Pakistani army during the Bangladesh War of Independence) highlighting the need for integrating the spiritualism of the East with the materialism of the West;
- the U.S. Institute of Education's Fulbright Scholarship Program, which made it possible for Ahmed to purse higher education in the United States;
- Gustave Gilbert, one of the Nuremberg Trials psychologists, who took a chance to admit Ahmed, without his having an adequate background in psychology, to the clinical psychology program at Long Island University, Brooklyn;
- the various eclectic courses taken at the University of Pittsburgh, reflecting the Boulder model of training of science practitioners—such as psychopathology courses by Peter Lang and Arnold Buss, which involved reading their article on cognitive deficits in schizophrenia highlighting sensorimotor deficits, and other readings that helped Ahmed to integrate psychodynamic therapy (Otto Fenichel's psychoanalytic theory of neuroses) with learning theory approaches to psychopathology by taking animal and human learning courses under Harry Fowler and James Voss;
- O. K. Moore's inspiring lecture on information processing as a naturally rewarding condition for social learning;
- Merle Moskowitz's course in History of Psychology, requiring the reading of Hans Reichenbach's *The Rise of Scientific Philosophy* (1961), which emphasized the importance of validating empirically any theoretical or practice assumptions, rather than relying on speculative thinking that cannot be consensually validated;
- David Lazovik's supervision of clinical practicum emphasizing the importance of empathic communication in therapy as the key to establishing a therapeutic alliance;
- John Cowles and Grace Lazovik's courses in statistics, emphasizing the role of measurement and statistics in data collection and the evaluation process; and

- Alan Fisher's course in neurobiology, with emphasis on chemical stimulation of the brain in influencing behaviors and highlighting brain–behavior perspectives.

Subsequently, Ahmed's interest in working with schizophrenia grew out of "process supervision" of psychotherapy with children and adults with schizophrenia at the Winnebago Mental Health Institute in Wisconsin, under the mentorship of Donald Derozier, who also introduced him to an article by Joseph Lyons (1958) ("The Psychology of Angels"), which, along with Ahmed's subsequent readings of *Interpretation of Schizophrenia* (Arieti, 1955) and *Existence* (May, Angel, & Ellenberger, 1958) provided him with insight and understanding of the "working of the schizophrenia mind," integrating information processing, existential perspectives, and learning theory approaches.

Ahmed's professional work in his early career with behaviorally disordered children in the Philippines, and his subsequent work with populations with developmental disabilities in the United States made him keenly aware of the multidisciplinary focus in mental health and the need for a collaborative approach to mental health interventions, involving education, psychology, psychiatry, neurology, mental health counseling, social work, and other disciplines. It also provided an early experiential base to test out the validity of positive redirection approaches and counter-conditioning techniques in dealing with "entrenched maladaptive behaviors," and helped to raise his awareness of how best to deal with these "behavior challenges" through a non-traditional alternative psychotherapy–consultation approach, which Ahmed was able to incorporate in his work with other psychiatric populations—such as schizophrenic, substance abuse, and geriatric clients—and which is reflected in the MICST model.

Ahmed's background of living with diverse religious faiths in his own family life, his exposure to philosophy training in his early university student life at Dhaka University in Bangladesh, and subsequent interest in astronomy helped him to identify and relate to clients around existential issues that all of us grapple with in our daily lives. Ahmed's upbringing in South Asia (British India, Pakistan, and Bangladesh) made him appreciate the value of resiliency and use of positive redirection in the face of adversities that are often the personal and collective experiences of people in that part of the world—the elements of which are highlighted in the MICST model.

Finally, Ahmed believes that his active involvement in the graduate psychology student training and supervision process at various inpatient and outpatient psychiatric settings in the United States, and at Ateneo De Manila University in the Philippines over a period of more than 40 years provided him with a two-way learning process, teaching and learning from his students, and helping him to keep his clinical knowledge current through these mutually beneficial interactions. This provided him with a great deal of motivation and inspiration for his continued professional growth, as is aptly reflected in this collaborative work with one of his former student externs, Professor Charles Boisvert, the co-author of this book.

Charles Boisvert's interest in schizophrenia grew out of his undergraduate work at Le Moyne College in Syracuse, New York and the opportunity to complete a clinical internship at St. Joseph's Psychiatric Hospital in downtown Syracuse. It was here that he saw at first hand clients with schizophrenia. During his first meeting with his internship supervisor, she handed him the first edition of E. F. Torrey's book *Surviving Schizophrenia* (1983) and told him it was important to read, but that it was only one perspective.

He observed tardive dyskinesia for the first time and wondered how and why that could happen. He observed patients talking to themselves and wondered what that was like for them. He observed patients smile when, for example, they asked him to go for a walk with them. He heard some tell jokes. He saw patients throw and catch the ball on the softball field and cheer each other on. They acted like softball players, not patients. He did not remember reading about some of these behaviors in his Abnormal Psychology Text. Mostly it described how disabled patients were and showed pictures of them looking disheveled and curled in a ball in the back corner of an inpatient ward.

He began to take a strong interest in a disorder that seemed so profoundly disabling in some ways, yet not in other ways—ways that could only be discovered by more direct contact with them. He was intrigued by what seemed to be clients' fluid movement between two different "reality perspectives"—one unique to them and the other common to all of us. They sometimes retreated to their private unique world and at other times seemed closely connected to the social world around them. How could that be? He soon learned that much of what clients said and did depended on what he said or did. They talked about symptoms if he asked . . . they talked about baseball if he asked . . . they talked about the news if he asked . . . If he did not talk to them, they sometimes talked to themselves. He went on to work with clients in community mental health centers for 12 years. His subsequent work with them further reinforced his belief that clients had skills, interests, and capabilities that were not always evident in typical clinical interactions. When he was introduced to the MICST model early in his doctoral training, he found that it was a natural fit with how he thought he could be most helpful to clients. The tenets and features of the model made sense.

He would like to thank all the clients with whom he has worked. They in many ways have had the most profound impact on shaping his ideas and beliefs about schizophrenia. In some ways they have served as mentors in their own right and helped generate many of the ideas discussed in this book. Their opinions, beliefs, knowledge, and insights are voiced throughout this book . . . they are all co-authors. In many ways this is their book, their voice, their expression of who they are.

There are also many people he wishes to acknowledge who have influenced his personal and professional development and who shaped his interest in the field of psychology and the development of ideas expressed in this book. A special thanks to his co-author Mohiuddin Ahmed, who served as an exemplary mentor and supervisor during his graduate school training and throughout his professional career. They have had the good fortune to collaborate on numerous projects, sharing ideas about the field of psychology, and keeping pace with each other's personal and family life. Dr. Ahmed has taught him that gaining knowledge and understanding is truly a collaborative effort, and that it is through partnership with others that people truly learn. The MICST model in many ways exemplifies this. He can only hope that he has incorporated some of Dr. Ahmed's wisdom and insights into his own clinical work.

The importance of teamwork and collaboration has also been reinforced through his own upbringing, growing up with three brothers (Louis, Tim, and Kevin) and one sister (Gerene). This paved the way for learning how to collaborate, work together, and not let individual differences and beliefs impede a common goal (all characteristics of the MICST model).

He thanks his graduate training clinical supervisors Richard Amodio, Edward Federman, Doug Gammon, John Garrison, and Ann Varna Garis for the many ways they shaped his clinical thinking and training, and for their insights and kernels of wisdom which to this day he still draws upon. He thanks his dissertation advisor David Faust for teaching him the importance of thinking critically and learning how to ask better questions rather than pursue unknowable answers.

He thanks his parents, both educators, for their love and encouragement over the years and for teaching him the value of education. They encouraged him to pursue whatever he was interested in and were truly the best teachers and parents anyone could ask for. His mother Marilyn's field of biology and the field of education of his father Louis have influenced him in many ways and helped shape his own educational and professional interests. Elements of this project reflect their influence both directly and indirectly.

Finally, our special thanks to our respective spouses, Josefina Resurreccion Ahmed, PhD, and Rachel Boisvert, LICSW. We both shared ideas about the development of the MICST model with them and received constructive feedback. We thank them for their emotional support and encouragement of our professional work, not to mention their infinite tolerance for our repeated discussions over the past few years about our goal of publishing a book. Most importantly, we are both fortunate to have them as life partners who have contributed immensely to our personal lives and professional growth.

Chapter 1

Introduction

This book presents a psychotherapy intervention model called *Multimodal Integrative Cognitive Stimulation Therapy* (MICST). The model emphasizes mind stimulation techniques and is designed for group work with clients with schizophrenia. The model can also be easily tailored to working with clients with schizophrenia in individual therapy, and can be applied to substance abuse clients as well as geriatric and physically compromised clients in nursing home settings. The MICST model is grounded in information processing and mind stimulation techniques and uses a positive psychology framework. The model is characterized by stimulating and enhancing clients' "intact" areas of memory and cognitive functioning so as to enhance their information processing and ability to engage in "reality-based" communication.

We present a therapeutic intervention model that makes intuitive clinical sense and is grounded in several years of clinical practice characterized by consistently high participation from group participants independent of their "cognitive and emotional disability." The model outlines a group protocol, which clinicians of all experience levels will find easy to adapt and implement in their ongoing clinical work with persons with schizophrenia.

The book begins with a brief discussion of the "historical development" of MICST and how this approach grew out of the authors' success in using the model in clinical practice with inpatient and outpatient clients with schizophrenia. Following this, we provide a brief historical perspective of schizophrenia, highlighting how schizophrenia has come to be understood as a "neurocognitive disorder." This understanding of schizophrenia provides the conceptual framework for discussing the central concepts of the MICST model: information processing and mind stimulation.

The book then describes the three core MICST group activities:

1. *body movement–mindfulness–relaxation (BMR)*;
2. *mind stimulation using group discussions*;
3. *mind stimulation using paper–pencil cognitive and self-reflection exercises.*

Chapters 3, 4, and 5 are devoted, respectively, to each of these core areas, with actual case vignettes to illustrate ways that these activities can be implemented when conducting MICST groups.

The book is designed to provide a theoretical and practical framework to teach clinicians the conceptual underpinnings of the model as well as to give directions to clinicians for implementing the various facets of the group. The rationale and goals for each of the group components are discussed as well as specific guides for implementing the different group activities. At the end of each chapter devoted to a core MICST group activity, we include *homework recommendations*, suggesting ways that clinicians can assist clients in practicing various skills and cognitive stimulating exercises. Following these three chapters devoted to the core MICST activities, Chapter 6 focuses on managing and evaluating (e.g., using various self-evaluation questionnaires) the group process.

Many of the MICST group activities can be modified or tailored to individual sessions with clients. Chapter 7 shows how the MICST framework, philosophy, and activities can be adapted to individual work with clients. Chapter 8 then discusses how MICST has been used with substance abuse clients and Chapter 9 focuses on using MICST with geriatric clients and populations with physical disabilities.

The back of the book includes several handouts, worksheets, and appendices. Some of these *handouts* are designed for clinicians and describe the core MICST group activities and the fundamental features and goals of MICST. These handouts can be used by clinicians to market the group and to inform colleagues and prospective clients about the nature of the group. Other handouts are for clients and include, for example, instruction sheets on practicing the relaxation exercises and redirection strategies to manage distracting thoughts. Various *worksheets* are also included such as goal-setting worksheets, a problem-solving worksheet, a coping strategies worksheet, a daily schedule worksheet, and a self-care recovery plan worksheet. Finally, the *appendices* include, for example, client feedback questionnaires, sample self-evaluation tools, and various paper–pencil mind stimulating exercises.

The Nature of MICST

The MICST model provides a set of core group activities that allow for flexibility in the actual clinical encounter. Providing this flexibility reinforces a fundamental characteristic of everyday psychotherapy practice; namely, that being spontaneous and innovative in the clinical encounter is more often the rule rather than the exception. We also believe that a "prescriptive manual" with highly structured guidelines, while appearing to be logically and theoretically consistent, and "structurally appealing," may have limited practical value in most inpatient and outpatient clinical settings serving persons with schizophrenia. In these settings, clinicians typically have limited resources, limited time, and competing job duties that often preclude them from implementing a highly structured curriculum or a "prescriptive" therapy protocol.

The MICST approach recognizes "the clinical reality" that no one specific theoretical and practical therapy intervention model has been identified that works uniformly well with schizophrenia populations, and that persons with schizophrenia often demonstrate variability in their cognitive skills, mood, and behavioral functioning at both intra- and interpersonal levels. As indicated by Roder, Müller, Brenner, and Spaulding (2011), "despite the prevalence and severity of cognitive impairment in schizophrenia, there is no single type or profile that characterizes the illness. Heterogeneity, in both the quality and severity of impairments, is the rule" (pp. 12–13).

MICST was designed for patients in long-term psychiatric inpatient facilities and for outpatient clients receiving services from community mental health centers (CMHCs). Given the variability in functioning that these patient populations display, for example, in their fund of knowledge, ability to recall factual information, and ability to understand and manage their mental health symptoms, it makes it difficult to design and implement a "sequential program" or curriculum requiring "mastery of skills" at each level. Additionally, capacity for new learning (analogous to laying new neural networks or connections as is implied in the learning of "new cognitive skills") may be "stress inducing" in already "stress compromised" persons with a history of schizophrenia. Factors such as cognitive rigidity and anxiety associated with "new" situations or "task expectations" may affect clients' learning of new tasks. Thus, clients may demonstrate particular difficulties in responding to approaches that focus primarily on learning new skills. Therefore, we believe that sequential learning of skills, which can require time-consuming remediation programs, may not be practical or useful to these particular patient populations for the reasons cited above.

The MICST model therefore is flexible in format and does not present a sequential or hierarchy-based program or "curriculum." We have avoided presenting the material in a way that is too prescriptive or curriculum-based. The MICST model emphasizes simultaneous stimulation of skills at various levels. Depending on what the clients in a particular group demonstrate, clinicians are encouraged to use their own judgment and intuition in determining what aspects of the MICST model to emphasize for any given group session. Our focus on cognitive stimulation for persons with schizophrenia stems from the view that all persons with schizophrenia, independent of the severity of their cognitive deficits, have some degree of intact cognitive skills and functioning, which may be underutilized or "unrecognized" by clinicians in typical interactions with clients.

The flexible MICST format provides every client with opportunities to demonstrate his or her own skill level, knowledge, and interests through the varied "mind stimulating" group activities. For example, a client may have considerable difficulty in accurately completing simple mathematical exercises—involving, for example, addition and subtraction—but may be able to recite poetry, accurately recall excerpts from literature, or recall other detailed and factual information. During the MICST group, this particular client may demonstrate his or her strongest skills during the discussion phase and not necessarily during the paper–pencil exercise phase. Alternatively, some clients may demonstrate, for example, poverty of speech and minimal contributions during group discussions, yet excel at paper–pencil exercises that are stimulating areas of "intact" cognitive functioning and exposing them to topics that are inherently interesting.

The model also allows clinicians to integrate their unique clinical training and expertise from other psychotherapy intervention models. That is, the traditional therapy approaches in which clinicians may be trained or are more accustomed to using can be easily blended in with the core MICST components in conducting groups or individual therapy sessions. The model encourages clinicians to learn to trust their judgment and to find ways both to adhere to the core group activities and to incorporate clinical material that emerges spontaneously in the group. We believe that this is how most clinical work evolves in actual clinical practice, that is by incorporating clients' spontaneous verbalizations and explorations into a theoretical structure and framework that is used to guide interventions.

The MICST approach teaches both clients and clinicians how to develop confidence and skills in managing the spontaneity of everyday conversations. The model also teaches clients how to use their own judgment, interests, and extemporaneous thinking to initiate and sustain meaningful conversations with others with the goal of promoting their well-being and competency to function in the social world.

We present the rationale that the traditional outcome evaluation "design" for psychotherapy, which follows an "ABA" design—i.e., A = pre-treatment or prior to intervention condition; B = change from baseline functioning where a treatment is provided and evaluated for efficacy; and A = baseline or desired state of functioning and cessation of the intervention—may not be a "viable" outcome model to use with persons with chronic schizophrenia. The "ABA" model assumes that the patient is able to internalize the treatment effects during the intervention phase (B) and that such internalized treatment effects will generalize following "withdrawal" or cessation of the intervention. These expected treatment outcomes may be unrealistic with persons with "chronic schizophrenia."

We believe that any given psychological intervention for these patients, if found to improve functioning, should follow the pattern of and rationale for how medication is conceptualized as an intervention for any chronic and persistent condition such as diabetes, hypertension, or "chronic schizophrenia." This way of conceptualizing treatment works from an "ABB" design rather than an "ABA" design, in that an intervention that is found to be effective is maintained in the patient's treatment regimen to promote continued enhanced functioning. In fact, medication management programs and associated community support programs offered through, for example, CMHCs have been instrumental in maintaining many hospital-discharged persons with schizophrenia in the community by operating under this type of "ABB" design. We need to provide clients with ongoing opportunities to practice cognitive and mind stimulation techniques no matter what their treatment or "recovery status" is. The recovery model can sometimes use the language of "graduating" from services, which can mean a reduction in services. Those clients who "graduate" or achieve a reduction in services will still benefit from ongoing cognitive stimulation opportunities to maximize their functioning.

Theoretical Foundation of MICST: Principles and Features

Some of the learning and social "principles" that have guided the development of MICST include:

1. principles of *operant conditioning* (i.e., behavior is influenced by reinforcement and reward consequences);

2. principles of *classical conditioning* or *counter-conditioning* (i.e., positively valued behavior when prompted and elicited or structured in one's environment displaces negatively valued incompatible behavior, as only one type of behavior can occur at any given time);
3. the *innate pleasures people have in exchanging information* about "factual" and other types of information or interests (e.g., when we go to a social gathering, we typically enjoy exchanging facts and opinions about various topics and interests);
4. the *high interest that people in all cultures demonstrate in engaging in problem-solving exercises* (e.g., games and puzzles);
5. the importance of having an *awareness of one's body movement in relation to one's physical and social surroundings* to promote adaptation;
6. the *"resiliency" that people can demonstrate* under all kinds of circumstances to "survive" and adapt;
7. recognizing that *all human beings have many "positive" characteristics and behaviors*, which may not be immediately evident, but can be elicited to improve functioning and adaptation (e.g., positive psychology principles); and
8. recognizing the importance of the *"principle of normalization"* (e.g., exposure to "real life" situations and activities), which has become an important principle guiding the mental health recovery movement.

The MICST model uses a variety of communication modalities and interventions and underemphasizes the more "traditional approach" in psychotherapy whereby the therapist may relate to the client by focusing on unique pathology, or "disordered" memories, or negative associations. A deficit-focused approach in psychotherapy may unwittingly generate a negative relationship framework between the therapist and the client and may reinforce clients' preoccupation with their own negative feelings and thoughts (Ahmed & Boisvert, 2006b; Boisvert & Faust, 2002). MICST has four underlying characteristics:

1. It uses a ***Multimodal*** approach.
2. It employs an ***Integrative*** framework of intervention.
3. It focuses on providing ***Cognitive Stimulation*** to access areas of intact cognitive and memory functioning.
4. It uses a *positive psychology* framework (Seligman & Csikszentmihalyi, 2000) to enhance self-esteem and well-being.

The *Multimodal* aspect of MICST refers to using both auditory and visual modalities (e.g., written exercises and handouts), as well as using a blackboard, easel, or PowerPoint-based handouts to illustrate concepts more effectively and facilitate discussions of various topics. Using multiple modalities of communication enhances "reality-based" discussions and goal-directed thinking.

The *Integrative* aspect of the model refers to using these multimodal techniques within a supportive relationship framework designed to integrate social skills practice, episodic (personal) and semantic (factual information and knowledge) memory exercises, discussions of current psychiatric treatment, and symptom management. Additionally body movement–mindfulness–relaxation (BMR) exercises are used to promote mindfulness and a greater sense of "reality" (see Ahmed & Boisvert, 2003b). The therapist also attempts actively to integrate discussions of psychological concepts such as brain–behavior relations, learning, and memory as well as various underlying cognitive issues affecting one's functioning. "Existential issues" or religious themes that are spontaneously brought up in the group are also discussed. We discuss experiences of "uncertainty" and adaptation as part of our universal human experience. This helps clients connect to the universal life experience, "normalize" their own feelings, and develop a sense of appreciation for "socially normative" forms of adaptation.

Cognitive Stimulation refers not only to discussing various topics that are spontaneously identified in the group, but also to cognitive skills training using written exercises to stimulate logical thinking, association, working memory, long-term memory, attention, and concentration (Ahmed & Boisvert, 2003b). The paper–pencil exercises also include self-reflection exercises through which clients assess their functioning and group participation. The self-reflection exercises are also designed to improve clients' motivation to work toward their personal goals by asking them specific questions about, for example, coping strategies and steps needed to reach their goals.

The *positive psychology* framework that underlies MICST refers to actively exploring and stimulating clients' "intact" cognitive (thinking and reasoning) and communication skills. This serves to promote clients' understanding of and active participation in a therapeutic milieu aimed at enhancing their functioning and limiting the effects of their "disability." The underlying assumption is that by promoting and accessing clients' positive traits, they will be able to limit or "displace" their preoccupation with or expression of "negatively valued" symptoms that can be frequently characteristic of schizophrenia (see Figure 1.1).

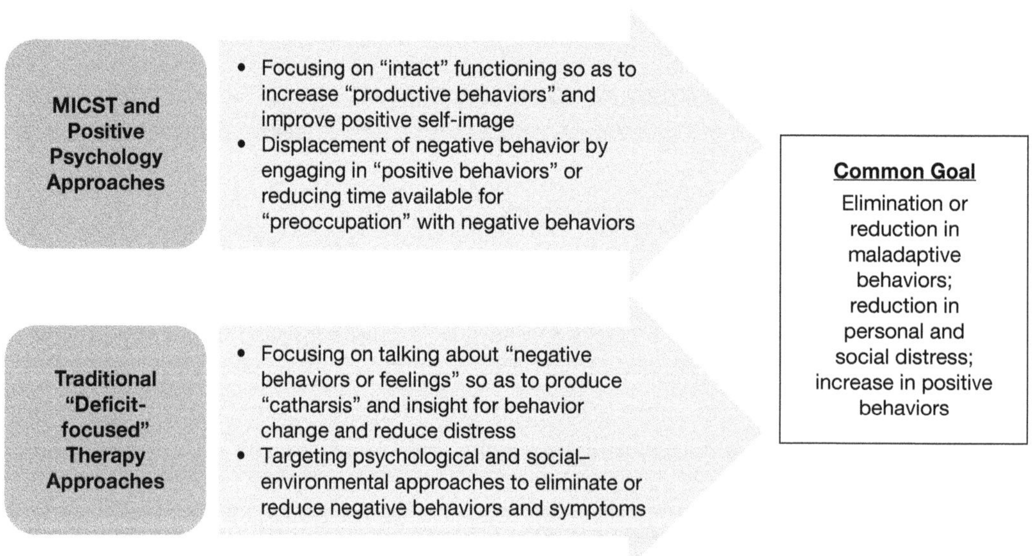

FIGURE 1.1 Contrasting "philosophical approaches" both aimed at achieving a similar therapy outcome

The fundamental features and "themes" of MICST (see Figure 1.2), which will be discussed in the upcoming chapters, include the following:

1. information processing is seen as the core to successful adaptation to the environment;
2. a positive psychology approach that stimulates the client's "intact" functioning and strengths and underemphasizes a "deficit-focused" approach;
3. positive redirection to factual and reality-based information;
4. sensorimotor stimulation, mindfulness, and relaxation training;
5. cognitive and memory stimulation;
6. incorporation of verbal and visual communication modalities;
7. use of feedback to reduce "cognitive rigidity";
8. incorporation of an existential perspective to facilitate discussions of spiritual issues and dealing with life's uncertainties;
9. active collaboration and support for medication management and other psychosocial interventions; and
10. assessment of outcome based on an "ABB" design.

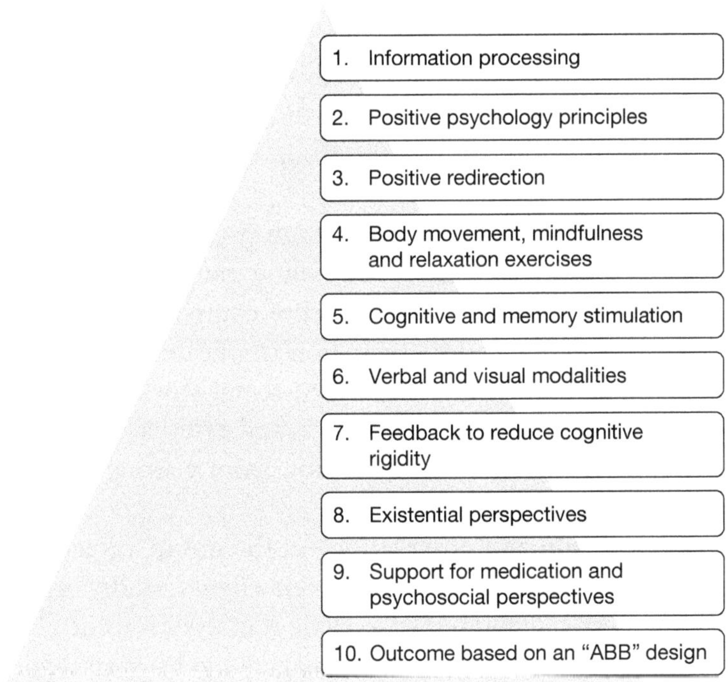

FIGURE 1.2 The fundamental features and core elements of MICST

Staff and Training Requirements to Conduct MICST

Throughout the development and practice of the MICST model, primarily psychology staff (licensed PhD psychologists, PhD/PsyD graduate students in clinical psychology), Master's students in counseling, and Master's-level mental health counselors and social workers) have been trained to conduct MICST. The nature of the MICST model requires an understanding of learning disabilities (developmental and acquired) and learning deficit issues that are often present in clients with schizophrenia. The model draws from principles of learning and neuropsychology and requires an understanding and awareness of each client's level of tolerance and skills for a given activity. The successful implementation of MICST is also maximized when clinicians have a broad knowledge base in mental health education and biological treatments, along with understanding milieu and team treatment issues, and current research in schizophrenia. In addition, a broad knowledge of general topics (e.g., geography, astronomy, history, philosophy) as well as current knowledge about medication treatment and the mental health service system are often needed to elicit or follow through with relevant discussions of various issues and concerns brought up in the group.

The clinician also needs to make spontaneous judgments and decisions as to the appropriateness of discussion topics and select appropriate paper–pencil cognitive exercises for the day. The clinician does this by taking into account group members' variable cognitive functioning, learning histories, and the current cognitive and emotional difficulties displayed. The clinician should also be comfortable in addressing existential anxiety and associated uncertainties of living, by focusing on a here-and-now approach, mindfulness concepts, and religious and spiritual themes. When appropriate, clinicians, for example, may use their science-based knowledge about astronomy, geography, history, and evolution when these topics emerge spontaneously during discussions, and may further pursue and facilitate discussions of these topics to help group members connect to the "reality of human existence."

We believe that any mental health clinician from psychiatry, psychology, social work, nursing, rehabilitation, or mental health counseling can be trained to conduct or co-facilitate MICST, or adapt MICST to their level of competency and expertise. In actual clinical practice, we have encouraged participation from direct-care staff, as well as other mental health professionals and disciplines (e.g., social workers, nurses, mental health counselors), along with psychology student interns and externs. In addition, the format of the therapy can easily accommodate participation from visiting students or other staff without disrupting the flow of the session.

Through their participation and observations in the group, direct-care staff can often gain a new perspective and understanding of their clients' skills, interests, and level of functioning, which otherwise would not be as evident in their routine clinical interactions. Furthermore, mental health workers and case managers can learn strategies to engage their clients in reality-based conversation by using cognitive stimulation techniques or redirection strategies when, for example, their clients may be exhibiting communication difficulties, "agitation," or "negative behaviors".

Targeted Populations

The MICST approach has primarily been used with clients with schizophrenia who are in long-term state psychiatric hospitals or who are receiving community support services through CMHCs. The nature of the model is such that it can easily accommodate a range of client profiles and levels of functioning within the schizophrenia spectrum as well as long-term psychiatric patients with bipolar disorder or severe personality disorders. It can also be easily adapted to individual work with clients (see Chapter 7).

The model has also been used with other psychiatric populations (e.g., substance abuse clients in residential programs (see Chapter 8) and geriatric and physically compromised clients in nursing homes (see Chapter 9)). In our clinical practice, when using aspects of the model with these diverse clinical populations, we have found that clients who may otherwise be reluctant to participate in traditional group therapy and discuss "treatment issues" become actively and positively involved in the various MICST activities. For example, clients seem to readily participate in the body movement–mindfulness–relaxation (BMR) exercises and in completing paper–pencil cognitive stimulation exercises and self-reflective thinking exercises. Chapters 8 and 9 present detailed case scenarios illustrating how MICST has been adapted in clinical practice to these diverse populations, and make a case for the potential application of various MICST model elements to these populations.

Chapter 2

The MICST Model and Schizophrenia

Historical Development of MICST

The MICST model was developed as a group intervention model by the senior author (Mohiuddin Ahmed) at a state psychiatric inpatient facility, based on his prior experience providing individual therapy to persons with schizophrenia in a community mental health center. Subsequently, the MICST group model was implemented in a CMHC, which formed the basis of the first publication on the group model in the *Community Mental Health Journal* (Ahmed & Goldman, 1994). Over the years, more groups were conducted using the MICST model in both inpatient and outpatient settings. This provided opportunities to gather a larger data set, much of which was collected in the process of routine clinical care, rather than as part of an "experimental design" study. This formed the basis of follow-up publications on the MICST model in *Psychiatric Services* (Ahmed & Boisvert, 2002) and *Professional Psychology: Research and Practice* (Ahmed & Boisvert, 2003b).

Since the early 1990s, a significant number of psychology graduate students and mental health clinicians, working under the supervision of the senior author in inpatient and outpatient settings, have participated in MICST groups and have collaborated, for example, in developing various paper–pencil exercises used in the group. Often these graduate students' first exposure to working with clients with schizophrenia was through the MICST group. Many of these students quickly developed a sense of "competency and confidence" in working with this challenging clinical population due to MICST's unique group structure and user-friendly format.

The MICST model has also been used with other psychiatric populations. For example, the success in adapting the MICST model to dually diagnosed substance abuse clients at a community mental health center was presented at the 23rd Cape Cod Symposium on Addictive Disorders in 2010 (Ahmed & Boisvert, 2010). Recently, MICST has been used in individual counseling sessions with psychiatrically compromised clients and clients with physical disabilities in nursing homes (see Chapter 9).

This chapter describes the core features and components of the MICST model and discusses the model in the context of engaging persons with schizophrenia more actively in the therapy process. First we provide a brief discussion of the historical background of schizophrenia, discuss current biological theories explaining the etiology of schizophrenia, and discuss how schizophrenia is currently viewed as a neurocognitive disorder. This understanding of schizophrenia as a neurocognitive disorder sets the stage for discussing how the core features of MICST are designed to stimulate neurocognitive functioning in schizophrenia. We also discuss how the MICST model has its own unique components and features compared to these other approaches used to treat schizophrenia.

Understanding Schizophrenia

A Brief Historical Background

Schizophrenia affects approximately 1% of the general population. This translates to approximately 3 million people in the United States and 51 million people worldwide (over the age of 18) who have schizophrenia (McGrath, Sukanta, Chant, & Welham, 2008). It is considered one of the most challenging mental illnesses, given that patients often display inconsistent responses to treatment and often need ongoing support and interventions (Horan, Harvey, Kern, & Green, 2011). This is partly due to the fact that people with schizophrenia show considerable variability in their pre-morbid functioning, prodromal characteristics, symptom profiles, course of illness, response to treatment, and overall adjustment (Heinrichs, 1993; Roder et al., 2011).

Emil Kraepelin (1883), the earliest modern theoretician on schizophrenia and the modern-day founder of psychiatry, believed that schizophrenia was characterized by progressive cognitive disintegration and rapidly declining cognitive functions (dementia praecox). Kraepelin believed that the primary disorder was not one of mood, but of thinking and cognition. He believed that schizophrenia essentially was a medical illness caused by biological dysfunction (e.g., chemical imbalances). In 1908, Paul Eugen Bleuler, a Swiss psychiatrist, was credited with coining the term schizophrenia (Bleuler, 1908). In his book *Dementia Praecox or the Group of Schizophrenias*, Bleuler (1911/1950) described schizophrenia as a group of disorders and challenged Kraepelin's etiological view of schizophrenia. He based his understanding of schizophrenia on his intimate personal experience in working with this population and challenged the notion of irreversible "dementia."

Bleuler viewed schizophrenia as a problem in "social relatedness," and identified the "four As" as characteristic symptoms of the condition. The "four As" comprised:

1. *associations* (disordered thinking in association and in mood);
2. *affect* (incongruent affect where one's thinking is at variance with one's mood, which leads to a "splitting of psychic functioning");
3. *ambivalence* (difficulty in making everyday decisions, which hampers one's ability to move toward personal goals); and
4. *autism* (preoccupation with one's inner fantasy world and thinking).

Bleuler believed that "the splitting of different psychological functions, which resulted in a loss of the unity of the personality, was the most important sign of the disease" (Fusar-Ploi

& Politi, 2008, p. 1407). Collectively these characteristic "four As" resulted in disconnection from the immediate social world and retreat into an "idiosyncratic reality" and inner world of fantasy and private logic. Bleuler also distinguished between "positive" and "negative" symptoms of schizophrenia, which he felt had meaningful diagnostic and prognostic value. The positive–negative symptoms distinction actually dates back to J. R. Reynolds in the mid-1850s and was further elaborated upon by J. H. Jackson (Berrios, 1985). Reynolds viewed positive and negative symptoms as being independent of each other, whereas Jackson thought the symptoms were closely connected (Berrios, 1985).

Arieti (1955) wrote a highly esteemed book on schizophrenia entitled *Interpretation of Schizophrenia* for which he received the 1975 scientific National Book Award in the United States. In the book he suggested that schizophrenia cannot be identified as an illness since it cannot be understood through the criterion of cellular pathology. He highlighted how "paleological thinking," characterized by predicative logic, dominates thinking in schizophrenia, whereby one generalizes to others by shared predicates, such as, "You have blue eyes, my cat has blue eyes—therefore you are my cat!" He essentially viewed schizophrenia as psychogenic and resulting from intense childhood anxiety, which forced the patient to construct a new reality due to the breakdown of and "injury" to normal ego defense mechanisms.

Other theoreticians have similarly conceptualized schizophrenia not as an "illness" *per se*, but as resulting from psychological, intrapersonal and interpersonal dynamics. For example, Freud, one of the most eminent thinkers and theoreticians in the field of mental illness, while not addressing schizophrenia *per se*, except under the rubric of psychoses and paranoia, emphasized how "psychotic thinking" is influenced by psycho-sexual conflicts of developmental origin. He described symptoms of hallucinations and delusions as individual adaptations to intense anxiety and stress (Freeman, 1977). Harry Sullivan, one of the many neo-Freudians, emphasized that interpersonal relationship conflicts between clients and their primary caretakers, contributed to clients' disordered thinking and behavior. He believed through his own clinical experiences that these problems were amenable to change through intensive individual psychotherapy and a supportive milieu focused on relationship building (Sullivan, 1962).

Laing and Esterson (1964) proposed that the so-called "atypical" behaviors in persons described as having schizophrenia were in fact a symbolic expression of intense personal distress in response to social–family upbringing where mother–child interactions were characterized by "double bind" communication (contradictory expectations and demands that the child cannot meet). Thomas Szasz (1961), in a somewhat similar vein, negated the notion of schizophrenia as an illness. He believed that schizophrenia was not like other medical illnesses, which often have an identified pathophysiological cause and course and are amenable to medical interventions. Rather, he viewed schizophrenia as a set of behavior patterns that are not culturally accepted or socially normative.

Mednick (1958) emphasized learning processes as contributing to the development of schizophrenia. For example, he emphasized the ease with which clients acquire conditioned emotional responses, along with their tendency to overgeneralize from a given situation and to display difficulty in performing complex tasks. Buss and Lang discussed schizophrenia symptoms from a learning theory perspective as well, and concluded that a fundamental sensorimotor deficit underlies psychological deficits in schizophrenia (Buss & Lang, 1965; Lang & Buss, 1965).

In many Eastern and other non-Western cultures, many people still believe in the external "spiritual" possession of the mind, which is responsible for influencing the person's non-normative behavior (e.g., hallucinations, delusions, or bizarre behavior) (Razali, Khan, & Hasanah, 1996). Individuals who exhibit these non-normative behaviors are sometimes viewed simply as "different," and tolerated by family and society. Some of them may join the wandering groups of "Sadhus" or "monks" or "street beggars" (similar to "street people" in some Western countries) roaming around the countryside or city.

Current Biological Theories of Schizophrenia

Advances in biological conceptualizations of schizophrenia have focused on a variety of biological processes and mechanisms that may contribute to the etiology of schizophrenia. Some of these biological mechanisms include genetic factors (e.g., chromosomal abnormalities), dysfunctional neurotransmitter systems (e.g., dopamine, serotonin, glutamate), neurodevelopmental events (e.g., disruption in neuronal migration), and neuroanatomical abnormalities (e.g., enlarged lateral ventricles, decreased cortical volume, and white matter pathology) (Keshavan, Tandon, Boutros, & Nasrallah, 2008; MacDonald & Schulz, 2009). However, no single biological model or hypothesis can satisfactorily explain the nature and etiology of the condition. This may be due in part to the heterogeneity of the condition, the variable expression one finds across persons with schizophrenia (Andreasen, 1999; Lakhan & Vieira, 2009; Roder et al., 2011); and in part to methodological problems that have made it difficult to link specific psychiatric symptoms to particular neurobiological processes (Mathalon & Ford, 2012). Modern-day psychiatry has found it meaningful to focus on different symptom clusters of schizophrenia such as "positive" symptoms (i.e., hallucinations and delusions) versus "negative" ones (i.e., avolition, anhedonia, alogia, affective constriction, social withdrawal). These symptom clusters are believed to have prognostic value, reflect different dysfunctional biological mechanisms, and have different treatment responses (American Psychiatric Association, 2013).

Dopamine Hypothesis

The Dopamine Hypothesis, which has been a viable hypothesis for schizophrenia since the early 1960s (Baumeister & Francis, 2002), has postulated that a dysfunctional dopamine system is the primary cause of the core positive symptoms of schizophrenia. Davis, Kahn, Ko, and Davidson (1991) modified the initial dopamine hypothesis, from a focus on excessive dopamine transmission in general to a focus on dysfunctional dopamine brain systems as accounting for the various positive and negative symptoms and behavioral manifestations in schizophrenia.

Specifically, the "revised" Dopamine Hypothesis has suggested that schizophrenia symptoms result from hyperdopaminergia (over-utilization of dopamine) in the mesolimbic brain regions, accounting for the positive symptoms, and hypodopaminergia (under-utilization of dopamine) in the prefrontal area/mesocortical brain regions, accounting for the negative symptoms (Baumeister & Francis, 2002; Howes & Kapur, 2009). These dysfunctional dopamine brain systems result in a "homeostatic imbalance" whereby the frontal lobes, characterized by hypodopaminergic activity, fail to exert inhibitory control over the temporal–limbic dopamine system, which in turn leads to hyperdopaminergia in the mesolimbic regions (Davis et al., 1991; Grace, 1991). Davis et al. (1991) proposed that the negative symptoms of schizophrenia, which are caused by frontal hypodopaminergia, are less responsive to anti-psychotic medication. Conversely, the positive symptoms, which resulted from over-utilization of dopamine in the mesolimbic brain regions, respond better to anti-psychotic drug treatments (Davis et al., 1991; Howes & Kapur, 2009).

Arnsten (2011) similarly presented evidence of compromised prefrontal lobe cortical function, characterized by significant loss in dendritic spines with subsequent reduction in dopamine and norepinephrine activity in this area and a corresponding increase of dopamine in the mid-brain. Arnsten (2011) hypothesized that prefrontal cortex dysfunction contributes to symptoms of cognitive deficits, thought disorder, delusions, and hallucinations. Arnsten, Mazure, and Sinha (2012) discussed how "stress experiences" in normal circumstances negatively affect the prefrontal cortex, the site for "concentration, planning, decision making, insight, judgment, and ability to retrieve memories." Specifically, they suggested that stress experiences redirect the flow of key neurotransmitters, such as dopamine and norepinephrine to primary emotional regulation sites such as the limbic system (amygdala and corpus striatum) (Arnsten et al., 2012). Correspondingly, the person with heightened stress becomes highly emotionally charged and aroused, with less capacity for "logical thinking," and rational self-control.

Howes and Kapur (2009) offered a further modified version of the dopamine hypothesis. They hypothesized that multiple factors such as genetic mutations, frontotemporal dysfunction, stress, and drugs interact to result in dopamine dysregulation and proposed that dopamine dysregulation and the "dopamine hypothesis" explain psychosis more than schizophrenia *per se* (Howes & Kapur, 2009). Keshavan et al. (2008) suggested that in general, the dopamine hypothesis seems to better explain and account for the positive versus the negative symptoms of schizophrenia and essentially does not account for the disorganized symptoms of schizophrenia. Drug studies do indeed support a "biochemical dopamine model" for psychosis by demonstrating, for example, that anti-psychotics are effective in blocking dopamine and subsequently reducing psychotic symptoms (Casey et al., 1960; Davis, Schaffer, Killina, Kinard, & Chan, 1980); and that drugs such as amphetamines increase dopamine levels in the brain and, when taken in excess, can induce a psychotic state or worsen positive symptoms in patients with schizophrenia (Laruelle et al., 1996). Indeed, some clients will get symptom relief, particularly relief from positive symptoms, through anti-psychotic drug treatment (Lieberman et al., 2005).

Beyond the Dopamine Hypothesis

Achieving "targeted regulation" of the dopamine system (e.g., decreasing dopamine utilization in the limbic system, while increasing dopamine utilization in the prefrontal lobes) through psychopharmacological interventions has not yet been accomplished. Research shows that for many patients, symptoms are not significantly reduced by medications that target dopamine (Lieberman et al., 2005). Many patients continue to have psychotic symptoms despite medication interventions and many continue to show schizophrenia-like behaviors despite a reduction in psychotic symptoms. The majority of persons with schizophrenia, even those who benefit from medication, continue to have residual symptoms and impaired social functioning and will most likely experience a relapse (Horan et al., 2011). Javitt and Coyle (2004) indicated that "two-thirds gain some relief from antipsychotics yet remain symptomatic throughout life, and the remainder shows no significant response" (p. 48).

We acknowledge that biological interventions are effective in managing some of the symptoms of schizophrenia, and in conjunction with "environmental support," can improve functional outcome, which ultimately varies from individual to individual. We, however, believe that the optimal management of schizophrenia depends upon the judicious use of biological interventions, not necessarily targeted at eliminating core psychiatric symptoms. Besides achieving a certain degree of agitation control and reducing clients' perceived "stress experiences," which is necessary and the first step in intervention, medications are not necessarily effective for many patients in reducing or eliminating atypical behaviors, delusions, or hallucinations. We believe that biological interventions, in general, can assist patients in optimizing their functioning by controlling their agitated and anxious state and by making them more responsive to the therapeutic and supportive social cues in their environment. However, conceptualizing the status of schizophrenia as a medically treatable and "curable" illness through specific biological and psychosocial interventions, has led, we believe, to some unsubstantiated claims of recovery over time and to an over-reliance and sometimes an overuse of medications aimed at "curing" the symptoms (Ahmed, Osser, Boisvert, Albert, & Aslam, 2007).

Whitaker (2005) presented evidence that the increase in the incidence of major mental illness, including schizophrenia, may indeed be an artifact of the inappropriate use of the medical model and an iatrogenic effect of anti-psychotic treatment. Interestingly, findings from the World Health Organization (WHO) found better outcomes for patients from "under-developed" versus "developed" countries. This research showed that patients from "under-developed" countries tended to be on medications for shorter time periods or were not treated with medications at all (Whitaker, 2008).

Schizophrenia: A Neurocognitive Disorder

A central theme that emerges from these causal models of schizophrenia is that patients with schizophrenia have deficits in processing information, navigating the personal and social world, and demonstrating goal-directed behavior (Green & Nuechterlein, 1999;

Laviolette, 2007; Sitnikova, Goff, & Kuperberg, 2009). Indeed, research has increasingly emphasized schizophrenia as a neurocognitive disorder (Green & Nuechterlein, 1999), characterized not only by positive and negative symptoms, but also by a variety of cognitive and information-processing deficits affecting attention, memory, problem solving, and difficulty in dealing with uncertainty in the perceptual world (Addington & Addington, 2008; Addington, Saeedi, & Addington, 2006; Braff, 1993; Goldman, Axelrod, & Taylor, 1996; Hoff & Kremen, 2003; Kalkstein, Hurford, & Gur, 2010; Morice & Delahunty, 1996; Roder et al., 2011; Spaulding, Fleming, & Reed, 1999).

Research has shown that compared to positive and negative symptoms, cognitive deficits impair daily functioning more, better predict functional outcomes (Green, 1996; Green, Kern, Braff, & Mintz, 2000; Horan et al., 2011), and change only minimally with anti-psychotic medications (Green, 2007; Horan et al., 2011; Keefe et al., 2007).

We take the position that schizophrenia can best be understood as atypical information processing associated with concomitant atypical neurocognitive functioning. Together, this atypical functioning contributes to the "positive" and "negative" symptoms and the disorganized behavioral manifestations of the condition.

We believe that there is a dynamic interaction process between brain and behavior (i.e., between mind and body) in that the underlying brain changes and dysfunction in schizophrenia patients contribute to changes in their behavior. Similarly, behavior changes lead to changes in the neural activity of the brain (see Figure 2.1). For example, Subramanium et al. (2012) demonstrated that a computerized training program increased activity in the medial pre-frontal cortex in a group of schizophrenia patients, who, otherwise, demonstrated low activation in that area. Thus, in common parlance, "the body affects the mind," and "the mind affects the body." Brenner, Roder, and Tschacher (2006) described the brain as an organ of transformation and suggested that "mental illness is the product of circular causality between neurophysiological, subjective, social, and other environmental variables constantly interacting with each other" (p. S11).

From a biological perspective, one can show how a given biological intervention can change overt behaviors, as the standard medication treatment model implies. For example, anti-psychotic medication can alter dopamine functioning in the brain (see Figure 2.1, arrow A) and subsequently alter behavioral manifestations of symptoms (e.g., reduce hallucinations) (see Figure 2.1, arrow C). Psychological and environmental interventions can lead to behavioral changes (see Figure 2.1, arrow B), which in turn can contribute to changes in brain functioning (see Figure 2.1, arrow C). Thus, when one conceptualizes brain–behavior relations as bi-directional, one can conclude the following: *changes in brain functioning can be achieved by either biological or psychological interventions, and changes in behavior can be achieved by either biological or psychological interventions.* From a psychological perspective, psychotherapy, psychosocial environmental interventions, or milieu interventions may lead directly to changes in brain functioning (see Figure 2.1, arrow D). Brenner et al. (2006) commented that "the results of quite a number of brain

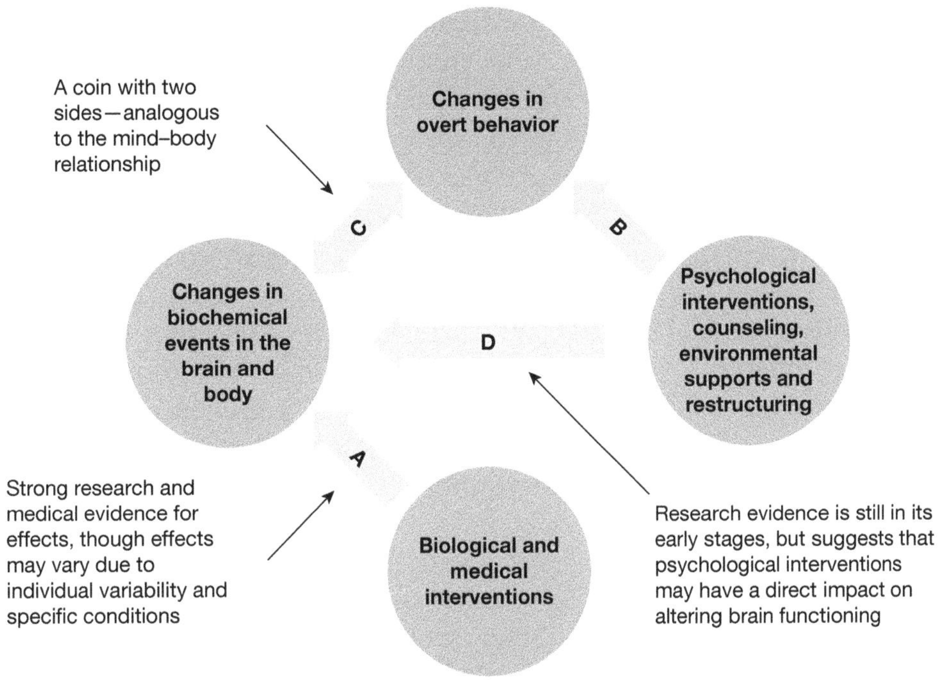

FIGURE 2.1 Relationship between brain–behavior functioning: a question of level of analysis

imaging studies during pharmacotherapy and/or psychotherapy suggested a 'top-down' effect of psychotherapy in that modifying dysfunctional cognitive-emotional schemata lead to [sic] a reduction in dysfunctions of subcortical brain regions" (p. S11).

While research continues to explore ways to improve the "targeted effects" of medication such as enhancing dopamine-related regulation in various brain regions, as well as exploring genetic factors and other vulnerability markers for schizophrenia, we believe that one of the primary research and treatment challenges is to develop more effective psychotherapy and therapeutic milieu interventions. Similar to biological interventions, these interventions can target and stimulate prefrontal cortex functions and stimulate "positive behaviors" so as to displace "negative behaviors" through specific activities. We believe that MICST is an adjunctive psychosocial intervention that provides a step in this direction and can augment traditional interventions for persons with schizophrenia.

Psychiatric Symptoms as Behavioral Habits

Although pharmacological interventions aimed at targeting specific dopamine systems may reduce psychosis in some patients by partially regulating these circumscribed dysfunctional areas, these same interventions may be limited in regulating the "experience of schizophrenia." That is, the "experience of schizophrenia" is not simply the totality of a patient's psychotic symptoms, but rather a way of adapting, processing information, and interacting that is only partially influenced by psychosis. Patients develop unique and habitual ways of thinking, behaving, and processing information, which helps them adjust and adapt to their environment.

Clients' unique "psychological stress" experiences along with their vulnerability to stress, possibly related to development factors (e.g., genetic, biological, and psychosocial environmental interactions) contribute to a preference for and preoccupation with internal fantasy and ruminations as well as difficulty tolerating everyday experiences and the "uncertainties in life." This can lead to an eventual breakdown of clients' perception of reality and contribute to the development of "atypical" behavioral tendencies.

The ongoing presentation of symptoms for "medication-resistant" patients may be better explained through "psychological–behavioral" principles such as "habits" of thinking and processing information. These patients will probably need ongoing milieu support and therapeutic opportunities to practice positive skills and to learn to displace or minimize the occurrence of these "habit-like" symptoms or "negative behaviors". Providing positive psychology approaches are likely to be useful in fostering other skills and compensating for the breakdown of the patient's stress-control mechanisms.

We take the position, that although "stress" associated with heightened agitation experiences may have been primarily responsible for producing "atypical behavior and thinking symptoms" in persons with schizophrenia, over time these behavior patterns and thinking processes get reinforced through practice (e.g., law of exercise)—that is, both through overt repetition of these behavioral habits and through the subsequent reinforcement and strengthening of underlying neural networks that support these "behavioral habits."

The Soteria treatment model has indeed demonstrated that a supportive milieu can achieve therapeutic benefits that can equal or surpass medication treatments (Mosher, Vallone, & Menn, 1995). That is, the model has demonstrated that clients can heal from psychosis without medication interventions or with low doses of medication combined with a supportive environment. The model emphasized a humanistic approach characterized by respect, dignity, normalization, safety, patient-directed treatment, elimination of labels such as "schizophrenia," and tolerance for extremes of behavior such as hallucinations and delusions as long as the client was not a threat to themselves or others (Alanen, de Chavez, Silver, & Martindale, 2009). The MICST model endorses many of these same characteristics.

Psychotherapy Treatment Approaches for Schizophrenia

Significant progress has indeed been made in maintaining persons with schizophrenia in the community. This was accomplished largely due to advances in medication practice (beginning with the introduction of phenothiazines in the 1950s and the atypicals in the 1990s). This resulted in a major shift in management of persons with schizophrenia from inpatient to community service programs. This development in medication management spearheaded federal funding for Community Support Programs (e.g., case management and psychosocial support vocational services, supported housing and other residential alternatives, along with access to 24-hour medical and psychiatric emergency support), as ancillary services to medication treatment.

Thus, along with research focused on discovering more effective medications to manage schizophrenia, research has also focused on developing more effective psychological, psychosocial, psycho-educational, and strengths-focused treatments (Huxley, Rendall, & Sederer, 2000; Mojtabai, Nicholson, & Carpenter, 1998; Penn & Mueser, 1996; Pfammatter, Junghan, & Brenner, 2006; Rapp & Wintersteen, 1989; Roder et al., 2011; Scott & Dixon, 1995). Other research has explored using a rehabilitation treatment model that focuses on optimal medication treatment and skills training to assist clients in overcoming social barriers and accessing resources within a recovery model (Anthony & Liberman, 1986; Horan et al., 2011; Kopelowicz & Liberman, 1995; Mueser, Bond, Drake, & Resnick, 1998).

Research suggests that traditional psychotherapy, however, has had mixed success for people with schizophrenia. Traditional psychotherapy often entails exploring personal issues and discussing emotionally laden topics involving "negative feelings and experiences" from one's past. Since the focus is often designed to probe clients' personal problems and deficiencies, it may elicit negative feelings, agitation, and "defensive" postures. Some research has suggested that traditional psychotherapy may be helpful for persons with schizophrenia (Karon, 1989; Karon & VandenBos, 1981; Mojtabai et al., 1998), and that some approaches such as cognitive-behavioral therapy may serve as a useful adjunct to medication treatment (Pinninti, Rissmiller, & Steer, 2010). Other research has suggested limited success with traditional approaches (Gottdiener & Haslam, 2002; Katz & Gunderson, 1990; Roth & Fonagy, 2005; Scott & Dixon, 1995). Other research has indicated that some insight-oriented approaches may even be harmful to some patients (Drake & Sederer, 1986; Mueser & Berenbaum, 1990). Researchers continue to recognize the importance of identifying psychotherapy approaches that can aid in patients' recovery (Lysaker, Wilkniss, Glynn, & Silverstein, 2010).

People with schizophrenia may have trouble tolerating heightened emotions and discussing in-depth personal or identity-related issues. Furthermore, some clients may have a limited response to traditional psychotherapy due, in part, to deficits in "verbal" information processing, attention, working memory, and social skills. Consequently, practitioners have used various other approaches to treat individuals with schizophrenia (e.g., psycho-education, problem solving, social skills training, cognitive-behavioral therapy, and computer-assisted therapy) (Ahmed, 1998; Ahmed, Bayog, & Boisvert, 1997; Beck, Rector, Stolar, & Paul, 2009; Haddock et al., 1998; Halford & Hayes, 1991; Hogarty et al., 1995; Liberman, Kopelowicz, & Young, 1994; Roder et al., 2011).

There is a wide body of literature indicating that group therapy can be effective for schizophrenia and is well suited for teaching clients interpersonal skills and coping skills, and for providing a supportive network (Herz & Lamberti, 1996; Kanas, 1996; Lehman, Carpenter, Goldman, & Steinwachs, 1995; Mason, 2000; Nightingale & McQueeney, 1996; Schaub, Andreas, Brenner, & Donzel, 1997). Often group therapy for schizophrenia is structured and task-focused to promote social functioning, interpersonal relations, cognitive functioning, and problem-solving skills (Brenner, Roder, Hodel, & Corrigan, 1994; Kanas, 1996; Pekala, Siegal, & Farrar, 1985; Roder et al., 2011; Yalom, 1983).

Cognitive skills training programs, such as Integrated Psychological Therapy (IPT) (Brenner et al., 1994; Roder et al., 2011) have been found to improve basic cognitive skills through structured sequential learning modules. Similarly, various forms of cognitive-behavioral therapy (Beck et al., 2009; Kingdon & Turkington, 2005) have demonstrated some degree of success in changing maladaptive beliefs and thinking (e.g., delusions and hallucinations) by using cognitive-behavioral strategies. Additionally, cognitive remediation programs and cognitive enhancement therapy have been successful in helping clients compensate for deficits in cognitive functioning (Eack, 2012; Hurford, Kalkstein, & Hurford, 2011; Wykes & Reeder, 2005; Wykes et al., 2007). Miran and Miran (1999) developed the "Adaptation of the Neuropsychological Therapeutic Community Treatment Model," which was founded on the principles of neuroplasticity. In a small study, the authors reported success in assisting clients with schizophrenia in improving their cognitive and interpersonal functioning to enable them to benefit from vocational and educational training programs.

Metacognitive therapy, a more recent variant of cognitive-behavioral therapy, provides a structured group training program to address clients' underlying "deficits" in thinking by making these thoughts "conscious" and by providing clients with reality-based thinking formats (Moritz & Woodward, 2007). Research in metacognitive therapy suggests that people with schizophrenia display cognitive biases, assumptions, and beliefs that are of a "pathological" or abnormal nature. For example, persons with schizophrenia tend to exhibit a bias against "disconfirmatory" evidence (i.e., not being able to incorporate "corrective feedback") and "cognitive rigidity" (Moritz & Woodward, 2007). Similar to cognitive therapy, metacognitive therapy attempts to modify underlying "maladaptive" beliefs and thought processes, and provide clients with alternative and adaptive ways of thinking that align more closely with the "normal" social world. In an article in *Scientific American Mind* (Kurtz, 2013), Kurtz reported on the positive impact of emerging social cognitive training programs in improving information processing in schizophrenia. For example, Kurtz reported on the work by Horan et al. (2012) that targets training and improvement in "emotional processing," to help clients "decipher emotional cues and take another person's perspective."

In the MICST model, we emphasis information-processing deficits, analogous to thinking deficits. MICST focuses on stimulating basic thinking processes that govern all of us, persons with or without schizophrenia. We believe that these basic universal thinking processes are not as easily accessible to persons who have schizophrenia, and that clients often do not have opportunities to exercise or stimulate these processes because of interference from ongoing psychiatric symptoms. As a result, atypical thinking processes that clients have developed for their individual adaptation become more pronounced. In our cognitive stimulation approach, we do not challenge clients' "atypical thinking." Rather, we provide clients with opportunities to practice adaptive thinking, and in the process, help displace or suppress "atypical thinking."

MICST: From Psychopathology Reduction to Psychopathology Redirection

Traditional medication management and psychological interventions have often identified symptom management or symptom elimination as a primary treatment goal. For example, medication often targets the dopamine system, which is hypothesized to contribute to both positive and negative symptoms of schizophrenia. Traditional psychotherapy such as psychodynamic, cognitive-behavioral, or psychosocial approaches have often focused on the goal of symptom reduction. This goal is often pursued by exploring the historical development of the client's symptoms, feelings, and belief systems with the understanding that the collaborative dialogue between the client and therapist will enable the client to "internalize the experience," gain insight, and achieve behavioral change. However, cognitive deficits that clients may demonstrate (e.g., impairment in prefrontal-lobe-related activities involving working memory, problem solving, reasoning) make it questionable whether or to what degree clients can "internalize" the verbal dialogue and the suggestions generated in more traditional therapy approaches.

Even though progress has been made in improving the quality of life of persons with schizophrenia through medication treatment and a range of psychotherapy service programs, many clients continue to experience psychiatric symptoms, making the goal of symptom elimination elusive. The MICST model emphasizes the need for consistently integrating any effective interventions into the therapeutic milieu or treatment program to assist clients in achieving optimal functioning. However, any targeted focus on symptom management, symptom elimination, or "problem areas" may unwittingly generate a "negative stress" experience in clients due to the focus on deficits and compromised functioning.

As we have postulated, clients' psychiatric symptoms may persist due to the symptoms taking the form of "behavioral habits" (analogous to Freud's conceptualization [1894/1962] of "psychotic defense" in the presence of overwhelming anxiety), which become strengthened over time through repetition. Many clients in inpatient facilities or CMHCs may have limited interests in hobbies and other productive daytime activities; this includes not having adequate opportunities for cognitive stimulation through, for example, reading, media, or social interaction. This can make their lifestyle not only different, but contribute to less satisfying activities, possible internal dissatisfaction with life in general, and increased psychological stress. Although a client's biological stress experiences may be partially reduced through psychopharmacological interventions, the psychological stress experience associated with the absence of many normal supports in the client's daily life can sustain the "stress experience," and in turn support or maintain the clinical symptoms ("behavioral habits") associated with these stress experiences.

The critical role that cognitive stimulation techniques and the therapeutic milieu can play in displacing some of these overt clinical symptoms and behavioral habits has not been fully recognized or appreciated. We believe that achieving a better understanding of this "stress–behavioral habit formation relationship" will lead to more effective interventions for persons with schizophrenia. The MICST model highlights the need for a therapeutic structure that promotes displacement of symptoms associated with behavioral habits by providing a variety of therapeutic activities. We believe that the MICST approach can serve as adjunctive support to clients' medication regimen, psychosocial rehabilitation services, and residential and day program support services.

Core Features of MICST

Information Processing: Using Visual Modalities to Enhance Auditory Processing

The MICST model operates from the assumption that information processing is at the core of our decision making and is the key function coordinating our thinking, emotions, and behaviors as we attempt to adapt to the environment (see Figure 2.2). Moore and Anderson (1969) hypothesized that information processing is intrinsically rewarding to promote learning of skills in one's environment without the need for any external reinforcement. That is, they contended that "information processing" activity (receiving information about the environment related to the activity that one is engaged in) by itself, may be a sufficient condition for reinforcement. Research has shown that information processing is often compromised in clients with schizophrenia (Addington et al., 2006; Green & Nuechterlein, 1999; Kalkstein et al., 2010), and as such, clients often benefit from interventions that serve to compensate for these deficits (Addington & Addington, 2008; Hurford et al., 2011).

Behaviors at variance with expected social norms and expectations of conduct may be viewed as "deficits in information processing" from a social perspective (see Figure 2.3). These "information processing" deficits may be characterized by difficulty in determining how to align one's behavior with the established social norms. Additionally, such deficits may contribute to a client's difficulty in managing their own personal distress as well as the distress of significant others which arises from trying to cope with the client's "atypical" behaviors. Furthermore, "deficits in information processing" often associated with schizophrenia may become more pronounced or exacerbated in the presence of increased emotional arousal or heightened agitation.

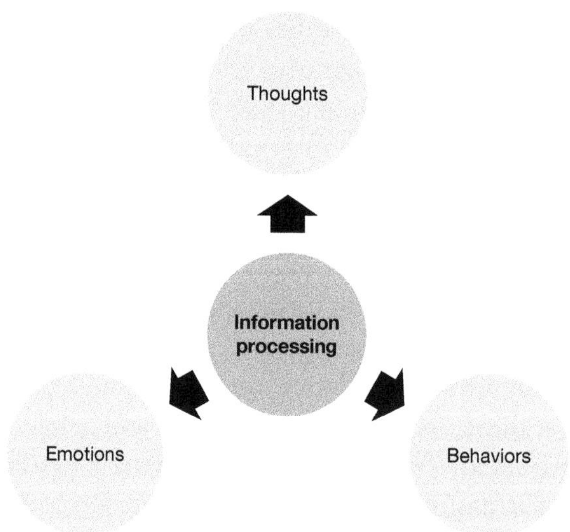

FIGURE 2.2 Information processing is the core function enabling us to adapt to the environment by coordinating our thinking, feeling, and behavior

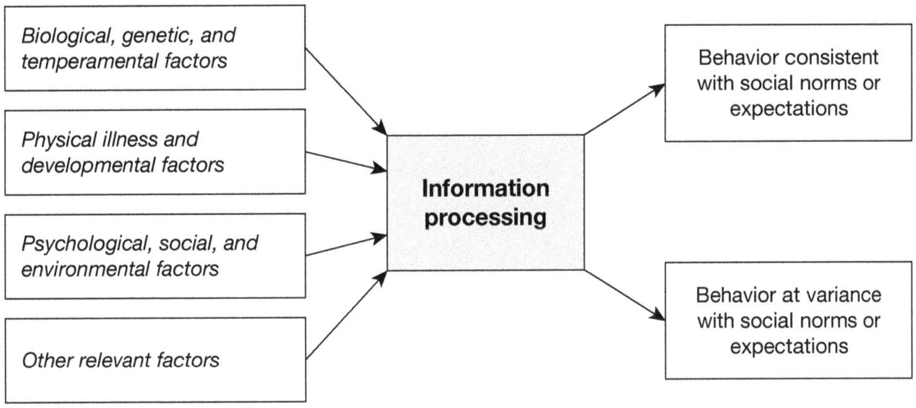

FIGURE 2.3 Our information-processing capabilities are influenced by a variety of factors and contribute to "adaptive" behaviors consistent with social norms or expectations, or "maladaptive" behaviors at variance with social norms or expectations. "Maladaptive" behaviors may lead to personal or social stress

Although all of our senses process information and assist us in adapting to the environment, human beings are by nature "visual creatures" and rely heavily on visual processing to navigate and respond effectively to the environment. In fact, a disproportionate amount of cortex in the brain is devoted to visual processing, compared to, for example, auditory processing (Garrett, 2010). For example, we all benefit from visual aids to assist us in processing information. Using PowerPoint and other visuals aids is customary and expected when one attends a presentation or conference. Similarly, an instructor, for example, would not typically teach a course without using visual aids. Students often optimize their performance in class by taking notes, reviewing written materials (e.g., handouts), and having access to visual modalities such as PowerPoint to supplement verbally presented material (Susskind, 2005).

In some of our prior work, we found that using visually presented materials enhanced communication in clients and engaged clients in more reality-based discussions (Ahmed, 1998; Ahmed et al., 1997; Ahmed & Boisvert, 2003a, 2006a). For example, we found that presenting the spoken word visually on the computer screen helped patients with schizophrenia stay more focused and enabled them to discuss their treatment goals more realistically and clearly. They were able to see their verbalizations on the screen and correct themselves when needed. Computer-facilitated dialogue was found to enhance communication during individual client sessions, and clients with schizophrenia benefitted from the opportunity to receive handouts (computer printouts) of the goals discussed in session (Ahmed, 1998). Ahmed and Boisvert (2006a) showed how visually augmenting traditional verbal interactions with clients enhanced their ability to engage more productively in discussing their treatment goals. In a condition such as schizophrenia, which is often characterized by, for example, auditory hallucinations, verbal processing can be compromised. Thus, relying solely on the auditory mode of communication can have its limits in achieving successful communication with clients.

Consider the following vignette of a client in a MICST group. The vignette highlights how using visual aids can enable clients to communicate more clearly and to access more easily their intact cognitive and memory functioning.

Clinical Vignette: Ethan

Ethan has a confused and at times "incoherent" presentation. He often cannot remember what he had for lunch and others have to remind him of the day's events. He frequently paced in the group home, was noticeably restless, and when first joining the group, often walked around the table during group activities. However, once the paper–pencil exercises were presented, he quickly went to his seat and focused on the exercises. He frequently worked without interruption for 3–4 minutes. He often got all the answers correct (see the worksheet below, where he answered 23 of the 25 questions correctly), and would ask for more exercises. When asked to share his responses, he would accurately read his responses back to the group. On one occasion he read his answer to a sports question and mentioned that he had played soccer in college and also that he had studied chemistry in college. No one in the group knew this including his case manager.

After attending the group for some sessions, Ethan no longer walked around the table during the group and could sit for the entire session. During group discussions, he still was confused and showed a marked poverty of speech, often answering in short phrases, but was able to complete the paper–pencil exercises, sometimes flawlessly. The paper–pencil exercises, which provided a "visual modality," seemed to focus his attention and enable him to engage more meaningfully in the group. These exercises also enabled him to practice using certain cognitive skills that were under-utilized and not evident during his routine verbal interactions with staff.

WORKSHEET

1. Name 3 New England states.
2. Which state is the largest?
3. Which state is the smallest?
4. In what country is Dublin?
5. Where is the equator?
6. Name 2 sections of the newspaper.
7. Name 2 members of a band.
8. This measures the mileage in a car.
9. Name a politician from R.I.
10. What is DNA?
11. Name 2 games in the Olympics.
12. What is a fathom?
13. What does CO2 stand for?
14. Name 2 ingredients in a cake.
15. Who was Hank Aaron?
16. Name a country in Africa.
17. Astronomers use this to observe stars.
18. What is penicillin used for?
19. The Pilgrims sailed on this ship.
20. Name two types of shell-fish.
21. Name a famous author.
22. This bodily organ makes insulin.
23. What is a silo?
24. What is a marsupial?
25. What is the study of life called?

The challenge to overcome behavior deficits or reduce personal or social stress requires that we learn new coping strategies or that we figure out ways of processing information in our social and physical interactions that produce more adaptive behaviors. The emphasis may vary from one clinical or behavior condition to another, but the unifying theme for all recovery and for psychological treatment is to help clients think and process information in ways to achieve more productive learning and coping. We next emphasize how "*mind/ cognitive stimulation*," the second core feature of MICST, plays an important role in this therapeutic learning process.

"Mind" (Cognitive) Stimulation

The second core feature of MICST is its focus on cognitive stimulation through three activities:

1. discussion of general knowledge, personal information, and mental health education, often using a blackboard, easel, or handouts to maximize group participation;
2. mind stimulation using paper–pencil exercises to address underlying skills that govern one's thinking, memory, logical association, attention, and concentration; and
3. personal assessment, using brief surveys and questionnaires, of goals, interests, and understanding of one's mental health treatment.

All of these exercises provide opportunities for clients to stimulate the various underlying cognitive functions of "the mind" that may be still intact, but under-utilized or under-recognized.

The MICST model focuses on accessing "areas of the brain" that are intact and that can lead to more logical and reality-based communication (see Figure 2.4). The deficit versus intact areas in the brain as labeled in the diagram below are not meant to represent actual anatomical areas in the brain that conform to these designations. Rather, the diagram is primarily meant to convey the concept that some brain areas or information-processing systems may be more or less functional than others. The diagram can be used as a teaching tool during a MICST group to convey this concept without having to use more complicated brain terminology or anatomy.

We use the concept of *mind stimulation* to acknowledge the historical and current wide use of the concept of "mind." The concept of mind is used to describe the entity that governs our internal thinking processes, which in turn guides our feelings and behavior. This acknowledges the fact that billions of human beings believe in the concept of a "mind" in their respective practice of a religious or spiritual faith or in their everyday thinking. In presenting the concept of "stimulating exercises of the mind," we do not limit our exercises primarily to stimulating the commonly accepted "cognitive areas" of attention, concentration, memory, logical association, reasoning, and problem solving. We encourage group members to think and talk about various other topics and subjects that affect them and all human beings: politics, sports, current affairs, geography, history, religious and spiritual values, astronomy, personal goals, mental health services, health-related issues, social and interpersonal relationships, and interpersonal communication.

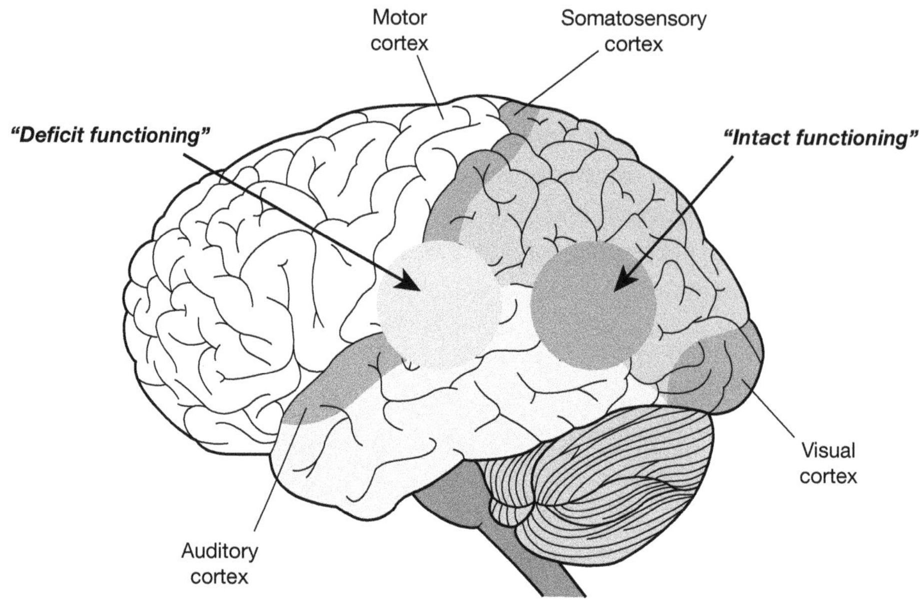

FIGURE 2.4 Hypothetical functioning of the brain characterized by areas that demonstrate "intact" functioning and areas that demonstrate "deficit" functioning

Essentially any topic of interest that is spontaneously brought up in the group can be addressed.

The general guideline to follow is that the discussion does not generate emotional stress or stimulate "negative memories," which may affect a group member's mood or increase his/her agitation. We believe that persons with schizophrenia have a vulnerability to stress and difficulty coping with "stress experiences." As such, discussions are kept relatively brief so that clients do not get distracted or preoccupied with negative internal experiences due to boredom or disinterest. However, the therapist needs to ensure that a reasonable degree of attention to the topic is sustained and that a multimodal approach is used as needed (e.g., oral discussion combined with visual aids such as writing information and responses on the blackboard and easel, using paper–pencil exercises, and providing handouts) to facilitate the discussion. In this vein, MICST is different from traditional therapy in that deliberate efforts are made to avoid discussing personal emotionally laden issues or conflicts, except in the context of group mental health education. We encourage members to follow up with discussions of their personal issues with their counselor, case manager, or psychiatrist.

The MICST approach helps clients to develop a greater appreciation of social reality and enhance their self-esteem by maximizing capabilities that may be under-utilized or under-recognized by clinicians due, in part, to the traditional "deficit-focused" approach aimed at managing symptoms or reducing psychopathology (see Figure 2.5, circle B). MICST helps redirect clients to circle A and minimize the focus on circle B and, as such, helps to reinforce positive coping strategies that enhance clients' ability to adapt successfully to the environment.

The mind–cognitive stimulation program we describe is conceptually different from other cognitive skills training programs, such as IPT (Roder et al., 2011), in that we do

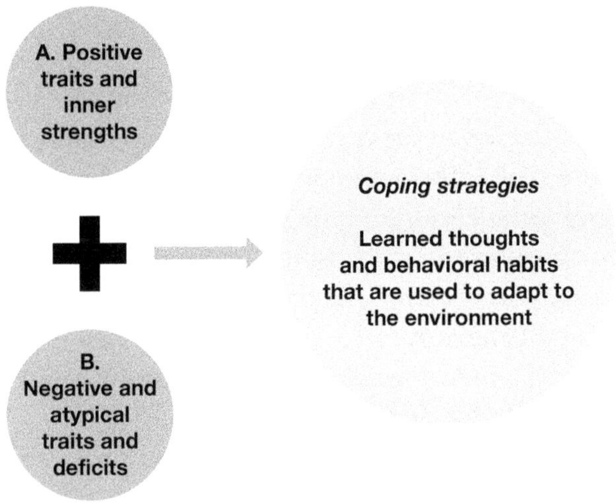

FIGURE 2.5 Our learned thoughts and behaviors are products of A and B and serve as coping strategies to help us adapt to the environment. If these coping strategies are eventually adaptive, they, in turn, reinforce the traits in circles A and B that were used to develop the coping strategies. MICST's positive psychology strategies are aimed at directing clients to circle A (positive traits and inner strengths) and minimizing the focus on circle B (negative and atypical traits and deficits). This reinforces clients using "A traits" compared to "B traits" in learning to adapt to the environment.

not set improvement in cognitive skills outside the group sessions as a central objective *per se*. Our primary objective is to demonstrate whether persons with schizophrenia can engage in a variety of mind-stimulating activities and improve their immediate ability to engage in reality-based discussions and interactions. The in-group observations of these interactions can provide valuable information on how to build structured and meaningful activities more effectively into clients' therapeutic milieu and treatment.

The mind–cognitive stimulation we describe is not to be confused with cognitive-behavioral therapies, which are often designed to challenge and change a client's maladaptive beliefs and thinking through a self-reflective dialogue between the therapist and client, or through paper–pencil self-reflection exercises. Also, unlike some of the more traditional cognitive-behavioral approaches, we do not try to "judge" or "evaluate" particular beliefs, but focus on stimulating basic thinking processes underlying mental and cognitive functioning. However, we believe intuitively that clients' involvement in mind stimulation exercises can have an overall positive effect in their everyday functioning outside the therapy sessions. For example, by engaging in mind-stimulation group activities, clients can become more aware of and more capable of using their intact thinking skills during both structured and spontaneous interactions outside the group.

The MICST model has a variety of goals aimed at teaching clients various skills, facilitating ways that clients can engage in more focused and reality-based discussions, and stimulating clients' intact areas of functioning. Below we list the core goals of MICST.

MICST Core Goals

1. *stimulate memory, association, logical reasoning* to help clients process information and communicate such information within "a reality-based framework";
2. *maximize benefits from therapeutic interactions*, mental health education, and milieu treatment available in the hospital or community setting;
3. *teach clients how to verbalize strategies for coping* and understanding mental illness symptoms affecting behavior;
4. *increase concentration and task involvement* and increase toleration of one hour of group interactions without disruption;
5. *promote deep breathing exercises* as a way to relax, promote attention to one's breathing process, divert one's mind away from "intrusive" psychiatric symptoms and "negative thoughts," and become more aware of "here and now" reality (a sense of "mindfulness");
6. *improve social skills* (e.g., learn to take turns, ask questions of other group members, show interest in following conversations in group, and reduce self-centered and self-preoccupying behaviors in the group setting);
7. *teach clients to relate to others through stimulating intact areas of cognitive functioning* by talking about events or recalling past accomplishments or achievements, practicing memory retrieval of factual information, sharing information, and getting feedback;
8. *teach clients to accept corrective feedback* on paper–pencil cognitive exercises, and through this feedback process reduce "cognitive rigidity" or agitation associated with "correction" of one's thinking and in the process improve self-image;
9. *help clients to verbalize specific areas in which the group has been helpful* and express positive benefits from continued participation, and in the process become mindful of activities necessary for further recovery and for maintaining clinical stability;
10. *improve clients' ability to process visually presented exercises and materials* that address various cognitive skills or mental health education topics.

MICST Core Group Components

The MICST group sessions typically last 50–60 minutes. There are three core MICST group components:

1. body movement–mindfulness–relaxation (BMR) exercises;
2. group discussions; and
3. paper–pencil exercises.

The group begins and ends with relaxation exercises. Following the relaxation exercises at the start of the group, clients participate in group discussions. The structured discussion often leads to spontaneous topics broached by group members, which can then lead to discussion of various general knowledge topics or topics such as stress management, the pros and cons of medications, and current events. Following the group discussions, paper–pencil cognitive stimulation exercises are completed.

Below we briefly describe the three group components and the approximate amount of time devoted to each. However, depending upon the interest and involvement of the group members, some group activities may be given more time. For example, if a particular discussion topic is of high interest and elicits strong group participation, the group leader may decide to spend more time on the discussion topic and possibly forgo the written exercises. It is left up to the group leader's judgment as to how much time to allocate to each component, based on the functioning of the group for that day. However, the BMR exercises are always used to start and end the group.

A: Body Movement–Mindfulness–Relaxation Exercises (BMR) (5 minutes: 2–3 minutes at the beginning and end of the group)

Members start and end the group with a 2–3-minute deep breathing relaxation exercise. Members stand and count aloud ten breaths. While taking these breaths, they are instructed to move their arms up while breathing in and down while breathing out. Members are taught to take turns in leading the exercise to experience the feeling of being a leader and a follower, and the value of adhering to a group structure. There are other variations of BMR exercises that can be used depending upon group members' level of participation. For example, the group facilitator can ask members to stand erect in a stretched position and engage in the breathing exercise, or ask them to watch one hand moving up and down slowly, as in Tai Chi, without stopping. The BMR exercises are used to help members learn to develop mental control and concentration by paying attention to subtle body movements and the breathing process, as well as to learn to use deep breathing as a way to promote relaxation and redirection from "troubling" thoughts and feelings. More importantly, the exercises promote alertness to one's immediate social environment, necessary for adaptation in everyday life experiences. We present more detailed discussion and demonstration guidelines in Chapter 3.

B: Group Discussions: *Mind Stimulation of Episodic Memory, Semantic Memory, Personal Interests, Existential Perspectives, and Mental Health Issues* (20–25 minutes)

Group members take turns talking about an activity in which they participated during the past week, and may at times discuss what they are doing for the day or what they have planned for the upcoming week. The discussion is framed in a short-term "past–present–future orientation" to facilitate recall of current and recent past memories. This exercise is designed to promote the group sharing process, using current activities and goals, to exercise memory functions, and to facilitate clients' verbal production and social dialogue using a reality-based and "here-and-now" framework. Any issues or interests that clients bring up may be generated into a group discussion topic and further elaborated upon during the group discussion phase.

Paper–Pencil Exercises: *Mind Stimulation of Attention, Logical Thinking, Reasoning, and Self-reflection* (25–30 minutes)

Members complete paper–pencil exercises (e.g., factual information, logical reasoning, word associations, comprehension, antonyms and synonyms) that promote associative reasoning, comprehension, logical reasoning, and memory stimulation, as well as task attention and concentration. The "neutral topics" help to focus concentration and attention and minimize symptom-related behaviors that can surface in conversations or activities that are more emotionally laden. Using visually presented information such as written exercises also helps to compensate for difficulties clients may have in processing verbal information.

Any client is eligible to participate in MICST, which has been designed to engage even the most challenging client. Historically, clients have been from group homes, community support programs, or inpatient programs. There is no particular exclusion criterion for the group. Clients without a diagnosis of schizophrenia (e.g., clients with bipolar disorder or a severe personality disorder) have on occasion participated in the group. However, the client populations have been relatively "homogeneous" given that MICST has been provided within CMHC community support programs or state hospitals which have their own "eligibility criteria" for services.

Using Co-therapists

We have found it important to routinely include case managers and other mental health clinicians as co-facilitators during MICST groups. This allows these mental health workers to gain a richer perspective on their clients and learn additional ways of engaging them in productive and meaningful discussions and activities. These clinicians often notice client strengths and interests that are not readily apparent in typical interactions outside the group setting. Also, mental health clinicians can help reinforce clients' skills and activities in between group sessions. We promote mental health workers' involvement in MICST to maximize the possibility of "generalizing therapeutic effects" outside the therapy session. MICST groups have also been used as "staff training placements."

Co-therapists, who may be case-workers, bachelor-level clinicians, or graduate students can serve the following roles:

1. support individual client responses throughout the group by providing positive feedback for participation;
2. assist with paper–pencil exercises for clients who may have learning difficulties or who may benefit from more individualized attention;
3. assist in researching (for example, via the Internet) group discussion topics, or in writing on the blackboard, whiteboard, easel, or PowerPoint handouts issues discussed in the sessions;
4. monitor the entire group process, provide redirection when needed, and reinforce group participation;
5. facilitate involvement from more reluctant or less active group members;

6. prompt group members during discussions by reminding clients of certain activities and events—when, for example, a client with whom the co-therapist is familiar, is having difficulty remembering events from his/her day; and
7. serve as a role model for social interaction and group norms.

MICST: An Adjunct to Medication and Psychosocial Interventions

The theoretical framework and clinical practice model we are presenting is not a substitute for biological interventions or other existing psychosocial clinical practice models. The focus of our book is not to challenge the usefulness of current biological treatments, other than highlighting the fact that many inpatients and outpatients with schizophrenia are on multiple psychiatric medications, and that there is not yet a universally accepted clinical practice medication protocol that consistently documents functional improvement. Similarly, we do not present evidence to substantiate any claim of the superiority or "efficacy" of the MICST model compared to other psychotherapeutic interventions.

Rather, we highlight a unique psychological intervention model as an adjunctive way of conceptualizing and practicing therapeutic interventions with persons with schizophrenia. We believe that the MICST model is compatible with other interventions and approaches, and that MICST has its own unique focus on highlighting and accessing clients' intact functioning and skills that may not be readily apparent or accessible through more traditional approaches. The acceptance of any model is governed by current knowledge in the field along with the perception of the "clinical usefulness" of the model. In this sense, each model has its own unique place and potential usefulness in clinical practice. We believe strongly that clinicians will find MICST clinically useful and effective in engaging clients in meaningful therapeutic interactions and activities.

Chapter 3

Body Movement–Mindfulness–Relaxation (BMR) Exercises

This chapter focuses on the body movement–mindfulness–relaxation (BMR) component of MICST. The BMR exercises consist of deep-breathing exercises coupled with rhythmic movement designed to achieve a state of relaxation and enhanced mindfulness. We start this chapter by explaining the concepts of body movement and mindfulness, and then explain the nature of and rationale for the BMR exercises. We provide *clinician instructions* on how to implement the exercises and present clinical vignettes to illustrate how clients have responded to these exercises in group sessions. We also describe the goals for these exercises in the context of the MICST model and conclude with *homework recommendations* to encourage ongoing practice of the exercises.

Movement

Awareness of the body moving in space, navigating the immediate physical and social environment, awareness of the present momentary existence of time, and anticipating and experiencing change, are all fundamental functions that are necessary for survival and adaptive behavior (Bartenieff & Lewis, 2002). Movement underlies our awareness of being alive, and it also provides us with information about our immediate physical and social environment. Across all human cultures, physical education and play activities have historically been identified as important components of socialization and physical growth, as well as necessary for emotional maturity and competency.

Research has shown that persons with schizophrenia demonstrate abnormal movements (Varlet et al., 2012) and disturbances in body ownership and agency (Thakkar, Nichols, McIntosh, & Park, 2011). For example, Thakkar et al. (2011) suggested that persons with schizophrenia may have abnormalities in temporoparietal networks implicated in body ownership and that body ownership disturbances may contribute to presentations of passivity. They suggested that clients' misattributions of agency to, for example, external sources, may manifest as "delusions of passivity" (i.e., someone else is controlling my actions). Varlet et al. (2012) noted that persons with schizophrenia demonstrate social motor coordination impairments, which may be rooted in various information processing and information transmission deficits. This is supported by early laboratory studies, which found that persons with schizophrenia have sensorimotor deficits impairing their ability to navigate the physical world (Buss & Lang, 1965; Lang & Buss, 1965).

Research has begun to highlight the role of the cerebellum in promoting not only motor coordination and muscular activities, but also its role—through its interaction with the cerebral cortex—in stimulating reasoning, memory, learning, and anticipatory responses necessary for adaptive behavior (Gallese & Lakoff, 2005). Some of these cerebellar functions may, in fact, be deficient in schizophrenia (Andreason & Pierson, 2008; Schiffman et al., 2009; Schmahmann, 2000; Sorensen et al., 2010).

From a clinical "observational perspective," people with schizophrenia often demonstrate poor gait and posture and may exhibit poor awareness of their own body movements. Additionally, they may exhibit deficits in their overall "social and environmental awareness," with associated difficulties in anticipating and effectively adapting to their immediate physical and social world. This lack of awareness of their own body movements may, in part, explain why some clients pay limited attention to their personal hygiene and show low motivation to engage in a "productive and focused day routine."

Research in the area of *embodied cognition* (Shapiro, 2011) suggests that our sense of self and self-esteem can be influenced by our perception of our body. One can hypothesize that poor attention to hygiene and self-presentation, which may be evident in persons with schizophrenia, can be both a cause and an effect of information-processing deficits. That is, clients may attend less to their appearance due to attentional impairments and consequently, the resulting appearance may serve to reinforce in clients lower expectations of their attentional capabilities and lead to lower "attentional output." This ultimately may create lower expectations in others of the clients' attentional capabilities. Clients may also exhibit poor anticipatory behavior (e.g., have difficulty anticipating social or physical happenings and as a result appear "absent minded"). Some of these behaviors characterize the hallmark negative symptoms of schizophrenia. Moreover, clients' anticipation of social and physical happenings may be compromised due to internal and obsessive preoccupation with "negative thoughts and feelings," which are often associated with positive symptoms of schizophrenia (e.g., delusions and hallucinations).

Mindfulness

Since the seminal book *Wherever you go, there you are: Mindfulness meditation in everyday life* (Kabat-Zinn, 1994), mindfulness has become a core component of psychotherapy practice and is now routinely integrated into many traditional forms of therapy (Baer, 2003; Didonna, 2009; Mace, 2008). Mindfulness strategies have been shown to increase well-being and self-awareness (Brown & Ryan, 2003), reduce ruminations (Coffey & Hartman, 2008; Kumar, 2010), and even improve management of psychotic-type experiences (Abba, Chadwick, & Stevenson, 2008). Mindfulness interventions have also been used successfully to help clients with schizophrenia manage psychosis (Chadwick, Taylor, & Abba, 2005) and anxiety (Davis, Strasburger, & Brown, 2007) more effectively.

Attending to the present moment is considered to be both a skill and an intervention in that one can teach clients to direct attention to the immediate moment and, as a result, enable them to displace or replace negative preoccupations. As clients, for example, use breathing as a vehicle to focus on the present (i.e., enhance mindfulness), they are by definition less distracted by internal preoccupations and can learn to focus their attention more effectively on the immediate moment.

Clients with schizophrenia, in particular, may benefit from mindfulness interventions. However, clients may need more "scaffolding" and environmental prompting to engage in mindfulness as they may be constitutionally prone to ruminating, which contributes to their tendency to seem preoccupied or sometimes unaware of their surroundings. The BMR exercises provide a structure through which clients can practice mindfulness and focus their attention on the immediate situation. The BMR exercises also interfere with clients' ongoing "rumination process" or obsessive preoccupation with internal thoughts. This is analogous to a "counter-conditioning principle," whereby an incompatible behavior, when it occurs, displaces the behavior in question. In this context, a "positively valued" behavior (i.e., movement and relaxation) displaces a "negatively valued" behavior (i.e., rumination).

BMR Exercises

The BMR exercises consist of asking group members to stand up with their feet about shoulder's width apart and knees slightly bent, almost in a skiing posture. The feet are firmly grounded, with a sense of one's body being connected to the earth. Group members are instructed to inhale with a closed mouth and exhale with an open mouth for a total of ten repetitions. A "form of Tai Chi movement exercise" is also added by instructing group members to move their hands up and down in a rhythmic fashion, with both hands in slow motion all the time (i.e., no stopping at all), which helps to maximize concentration and attention. Specifically, group members are instructed to raise their hands with palms up and elbows slightly bent when inhaling, and to lower their hands with palms down and elbows slightly bent while exhaling. One can introduce visual imagery such as: "As you look up, you see the blue sky and birds flying, and you are feeling great." When a client is leading the exercise, it is best just to use the ten counting repetitions and not require that the client introduce visual imagery unless he or she is comfortable doing so.

One can also use a modified movement exercise by asking the group members to stand firm, move only one hand up and down without stopping and watch the hand move, and then do the same exercise with the other hand. This promotes awareness of the movement of one's body part and fosters more focused attention and concentration. It also promotes a sense of contentment and "feeling good" by seeing and experiencing one's own body movement (i.e., the hand moving up and down without stopping). The range of motion should be at each individual's comfort level, as some clients may have limitations in their movement ability due to, for example, arthritis or medication side effects. The purpose of this exercise is different from physical therapy exercises, in that the primary goal is to induce a sense of contentment and positive feelings associated with the experience of one's body, independent of any physical limitations. The exercise helps to reaffirm positive feelings that one is "alive and on this earth" and to promote a feeling of contentment in experiencing the movement of one's body.

Following the BMR exercises, clients are often instructed to look around and notice different things in the room as well as to note the presence of different group members. This helps to promote "mindfulness." Group members are encouraged to be aware of being "alive" and to be aware of the "present reality" of their existence. At times, this can also be used by the therapist as a discussion topic to describe the process of "existential living." "Existential living" can be discussed as something all of us experience—a series of momentary experiences we all go through and which give us a sense of connection to all human beings. This can also lead to discussing "what is real and present" versus "what is not real and not present."

The group leader can also explain how the BMR exercises promote goal attainment by specifying the steps needed to achieve a goal and evaluating the completion of the goal. The group leader may decide to continue with a discussion of clients' individual treatment plans, how treatment plan goals are conceptualized, how the steps to achieve a particular goal are specified, and how one evaluates the attainment of a goal.

The BMR exercises provide a technique for increased awareness of one's immediate "living existence" by making the group members more aware of their own body movements, and thereby enhancing their perception of the immediate physical and social reality. In the process, the exercises promote adaptive behavior for the immediate situation clients are experiencing. In addition, heightened agitation and anxiety symptoms that many persons with schizophrenia demonstrate may be reduced or managed more effectively by learning and practicing mindfulness and relaxation through the BMR exercises.

Goals for the BMR Exercises

- to provide a positive and "goal-directed" mental set for the beginning of the group and to use this same exercise to signal the end of the group, enabling clients to leave the group with a positive feeling;
- for clients to learn how to focus on inner body cues and learn to relax through a brief and "easy-to-implement" exercise;
- for clients to learn how to focus on a specific activity, which can redirect attention from internal ruminations and preoccupations with "psychiatric symptoms";
- to provide clients with a practical experience in leading the group through modeling a "peer group leader" (members rotate in this role), which promotes assertive communication in social interactions and a positive self-image;
- for clients to learn how to practice a relaxed and assertive body posture by standing firm and erect, and to feel more comfortable and confident in the immediate social environment;

- for clients to become more "mindful" of the present moment and the reality of the immediate physical and social world, and in the process, enhance their capacity to adapt to the present structure of the group routine;
- for clients to practice goal attainment by following the structure and "goal" of the exercise (i.e., counting from one to ten), which helps them to link how their individual treatment plans are formulated and expectations of steps they need to take to reach a specific goal;
- for clients to learn to practice BMR exercises outside the group session for ongoing relaxation and control of agitation symptoms.

Conducting the BMR Exercises

CLINICIAN INSTRUCTIONS

The group leader briefly explains the rationale for the exercises by stating or paraphrasing the following:

"WE WILL BEGIN WITH A DEEP BREATHING EXERCISE TO HELP US RELAX AND BECOME AWARE OF OUR BREATHING AS WELL AS OUR BODY MOVEMENTS. THIS EXERCISE REMINDS US THAT WE ARE ALIVE AND ARE CONNECTED TO THE EARTH. WE WANT TO PRACTICE BEING AWARE OF OUR BREATHING, OUR BODY MOVEMENT, AND THE IMMEDIATE PRESENT MOMENT. IN THE PROCESS, WE BECOME MORE ALERT, THINK MORE CLEARLY, AND LEARN TO RELAX AND NOT FEEL STRESSED."

The group leader then describes the exercises:

"WE WILL PERFORM THE BREATHING EXERCISE TEN TIMES BY COUNTING OUT LOUD TO TEN. COUNTING PROVIDES US WITH THE STEPS NEEDED TO REACH OUR GOAL OF TEN REPETITIONS."

"PLEASE STAND UP. WHILE STANDING UP, SLIGHTLY BEND YOUR KNEES TO FEEL THE WEIGHT OF YOUR BODY GROUNDED TO THE EARTH. YOUR STANCE SHOULD BE SIMILAR TO SOMEONE IN A SKIING POSITION."

(The leader demonstrates the posture: see Figure 3.1 below.)

"WITH YOUR KNEES SLIGHTLY BENT, BREATHE IN THROUGH YOUR NOSE WITH YOUR MOUTH CLOSED, AND THEN BREATHE

OUT THROUGH YOUR MOUTH KEEPING YOUR MOUTH SLIGHTLY OPENED."

"AS YOU FOCUS ON YOUR BREATHING, NOTICE WHAT YOU ARE DOING AND HOW YOU ARE WORKING TOWARD YOUR GOAL OF TEN REPETITIONS."

"LET'S PRACTICE THE BREATHING AND COUNTING. WE WILL COUNT OUT LOUD EACH COMPLETE REPETITION UNTIL WE REACH TEN . . . READY . . . GO."

"NOW, WE ARE GOING TO DO IT SLIGHLY DIFFERENTLY. THIS TIME YOU WILL ALSO MOVE BOTH OF YOUR HANDS PALMS UP AS YOU BREATHE IN THROUGH YOUR NOSE, AND MOVE YOUR HAND PALMS DOWN WITH BOTH ELBOWS POINTED DOWN AS YOU BREATHE OUT THROUGH YOUR MOUTH. THE MOVEMENT OF YOUR HANDS SHOULD ALWAYS BE CONTINUOUS."

(The leader demonstrates the movements: see Figure 3.2 below.)

"LET'S DO THE FULL EXERCISE NOW. WE WILL COUNT OUT LOUD EACH COMPLETE REPETITION UNTIL WE REACH TEN. REMEMBER AS YOU BREATHE IN WITH YOUR MOUTH CLOSED, RAISE YOUR HANDS. AS YOU BREATHE OUT WITH YOUR MOUTH SLIGHTLY OPENED, LOWER YOUR HANDS. READY . . . GO."

FIGURE 3.1 Person in standing/skiing position

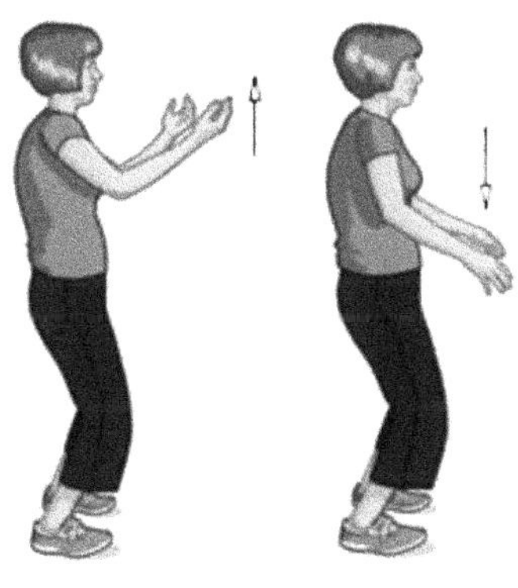

FIGURE 3.2 Person raising hands up and down

Note: *The group leader can add this alternative "one hand arm movement" version as needed. When asking members to stand with knees slightly bent, instruct them to move only one hand during the arm movements, but always maintaining focus on the moving hand (the group leader may need to demonstrate). Again, have the members do the exercise for a count of ten breathing repetitions.*

Optional: *Additional comment to be added if using the "one hand" version:*

"THIS EXERCISE HELPS US TO FOCUS ON OUR BODY MOVEMENT MORE DEEPLY, TO FEEL GOOD TO SEE HOW OUR HAND IS MOVING UP AND DOWN, AND FEEL GOOD TO BE ALIVE IN THIS WORLD. WE ARE HAVING AN EXPERIENCE OF TOTAL CONCENTRATION DURING THIS EXERCISE, AND WHILE WE ARE DOING THIS, WE ARE NOT THINKING ABOUT ANYTHING ELSE. WE ARE LEARNING TO TAKE A BREAK FROM OUR TROUBLESOME THOUGHTS. IT IS TEACHING US HOW TO LEARN TO PUSH AWAY NEGATIVE THOUGHTS AND CONCENTRATE ON SOMETHING POSITIVE. THIS IS HOW WE PRACTICE DOING DIFFERENT THINGS ON A DAILY BASIS, PUSHING OUR ANXIOUS AND TROUBLING THOUGHTS AWAY AND FOCUSING ON SOMETHING THAT MAKES US FEEL GOOD."

Optional: *The leader can reiterate the following before or after the BMR exercises:*

"BY FOCUSING ON THIS ACTIVITY AND PRACTICING OUR BREATHING, WE ARE PAYING ATTENTION TO OUR BODY AND THE PRESENT MOMENT. WE ARE NOT PAYING ATTENTION TO NEGATIVE THOUGHTS OR FEELINGS THAT SOMETIMES BOTHER US. WE ARE FEELING GOOD THAT WE ARE ALIVE AND CAN NOTICE OUR BODY WORKING AND MOVING. AS WE LOOK UP WHEN WE INHALE AND EXHALE, WE FORGET ABOUT OUR PERSONAL PROBLEMS AND SEE OURSELVES CONNECTED TO THE UNIVERSE AROUND US."

"WE ARE LEARNING TO PRACTICE A RELAXED AND ASSERTIVE BODY POSTURE, STANDING TALL AND ERECT, AND TO FEEL COMFORTABLE IN THE CURRENT SOCIAL ENVIRONMENT. WE ARE ALL PRACTICING THIS AS A GROUP AND WORKING TOGETHER."

"WE ARE ALSO LEARNING HOW TO PRACTICE REACHING A GOAL THAT WE SET UP. THAT IS WHY WE DO THIS EXERCISE TEN TIMES, AND COUNT EVERY TIME WE DO IT. THIS IS SIMILAR TO STEPS WE HAVE TO TAKE TO REACH A GOAL AND BEING ABLE TO FEEL GOOD WHEN WE REACH THE GOAL WE SET OUT TO DO."

Optional: *At the end of the BMR exercise, the leader can say:*

"NOW, WHILE YOU ARE IN A RELAXED NORMAL POSITION (STANDING), I WANT YOU TO LOOK AROUND AND NOTICE FIRST EACH MEMBER OF THE GROUP PRESENT. THINK ABOUT THEIR NAMES, IF YOU CAN, THEN LOOK AT ALL THE DETAILS IN THE ROOM: NOTICE THE FURNITURE, PICTURES HANGING, DOORS, AND WINDOWS ALL AROUND YOU."

"LOOK BEHIND YOU, SO THAT YOU ARE NOW KEENLY AWARE OF YOUR IMMEDIATE SURROUNDINGS. THIS WAY WE ARE AWARE OF OUR PRESENT IMMEDIATE SOCIAL AND PHYSICAL ENVIRONMENT, AND IT AUTOMATICALLY GUIDES OUR MIND TO HELP US FIGURE OUT WHAT TO DO. AS WE FOCUS ON OUR SURROUNDINGS, WE DO NOT GET CAUGHT UP IN THINKING ABOUT OUR PAST OR FUTURE, WHICH IS NOT THE REALITY AT THIS MOMENT. A LOT OF TIMES IN OUR LIFE, WE CAN FORGET TO BE PRESENT-ORIENTED. AS A RESULT, WE MAY NOT FUNCTION AS WELL AS WE COULD IN A GIVEN SITUATION."

Note: *Group members may rotate in leading the BMR exercises for each group session. When a client leads the BMR exercise, it is best to eliminate any visual imagery and have the client focus rather on just counting through the ten breathing repetitions.*

Practicing the BMR exercises at the beginning of the group provides a structured framework to initiate members' participation in the group and to ease their transition into the other group activities. Many persons with schizophrenia can demonstrate an "independent" way of thinking and behaving, with a history of "authority conflicts," or resistance to following group social norms. This structured group exercise practiced at the beginning of the group prepares clients for participation in the group with a positive frame of mind, and helps them leave the session in the same way, as the exercise is also practiced before leaving the group.

Independent of any physical discomfort, other difficulties, or a "negative" attitude that some clients may exhibit, we encourage them to participate in the BMR exercise to their ability level. The therapist focuses on demonstrating the technique, rather than on evaluating or correcting individual group members' level of participation. Clients are praised for whatever aspect of the exercise (partial or full) they are able to perform.

Taking turns in initiating and following the group exercise also promotes adherence to a given therapeutic structure and highlights the value of following and accepting a group routine. Leading the exercise also allows the client to experience a sense of renewed self-confidence and to get real-life practice in playing an assertive social role, an opportunity which is often lacking in their daily life. For clients who otherwise habitually act as socially withdrawn and "timid," we have observed notable behavior changes characterized by clients learning to adopt "a more assertive posture" and learning how to increase their verbalizations in the group.

Below we include two clinical vignettes, which describe situations whereby clients, in spite of limitations and difficulties in responding fully to other aspects of MICST group activities, were able to respond positively to the BMR component and benefit from group participation.

Clinical Vignette: Tammy

Tammy has a long hospitalization history with a diagnosis of paranoid schizophrenia with forensic involvement. She is generally verbally underproductive during most of the group sessions. She responds to questions by nodding or using one-word phrases. She may say "Yes" to questions asked, but will indicate "No" by non-verbal gestures.

Tammy will not respond to any questions related to personal opinions or memory, but does reasonably well on paper–pencil exercises involving neutral topics, such as questions requiring her to recall general information or facts and problem-solving-type questions. Her difficulty in verbalizing any comments related to her mental illness symptoms or verbalizing a commitment to a specific discharge plan presents a barrier to her community placement.

During the MICST group, however, Tammy does extremely well in practicing the BMR exercises. She is able to demonstrate a very relaxed posture and exhibits a high level of concentration in performing the exercises. Over the years, her mood has become more positive. She is considered to be clinically stable, and her level of privileges has increased. Her quality of life within the hospital setting has improved as indicated by her increased level of participation in a variety of activities compared to baseline.

For this client, practicing deep breathing exercises gives her a sense of connection to the group process, even though her personal memory is disordered. She is able to follow a routine with a structured task, such as deep breathing exercises or paper–pencil exercises, but is unable to participate actively in traditional conversational and theme-focused therapy.

In spite of Tammy's "paranoid stance," "non-cooperative" attitude, and conscious or subconscious withholding of information related to her personal opinions or treatment plan issues, she is able to participate meaningfully in some aspects of the group treatment, showing clinical stability and progress over time.

Clinical Vignette: Coby

Coby has a history of a mild learning disability and substance abuse, as well as several psychiatric hospitalizations with follow-up care in a community mental health center. Coby has had difficulty adhering to any treatment regimen, and was homeless before being admitted to a residential program. He has difficulty in participating in group discussions, and gets easily confused when personal questions are asked, but at times will ask relevant questions. He does well with paper–pencil exercises with guidance and support, and does extremely well with the BMR exercises, maintaining a relaxed posture.

Despite his school learning difficulties and failure experiences, compounded by the fact that his learning disability issues were unrecognized, Coby responded very positively to the MICST group setting, which reminded him of a supportive classroom learning environment, which he probably missed or longed for.

Over a period of time, Coby showed slow and steady progress in participating in all phases of group activities, but was most productive during the BMR exercises and paper–pencil exercises. He showed difficulties in participating in group discussions which required oral communication. This may have been due to his schizophrenia symptoms in combination with his learning issues which were characterized by difficulties in organizing and expressing thoughts and emotions verbally. Nevertheless, his level of participation in other aspects of the MICST group was high, and he would not have been responsive to more traditional conversational modes of psychotherapy.

Most of the clients participate to the best of their ability during the BMR exercises. Even though some may have difficulty coordinating breathing with rhythmic hand movements, often reflecting side effects from long-term use of anti-psychotic medication or the deficits in sensorimotor functioning associated with schizophrenia, many take obvious pride in participating in and leading the exercises. From time to time, members are asked how the BMR exercises have been helpful. Clients are able to verbalize how the exercises set the tone for the group, provide them with relaxation training, ensure circulation of air and oxygen to the body, help improve their focus on the present, improve their concentration, and help to redirect their mind from "troubling thoughts."

Client Feedback and Reflections on the BMR Exercises

Below are session examples in which the group members contributed their own ideas in responding to the question "Why do we do the deep breathing (BMR) exercises?"

Please note that this kind of discussion has been repeated in the group to reinforce the benefits of the BMR exercises. The ideas expressed have some commonality across the three group samples provided below. The therapist usually wrote the responses on the blackboard for everyone to see and reflect on, and at the time, had to paraphrase some responses for clarity. This process of sharing provides the contributing group members with a sense of "ownership" of the ideas written on the blackboard and enhances their positive self-image.

Session Example 1

1. "Rejuvenate"
2. "Concentrate"
3. "Increase IQ" (thinking power)
4. "Preparation for group . . . ending group"
5. "Oxygen to the brain . . . circulation of blood"
6. "Diminished tension/muscle tension"
7. "Push away bad thoughts"
8. "Be positive . . . think positive"
9. "Soul searching"
10. "Meditate"
11. "Clearing of thoughts"
12. "Eliminate stress"
13. "Focus."

Session Example 2

1. "Feel more alert"
2. "Feeling more receptive," "Knowing what is going on in your environment," "Helps you feel well rested"
3. "Clean slate"
4. "Fresh mind," "Leave confusion and misunderstanding behind"
5. "Stop depressing thoughts"
6. "Think positive," "Focus thoughts on positive things rather than on the negatives"
7. "Relaxation/meditation"
8. "Helpful in setting goals"
9. "Experience of success."

Session Example 3

1. "Relax (body then mind)"
2. "Focus on (one thing)"
3. "Think about God or Supreme Being
4. "(Mantra) or soothing word repeating"
5. "Mental exercise"
6. "Different types of postures"
7. "Set time limit"

8. "Restore/replace normal thoughts"
9. "Different types of meditation."

One can see from the responses how group members can collectively articulate and express insightful and sophisticated thoughts about a therapeutic issue and topic. This shows that many clients, in spite of their overt "expression of disability" in thinking and articulation, when given an opportunity through a particular therapeutic "structure" or environment, can access their own intact capacity for reasoning and insight and express this in a profound and clear manner.

Additionally, it illustrates that achieving insight and understanding of their emotional difficulties and gaining knowledge of coping strategies, which is often the focus of traditional psychotherapy, may not be a necessary therapy goal or the most productive use of therapy. That is, clients may already have adequate insight and knowledge in these areas. Rather, it is more likely that their diminished capacity to act upon this knowledge and to use effective coping strategies consistently may be due, in part, to other issues such as possible entrenched idiosyncratic habits of feeling and behaving due to chronic internal stress and agitation experiences, and a lack of opportunities to practice these "dormant" skills through mind stimulation activities.

Stimulating the cerebellum through the BMR exercises may help to promote not only movement, but also "cognitive stimulation" and the emergence of "insightful" ideas expressed in the context of a therapeutic group structure. Research shows that the cerebellum is increasingly being identified as an important "site" for reasoning and thinking besides being a known site for motor coordination and movement (Gallese & Lakoff, 2005).

Therapists, in explaining the value of the BMR exercises, emphasize the value of positive redirection. The therapist highlights how schizophrenia symptoms frequently manifest in obsessive ruminations of specific thoughts in which clients often find themselves absorbed. This can lead to clients losing the capacity to be aware of their environment and to redirect themselves successfully to current tasks or social cues. Thus, the simple BMR exercises are used not only to practice redirection, but also to provide a basis for discussing and understanding one of the core symptoms of schizophrenia—ruminative thinking. The exercises promote logical thinking and insight that may lie nascent and "inaccessible" to them. Finally, considering the variable functioning of clients, and difficulties they may have in sustaining attention and movement over more prolonged periods, the exercise is kept brief. This allows most, if not all, of the clients to experience some degree of success in performing the exercise.

Since clients are able to articulate the benefits of the BMR exercises, and given that the exercises can easily be taught to outpatient counselors or mental health workers in inpatient facilities, we recommend that the BMR exercises become incorporated into clients' daily routine to promote positive feelings and confidence, and to help them minimize agitation or restlessness. We conclude with *homework recommendations* on how to incorporate the BMR exercises into clients' daily routine.

HOMEWORK RECOMMENDATIONS

General Recommendations

- A handout describing the BMR exercises can be given to each client to help guide the practice of the exercises in between group sessions (see *Handout 4: BMR Exercise Instructions*). The time and schedule for individual practice of the exercises can be determined based on the client's style and motivation and on recommendations from mental health staff.
- Ideally, the exercise should be practiced 1–2 times a day. Clients may be instructed to practice the exercises on a routine basis as well as use the exercises to control agitation and anxiety symptoms as needed. Routine daily practice will allow the formation of a "habit," which clients can later "activate" whenever they feel distressed.
- To maximize staff cooperation in reinforcing follow-up practice, a brief in-service training on the facets of mindfulness and BMR exercises can be provided to staff. It would be helpful to have the support of administrative and clinical staff to ensure ongoing success in implementing the exercises within the clients' treatment.
- Specific instruction for group practice can be given to the residential manager or mental health counselor. The instructions can outline when and where to practice as well as highlight the rationale for performing the exercises.

Specific Recommendations for Individual Practice

- Encourage clients to chart their daily practice using *Worksheet 1: BMR Charting Record.*
- The charting can be used to evaluate compliance and progress and to record the benefits achieved from the exercises.
- Post the practice guide and monitoring chart in the client's room.
- Encourage the client to practice the exercises independently 1–2 times a day.
- Encourage the client to report practice back to the group as needed to reinforce the intervention and to share experiences with other group members.
- Review the practice schedule with the client as needed.
- Practice the exercises with the client once a week and discuss the benefits of and rationale for the exercises (similar to ongoing medication check-ins and discussions of the benefits of medication compliance).

Other BMR-type Exercises: Psychomotor Exercises

- Clients may be encouraged to practice using a stress ball by catching it one hand at a time or squeezing the ball for some sensorimotor stimulation. This complements the BMR exercises practiced in the group setting. Staff can also engage in "creative interactions" involving a stress ball whereby clients are instructed to catch the ball when their name is called. This helps clients develop body movement awareness and anticipatory behavior, which is essential to adaptation.

- In the same vein, "hands on" exercises, such as gardening, fishing, working on puzzles, as well as psychomotor movement exercises involving "light sports" like table tennis or walking, should be promoted as part of the client's routine.

Chapter 4

Group Discussion Exercises

Mind Stimulation of Episodic Memory, Semantic Memory, Personal Interests, Existential Perspectives, and Mental Health Topics

This chapter discusses the various ways that group discussions are used in MICST and the rationale and goals for the discussions. The group discussions are used to assist clients in sharing thoughts, ideas, knowledge, and questions across a potential broad range of topics. A primary aim of the group discussions is to provide clients with a framework to stimulate their episodic memory, long-term and semantic memory, share their personal interests and knowledge, and increase their awareness of interpersonal communication rules. Another important goal is to use the group discussions to enhance clients' positive self-worth through providing them with opportunities to communicate and share their knowledge and personal interests. The group discussions are also designed to actively stimulate and access clients' dormant but intact cognitive skills. We provide a set of *clinician instructions* for how best to shape group discussions into reality-based discussions, and conclude with *homework recommendations*, suggesting various ways that clinicians can assist clients in engaging in meaningful mind stimulating activities outside the group sessions.

In the process of focusing on specific group discussion topics, clients learn to displace their preoccupations with self-ruminating thoughts, and to reduce their sense of isolation. The format of the group discussions also facilitates clients' willingness to accept feedback about their thinking and to incorporate new ideas and information. They also learn to develop a sense of "feeling good" about sharing their thoughts and knowledge. This is analogous to our everyday experiences, when, for example, we meet friends or go to social gatherings and enjoy talking about different topics and sharing our thoughts and ideas. In addition to being structured like a therapy group session, MICST also incorporates elements of a structured classroom learning environment. Many clients often refer to the group as "class" in a positive way, in spite of the fact that some of them may have had poor school learning histories; they appear to look forward to the group meetings as a forum for a positive learning experience that they may have missed in their lives.

The discussion topics are usually based on clients' spontaneous verbalizations during the sessions. This gives clients a "sense of ownership" of ideas and makes the discussion topics relevant to their personal lives. Clinicians need to be astute in extracting a given idea or spontaneous thought expressed by a client and turning this into a structured discussion topic. The goal is to use the topic to facilitate participation from all group members so as to enhance knowledge and information (we provide examples later in the chapter to illustrate how discussion topics can be extracted from clients' spontaneous verbalizations). The topics are often varied, reflecting a wide range of clients' knowledge and interests. Also, particular attention is paid by the therapist to identifying when a topic broached by a client's spontaneous "utterances" may lead to a discussion of a mental health topic or theme.

Social skills "training," interpersonal communication "training," and learning about mental health coping strategies are done through modeling and discussing facets and aspects of communication as needed rather than through, for example, following a social skills or mental health coping skills curriculum. As such, the therapist does not ordinarily come to the session with a "definitive agenda" for discussing certain topics, but rather is open to exploring spontaneous topics.

Throughout the group discussion phase, the therapist uses clinical judgment to determine whether the discussion of a particular topic is going to be "clinically" helpful to the group. This is where the therapist's clinical training and skills come into play, in deciding what to highlight versus what to ignore, all the while keeping in mind the group members' interests and the potential benefits each can derive from the discussion. For example, a client in the course of a discussion may make reference to sleeping difficulties, attending a treatment plan meeting, participating in a family visit, or meeting with his/her psychiatrist. The therapist may then "on the spot" decide to shape one or more of these issues into a discussion topic.

This "selecting" of topics and discussion themes, we believe, parallels the role that therapists often play in directing conversations in traditional therapy sessions. For example, even in "non-directive" therapy sessions, the therapist often highlights certain utterances, ignores others, and uses the client's spontaneous reporting to guide the therapy. This process of selecting a particular utterance for a discussion topic is analogous to what we consider the "*browsing technique*," which one uses in researching topics on the Internet. The therapist is exploring the knowledge base of group members in an active and "adventurous" manner to determine what knowledge and skills may be accessible through prompting, browsing, and stimulating clients' interests and knowledge.

The therapist uses clinical judgment to determine how long to sustain a discussion topic without group members losing interest or becoming "stressed" or uncomfortable. Also, the therapist determines when to change the discussion topic or move on to other structured group activities. Some clients may, at times, express difficulties in staying focused on a discussion topic, and may show restlessness, agitation, or disruptive behavior tendencies. Instead of asking a client, for example, to leave the group, the therapist or co-therapist usually redirects the client to paper–pencil cognitive exercises or another structured exercise such as reviewing the pictorial content of a book. The therapist will later attempt to direct the client back to the discussion when the he or she appears amenable to it. The goals for the group discussions are listed below.

Goals for the Group Discussions

- *promote social interaction and communication*, recognizing that persons with schizophrenia often appear preoccupied, and sometimes have difficulty paying attention to their social surrounding or interactions with others;
- *raise self-awareness* through discussions and group interactions that will enable clients to pay more attention to personal hygiene and daily goals, both of which are important in the recovery process;
- *enable clients to practice basic social communication skills*, such as asking questions of other group members and learning to pay attention to what the other members are saying;
- *encourage clients to practice recalling personal events*, as episodic memory (information about one's personal history) is often impaired, and help group members practice communicating events and information in ways that others can understand;
- *promote "here and now" discussions* and reporting of current activities to help clients focus on the immediate environment and present life circumstances, and in the process, displace habitual preoccupying "negative thoughts and feelings" from the past;
- *promote discussions of various general knowledge topics* as a way to stimulate long-term and semantic memory and other "intact areas" of memory;
- *create enthusiasm for practicing "information exchange"* about factual matters, which promotes reality-based conversations and enables the client to experience normal feelings of "elation," countering "anhedonia," which can be a characteristic symptom of schizophrenia;
- *promote discussion of mental health-related issues* from a therapeutic learning and coping perspective in a format that allows sharing, reflection, and participation;
- *help clients to accept a sense of duality of living experiences*, with a sense of "comfort" with both their inner world of fantasy (characterized by "autistic-like withdrawal" or private idiosyncratic beliefs), and their immediate social and physical world; and in the process, help them learn how to practice switching from one world to the other in the group setting. This strengthens clients' capacity for "positive redirection" from "autistic preoccupation," through the "structure" of the group activities;
- *enable clients to practice using communication rules* to help others understand what they are talking about by distinguishing between their own private and "atypical thoughts," which others cannot understand and their more logical ideas and thoughts, which can be consensually validated, communicated more clearly, and understood in the group setting;
- *promote discussions of spiritual and faith issues* and existential perspectives of living to help clients discuss universal "uncertainties of living," and to provide a sense of connection to other human beings;
- *help clients to learn to accept "corrective feedback"* to their thinking and knowledge base, making them amenable to suggestions and feedback from others, and in the process, reducing "cognitive rigidity."

The therapist may highlight the rules of communication by using a Venn diagram (see Figure 4.1 below) to illustrate atypical and personal thoughts that cannot be communicated effectively to others versus thoughts that are logical and can be consensually validated and communicated effectively to others. This strategy has been very helpful in diverting a discussion about a client's atypical thoughts or experiences (e.g., delusions or hallucinations), without passing a value judgment on the client.

The therapist does not label thoughts and feelings as "delusions" or "hallucinations," but rather labels them as "atypical experiences" that are difficult to communicate to others and difficult for others to understand. A primary goal of the group discussion is to find a common point of reference or a "consensual" communication framework that will facilitate reality-based conversations.

Clients may be encouraged to discuss their "atypical thoughts or experience," if they are important, with their mental health counselor in follow-up individual sessions. However, at times, a client's reporting of "atypical experiences" (e.g., auditory or visual hallucinations) can be used to facilitate a psycho-educational discussion of the best ways to manage these symptoms in the context of current knowledge in the mental health field.

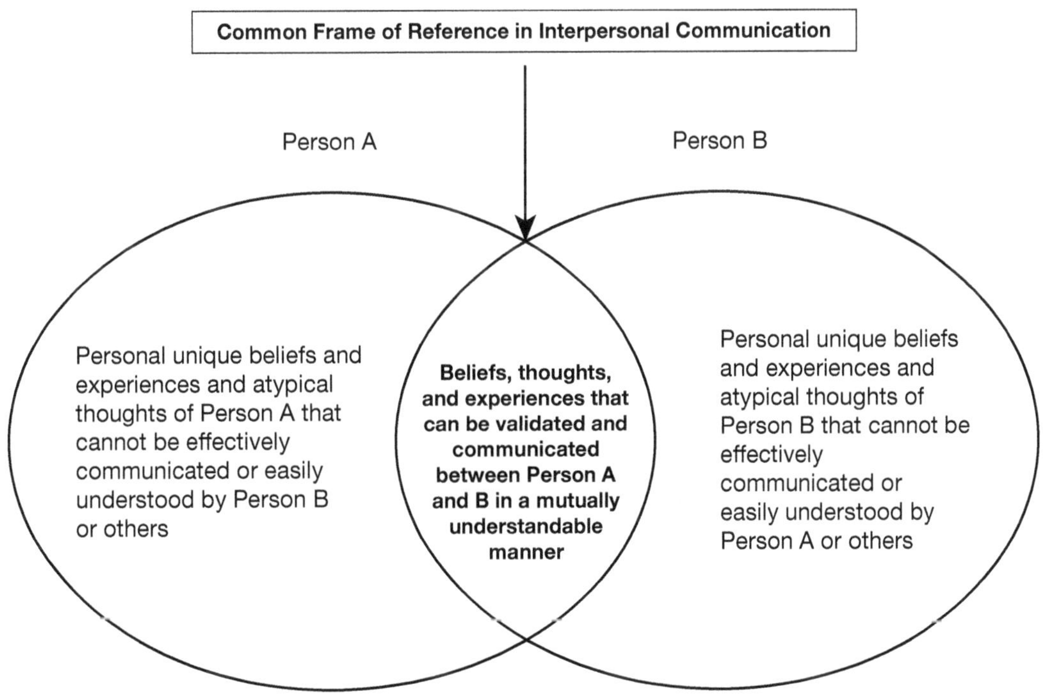

FIGURE 4.1 Venn diagram used to redirect group members to reality-based conversation by illustrating "rules of communication" and the goal of achieving "consensually validated" and "mutually understandable" communication

The discussion phase of the group is characterized by three components, each of which is described below.

Three Components of Group Discussions

Discussion of the Past Week's Activities

The group discussion phase usually starts by asking group members to report on their past week's activities. This discussion can occur in the following ways:

1. the group leader asks each group member in turn to report an activity from their past week; or
2. the group leader asks one member to report an activity from their past week, and then that group member asks any other group member to report on his or her week. The process continues until all group members have been asked to report an activity from the past week.

At times, group members can also report on an activity they plan to do in the upcoming week to help them with goal setting and planning activities. During the reporting, the therapist can take note on an easel or blackboard of a topic broached that could lend itself to a more formal discussion.

The group discussion is structured and operates from a short-term *past–present–future* framework to help clients stay focused on the here and now of their current life experiences. For the sake of time management and "relevancy," the therapist uses active redirection strategies when clients may be spending too much time on a topic or reporting too much detail.

Examples of activities and topics that clients have discussed during the reporting of their past week's events are as follows:

- family visit or contact;
- special activities in the residence;
- day program activity attendance;
- treatment team meeting attendance;
- birthdays;
- holidays (recent, past, or upcoming, preparation, gift buying);
- personal physical health issues (e.g., sleeping problem, physical discomfort, dental or other medical appointments);
- personal mental health issue (e.g., bothersome symptoms, medication change);
- discharge goals (e.g., "I want to get out of the hospital" . . . "I want to move to another residence" . . . "I want to go back to live by myself");
- sports watched;
- television shows or movies watched;
- current news events;
- vocational or volunteer work activities.

Discussion of General Knowledge Topics

The second component involves discussing any general knowledge topic that a group member may bring up spontaneously while discussing his or her past week's events or during other discussions in the group. The group leader may use this general knowledge topic to stimulate clients' interest, logical associations, memory, knowledge base (e.g., semantic and "intact" memory), to affirm their connection to the social world, or to promote motivation for "social exchange of information." In our everyday life, all of us routinely stimulate our knowledge base by engaging in activities such as reading newspapers, magazines, or books, listening to the radio, or watching TV. We also commonly exchange knowledge about various topics of interest such as politics, current events, books, TV shows, entertainment news, or sports. During group discussions, the therapist actively infuses some degree of natural enthusiasm and excitement that we often feel when participating in these types of discussions during our everyday social interactions.

At times, the clinician may not have the relevant information or knowledge about some of the questions and issues raised by group members. The MICST model does not require the therapist or group members to be knowledgeable about all the different topics discussed in the group. However, this should not prevent the therapist from partially addressing these topics. It is imperative that the clinician, in these encounters, does not become defensive, but remains open to exploring different topics, without implying that he or she has full or complete knowledge about the topic. This way, independent of his or her knowledge, the clinician will be comfortable following the lead taken by a group member in further discussing the topic. This allows clients who may have knowledge about a topic to share this knowledge and teach other group members, and in the process feel positive about contributing to the group.

It is best for the therapist to explore what knowledge of the topic exists in the group by using a didactic format. The clinician can then monitor the discussion to ensure that the other group members can benefit from the discussion within the "therapeutic guidelines" of MICST. The therapist can act as a facilitator, and if needed, can suggest that a group member or a co-leader (e.g., a student therapist or a mental health worker) research the topic further and bring back information and possibly handouts on the topic to the next group session (see *Worksheet 8*: *Data Collection Worksheet for a Topic*).

At times, some group members may allude to the "existential perspective of life" by reporting on personal losses or current life changes. The therapist may then facilitate a discussion on universal "existential issues" such as dealing with life's "uncertainties." The therapist may also take this opportunity to discuss various religious faiths or, for example, science-based knowledge about astronomy. In presenting this science-based knowledge about the universe, the therapist makes a point of not contradicting any group member's personal religious faith, but highlights how many human beings face the world of uncertainties by practicing different forms of religion to deal with this experience. The therapist supports individual clients' preference for or practice of a religious faith to help normalize the reality of human beings using different ways to cope with life's uncertainties.

Below is a sample of topics discussed during 15 different sessions of a MICST group. In many of the sessions, the therapist played an active role by initiating a discussion of a topic based on the spontaneous utterances of clients during the group.

Sample General Knowledge Discussion Topics

Session 1. Ancestral origin: the type of work parents did for a living, remembering ages of siblings, and other pertinent family information.

Session 2. Geography/astronomy: capitals of U.S. states and countries, astronomical facts, recent discoveries.

Session 3. Educational attainments of various group members: favorite academic subjects, and subjects that were challenging in various phases of one's schooling (e.g., elementary, secondary, high school).

Session 4. Miscellaneous topics: automobiles owned by clients or family members, individual work histories, and brain functioning and anatomy.

Session 5. 1) Map reading skills; 2) Demonstration of a Tai Chi exercise that two group members observed at a Senior Center.

Session 6. 1) World Series record of New York Yankees and Boston Red Sox baseball teams (reflecting a group member's sports interest); *2) Uncertainty in living:* the sun's revolution around the galactic center and what it means related to our own uncertainties in living and our religious faith.

Session 7. World religions, and science-based knowledge about cosmic history: (the therapist makes a point of not challenging or contradicting any one's religious faith, but highlights the fact that many human beings practice some form of religion as part of their faith to deal with the uncertainties of living; astronomy and cosmology subjects are presented as science-based information, different from faith-based knowledge, which cannot be subject to the same "verification" process).

Session 8. Hobbies clients had as children and adolescents, such as collecting coins, stamps, and playing a musical instrument.

Session 9. 1) Sports that group members played; 2) Alcohol or substance abuse in adolescence or adulthood.

Session 10. Meaning of the words "accomplishment" and "inspiration" (from a paper–pencil exercise completed in the prior session), as they relate to one's personal life and experience.

Session 11. Significance of Memorial Day: World War II and other historical events.

Session 12. Travel experiences of group members and discussion of international travel and the currency of different countries (topics generated by the therapist reporting on his recent travel experiences).

Session 13. Martin Luther King Day: what did Martin Luther King stand for, issues of discrimination and acceptance of diversity and how these relate to mentally ill people.

Session 14. Election, voting, and history related to democratic movements, and difference among political systems: socialism, communism, democracy.

Session 15. Interpretation of religious statements: symbolic meaning versus literal meaning; different types of religion; and need for tolerance of diverse faiths.

The list presented is not exhaustive in capturing all the different MICST discussion topics over the years. However, it illustrates the diversity of topics that can be discussed and the various topics that are of interest to clients. Please note that the themes mentioned above may get repeated in different sessions, depending on the interests of group members and the benefits they are deriving from the cognitive and memory stimulation arising from the topic. We have been impressed by the depth of knowledge and recall of facts that many clients demonstrate across a range of topics and subject areas. This depth of clients' knowledge may not be obvious or known even to those with whom the client has regular contact. This may be due, in part, to the tendency of family members or staff to focus encounters with clients on "symptom management" and not use the encounter to discuss other topics that would elicit more readily the depth of the client's general knowledge or interests.

Discussion of Mental Health Topics and Issues

Mental health issues are also discussed in a similar manner to general knowledge topics. The clinician generally extracts the specific topic from clients' spontaneous verbalizations during a group discussion. Often the clinician may note the relevance of the mental health topic during a particular discussion, and facilitate an expanded discussion later on during the group. At times, depending upon the "readiness" of the group, the clinician may immediately launch a discussion of the mental health topic raised and shorten the discussion of clients' past week's activities or curtail a general knowledge topic that may be in progress.

Mental health issues are discussed in a psycho-education format whereby, when any mental health issue is raised, it is treated as a "group issue" rather than a "personal issue." All group members are encouraged to participate to help normalize clients' experiences and to provide an environment of support through sharing of similar experiences. The group leader often uses a blackboard or easel to write down group members' responses to specific questions that the group leader believes will elicit maximum feedback and reflection from group members. Often, to maximize the discussion flow, the clinician may need to paraphrase clients' statements, ensuring that he or she has the client's full agreement to the paraphrased statement. The clinician can expand the discussion by drawing on his or her knowledge about the subject.

Any mental health issue mentioned spontaneously by a client in the course of reporting can be used as an expanded discussion topic. Some examples of client "utterances" that may be expanded upon include: "I did not sleep well last night," "I am depressed," "I had a medication change," "I had a treatment team meeting," "I saw my psychiatrist," "I want to go back to living by myself," "I had a bad experience in hospital . . . they shocked my brain," "I don't like the medication I am taking . . . I feel like getting off of it," "I want to get a job." These utterances can be used as discussion points by soliciting information from other clients, or by making it a collaborative discussion with guided input from various members.

Mental health topics are discussed for a limited time, in view of the fact that clients with long-term mental illness often have difficulty attending to and processing auditory information over a prolonged period without interference from internally produced associations or preoccupation with "psychiatric symptoms." In addition, focusing on "negatively perceived topics" such as one's mental health symptoms or personal deficits may trigger negative associations and feelings.

The clinician can also choose intentionally to introduce a topic by making his or her own associations to the clients' verbalizations, or by bringing in a topic that the clinician believes is relevant and helpful to the particular group. Mental health staff who are co-facilitating the group or who may periodically sit in on a group session can also assist in this process and bring in topics that may be unique to the particular group or the particular group setting (see Appendix A for a list of sample mental health topics discussed during MICST sessions).

Sample Client Responses to Mental Health Discussion Topics

(The examples below represent the actual statements and reflections made by group members, with occasional input from the clinicians to clarify a specific thought expressed by a client.)

Sample Topic 1: Depression

"What are the typical feelings of depression?"

- "Loss of self-esteem"
- "Withdraw and stay in bed"
- "Loss of appetite"
- "Slowed and mixed up thoughts"
- "Feeling down on myself"
- "Feeling lousy"
- "Feeling angry"
- "Eating or sleeping excessively"
- "Not wanting to take care of myself"
- "Hopelessness . . . nothing will go right."

"How do I know that I am depressed?"

- "Sleeping too much"
- "Not caring"
- "I am very sad"
- "Paranoid"
- "Fatigue"
- "Loss of appetite"
- "Iratated" [Irritated]
- "Being silent"
- "Eating too much"
- "Diminished, narrow perspective"
- "Keep using telephone"
- "Don't feel like doing too much"
- "Not caring of cleanliness . . . good hygiene!"
- "Everything seems to be hard or impossible to accomplish"
- "Staying in seclusion in room"
- "Not talking to anyone"
- "Tired"
- "Hearing voices"
- "Drained"
- "Loss of sleep"
- "None"
- "Quiet"
- "Day dreaming"
- "Somewhat negative outlook"
- "Put off showering"
- "Stop caring about accomplishments."

"What Can I Do to Prevent Myself from Getting Depressed?"

- "Go out on grounds pass"
- "Listen to music"
- "Play board games"
- "Use deep breathing"
- "Meditation"
- "Sleep enough"
- "Pay all my debts for the month"
- "Fix up body with pain killer[s]"
- "Keep active, accomplish things you like"
- "Keep a good amount of money"
- "Try to get involved in positive activities and programs"

- "Talk to people . . . Speak to people so you won't get ignored"
- "Hang out with a buddy"
- "Take a shower"
- "Take medications that are prescribed"
- "Get plenty of sleep"
- "Exercise"
- "Think happy thoughts"
- "Eat right"
- "Take meds."

"What Can I Do to Minimize Depression Once I Have It?"

- "Get out of my room and join Day room"
- "Motrin for headaches or other pains"
- "Participate in groups"
- "Talk with friends"
- "Eat right"
- "Take meds"
- "I don't know what to do"
- "Realize what it is"
- "Meditation"
- "Shower"
- "Try to enhance my perspective"
- "Take advice and keep on learning to cooperate"
- "Get busy with something to accomplish things you like or need to do"
- "Take medication till further notification"
- "Have visits"
- "Laugh"
- "Talk to someone"
- "Listen to music"
- "Read"
- "Watching TV"
- "Use deep breathing"
- "Exercise"
- "Walk."

Sample Topic 2: Psychiatric Symptoms

"What Are the Manifestations of My Psychiatric Symptoms?"

- "Loss of self-control"
- "Body movements"

- "Poor concentration"
- "Suspiciousness–paranoia"
- "Mood swings"
- "Hyperactivity"
- "Low motivation"
- "Difficulty in talking or listening"
- "Hearing voices"
- "Thoughts racing"
- "Memory difficulties"
- "Thinking about the same thing"
- "Anger control problem"
- "Anxiety"
- "Low self-esteem"
- "Compulsivity"
- "Delusions"
- "Restlessness."

Sample Topic 3: Stress

"What Are the Causes and Effects of Stress in One's Life?"

(Note: some of the client statements below were paraphrased by the group leader for clarification.)

- "Worrying about performing"
- "Boredom"
- "Sleeplessness"
- "Worrying"
- "Thinking too much about something"
- "Having goals and expectations too high or difficult to meet"
- "Anticipation of what is going to happen, mostly thinking about bad things"
- "Inner tension"
- "Having no money"
- "Agitation."

These responses reflect how, given a supportive learning and teaching environment, clients, in spite of the cognitive and emotional limitations associated with long-term mental illness, can still verbalize issues and concepts to a degree that shows capacity for reflective thinking and insight. This capacity for reflection and insight may not be readily evident in typical conversational therapy with clients or during clients' day-to-day interactions with their peers and staff members.

Below are clinician instructions and guidelines for facilitating the group discussions. The group leader is encouraged to facilitate group discussions using the following strategies.

CLINICIAN INSTRUCTIONS

1. Browse the "Information Internet" of the Client

"Browse" the various topics that the client either alludes to or introduces during his or her spontaneous verbalizations during the group. Decide which topics or issues may lead to a more expanded or reality-based discussion. From past group discussions, use what is known about a client's knowledge base to stimulate further discussion topics in this area. Clients may be called upon at times to share their knowledge of a topic.

Any mental health or general knowledge topic mentioned, such as "I have been feeling depressed," "I am not doing well with my medication adjustment," "I had a treatment team meeting last week," or other interests mentioned such as sports, travel, religious practice, and hobbies can lead to an expanded discussion of the topic in the context of mental health education, general knowledge, or personal history recapitulation.

2. Click onto "Reality-based Links" (RBLs) from the Clients' Verbalizations

RBLs are the more logical thoughts or utterances that are imbedded in a client's verbalizations and linked to "intact" and logical thought processes. These links, when "clicked on," will more likely lead to information that can be consensually validated and agreed upon by other group members; RBLs will also be clues to a client's knowledge base and reflect potential discussion topics.

"Clicking" onto these links will elicit more intact thoughts and memories which the client can more easily expand upon. Deliberately "clicking" onto these links will also help clients focus and shape their thoughts into a more reality-based discussion.

Consider how the therapist clicks onto the reality-based links in the following examples:

Example 1—Clicking onto one link

Therapist (Th): *What did you do this past week?*

Client (Ct): *I don't know . . . I'm doing nothing . . . I keep getting the opposite . . . my lunch is never too strong . . .* ***my sister asked me to go to my niece's soccer game*** *. . . it's all the same . . .*

RBL 1: ***My sister asked me to go to my niece's soccer game***

The therapist can "click" onto this link and see if it brings the client into a more focused and reality-based discussion, despite the client's initial confused presentation.

The therapist could now follow up with:

Th: *Did you ever play soccer?*
Ct: *Yes, in high school.*
Th: *What did you like about soccer?*
Ct: *It was fun. I played goalie.*
Th: *Who else played a sport in high school . . .?*
Th: *How does playing sports and exercise help us . . .?*

This can now lead to an expanded discussion about the value of exercise, or it may lead to a discussion about sports that other group members enjoyed playing. The goal is to extract a theme that can lend itself to a meaningful and reality-based group discussion.

Example 2—Choosing among Multiple Links

Therapist (Th): *What did you do this past week?*
Client (Ct): *I don't know . . . I'm doing nothing . . . I keep getting the opposite . . . my lunch is never too strong . . .* ***my sister asked me to go to my niece's soccer game (1)*** *. . . it's all the same . . .* ***I am always worried something bad is going to happen (2)*** *. . .*

In this exchange, the therapist may choose to "click" onto RBL 2.

RBL 2: ***I am always worried that something bad is going to happen . . .***

The therapist could now follow up with:

Th: *Do other people sometimes feel worried too?*
Ct 2: *Yes, I do sometimes.*
Th: *What events cause us to be worried?*
Ct 3: *I feel nervous walking alone in the city.*
Ct 4: *I worry when I don't know for sure if my father is going to visit me on Sunday.*
Th: *We all have to learn how to cope with life's uncertainties. When we worry, what can we do that will help us cope better?*

The therapist could follow up with a discussion of coping and ways to deal with life's uncertainties. As the topic of anxiety is introduced, group members begin to share their experiences and learn about the universal nature of anxiety and that they are not unique because they feel anxious. The discussion can lead to exploring coping strategies and group members can share strategies and skills they have learned. This can lead to an expanded discussion of coping and remind group members of ways that they can more effectively manage anxiety or worry.

Example 3—Clicking onto a Link within a Link

Therapist (Th): *What did you do this past week?*
Client (Ct): *I don't know . . . I'm doing nothing . . . I keep getting the opposite . . . my lunch is never too strong . . .* ***my sister asked me to go to my niece's soccer game (1)*** *. . . it's all the same . . .* ***I am always anxious and worried something bad is going to happen (2)*** *. . .*

The therapist could now follow-up as before with an inquiry about soccer using **RBL 1**:

Th: *Did you ever play soccer?*
Ct: *Yes, in high school.*
Th: *What did you like about soccer?*
Ct: *It was fun. I played goalie, but* ***I was not as good as others*** (3) . . .

RBL 3 is elicited as the client engages in a more expanded discussion of RBL 1.

The therapist can now "click" onto RBL 3: ***I was not as good as others . . .***

Th: *Sometimes when we play things we may feel that we are not as good as others and this can make us feel down.*
Th: *Sometimes it is more enjoyable to participate in an activity just for the sake of enjoyment and to not compare ourselves to others. We all have different talents and abilities.*

RBL 3 is expanded upon through a follow-up group discussion addressing common life experiences and feelings and how people cope with these feelings. A discussion continues addressing themes of: recognizing one's limitations and strengths, recognizing variability in one's functioning, learning to participate in activities just for the sake of enjoyment without comparisons to others, and ways to avoid getting stuck in one's negative feeling mode.

Example 4—Clicking onto an Episodic Memory Link

Therapist (Th): *What did you do this week?*
Client (Ct): *I went to the day program. Not much. They have books to read. I don't like the lunch.*
Th: *What kind of books?*
Ct: *Different types. I like to read about presidents. JFK was my favorite. The books are dirty sometimes like my apartment. I keep spilling things all over my coffee table.*
Th: *JFK was a famous president.*
Ct: ***Yes, I remember that I was working at a restaurant when I heard the news that he was shot. I used to be a waitress. (episodic memory link)***

The therapist "clicks" onto the episodic memory link (EML): **Yes, I remember that I was working at a restaurant when I heard the news that he was shot. I used to be a waitress.**

Th: *What did you do for that job?*
Ct: *I met lots of different people and really liked working weekends because it was busy and I made lots of tips.*
Th: *What other types of job have people had and why is working good for us?*

The EML is expanded upon through a follow-up group discussion addressing group members' work experiences and the importance of engaging in a productive day routine for mind stimulation and social engagement (*Handout 3: What Is Mind Stimulation?* can be provided to clients).

3. Operate Out of a "Reality-based Framework"

Recognizing the difficulties that many people with schizophrenia have in communicating with each other through a "reality-based framework" and their tendency to bring in tangential associations or "intrusive" thoughts, the therapist focuses discussions on the here-and-now and concrete events that clients are participating in. Group members are encouraged to talk about activities and events from the past week so that the discussion of issues and events are specific and reality-bound.

The therapist makes an ongoing effort to shape and facilitate conversations through a "reality-based" framework, helping clients stay focused on information and issues that can be "consensually validated" and understood by all group members. Efforts are made to identify universal themes that all clients can relate to and for which all clients can share relevant experiences that contribute meaningfully to the group discussion.

4. Actively Use Redirection Strategies

If "delusional material" is brought into the reporting process, only relevant associations are extracted that could lead to reality-based discussion, while acknowledging group members' desire and intention to share information with others (see Figure 4.1—Venn diagram, above).

Throughout the discussion phase of the group, the group leader actively redirects the conversation to themes and issues that are logical and that lend themselves to a shared discussion (see Figure 4.2 below—redirection strategies). These redirection strategies are also used to minimize preoccupation with "pathology" and to facilitate clients' ability to engage in more focused reality-based discussions.

5. Involve All Group Members at their Level

Clients' participation level varies according to their ability level and interest. Some group members may need more active prodding. The group leader can use co-therapists as needed to work individually with those clients who may need more prompting or support to participate in discussions. Throughout the discussion phase, group members are encouraged to ask each other questions or respond to comments, which helps provide social skills training through modeling how to initiate social conversations, listen to others, and sustain conversations.

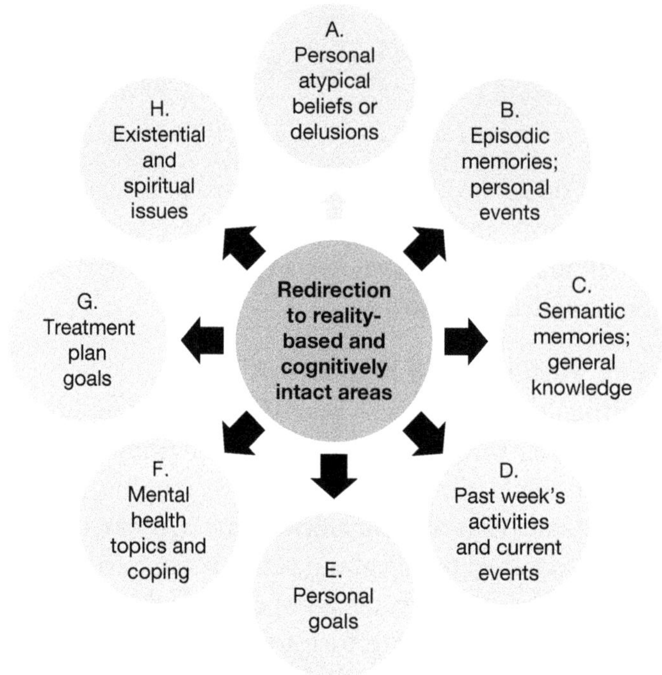

FIGURE 4.2 Redirection strategies: therapist's rotating focus to engage clients in reality-based discussions. The therapist focuses on accessing information in circles B–H and minimizes accessing information in circle A

Clinical Vignettes

The following vignettes are derived from actual cases and illustrate the various ways that clients may participate in group discussions. The vignettes are followed by *homework recommendations* that clinicians can use with clients.

Clinical Vignette: Stew

Stew is an inpatient client with a diagnosis of paranoid schizophrenia, who minimally participates in the relaxation exercises. He communicates a great deal of ambivalence in joining the relaxation exercise. For example, he may stand up with the group, but typically not practice the routine that everybody is asked to do. He will also not do any paper–pencil exercises, but will spend time, when asked or prompted, in browsing or reading some general knowledge or science-related materials that are available in the group room for members to look at or read prior to the formal start of the group. After reading these materials, he may report what he has read when asked to practice his reading comprehension, memory, and reality-based conversation using a factual frame of reference. In addition, Stew will participate actively in reporting about his past week's events or in discussing issues for the day. He often responds to questions orally when the paper–pencil exercises are reviewed, even though he may not complete any of the written exercises. He does best with one-to-one staff support and prompting during the group.

Clinical Vignette: Gil

Gil often talks to himself, and appears preoccupied with his own thoughts, but follows the group home routine by responding to staff requests and guidance. In the MICST group, Gil will comply minimally with the relaxation exercises, and will not participate in the paper–pencil exercises, except for doodling or writing incoherent statements or words of his own. However, he will actively participate in general knowledge discussions, displaying a high level of pre-morbid intelligence and academic learning attainment (he attended a prep school). This client also has an excellent memory for songs, poems, and Bible verses and will often respond positively to the group leader's suggestion to start or end the group by reciting a poem or Bible verse, or singing a song. Using general knowledge discussions and long-term memory exercises through recitation of poems or Bible verses and singing songs provided Gil with a meaningful level of group participation even though he would often become tangential and disorganized when talking about mental health or personal issues.

Clinical Vignette: Mic

Mic often engages in self-talk in public and will not participate in many of the structured group activities (e.g., deep breathing exercises or paper–pencil exercises, except for doodling). But when discussing mental health issues, he often will express anti-establishment and anti-medication views, while overtly complying with medication and other prescribed treatment or group routines. He will often respond to oral questions or participate in the feedback on the written exercises, and does extremely well in discussing various topics and themes that the therapist might choose to focus on, based on some other client's utterance. He shows a wide range of knowledge and information about a variety of topics. While discussing certain topics, this client is able to talk about issues in a logical manner, showing capacity for reasoning, logical association, and "intact memory" for facts and general knowledge, which otherwise may not be apparent to others in his daily interactions. If one were to focus on his present feelings or ask personal probing questions, he might talk rather incoherently. Traditionally, in a verbally mediated symptom-focused therapy, this client would be considered inappropriate. But using the MICST model, this client can function reasonably well in the therapy sessions, when clinicians access his strengths and interests by relating to and stimulating aspects of his mind and memory that are reasonably intact.

HOMEWORK RECOMMENDATIONS

The case manager or mental health staff attending the MICST group can facilitate homework and help prepare handouts if needed. The time and schedule for the exercises can be individualized based on the client's style and motivation and based on recommendations from mental health staff.

- Mental health issues: Group members may be asked to write down information discussed in the group or may receive a handout of the discussion topic for that day, such as how to cope with depression or anxiety. Clients can review this handout after the group to reinforce mental health knowledge and coping strategies.
- General knowledge issues: Group members may be given an article that was published or a handout from the Internet on a topic that was discussed in the group. Group members can continue to research this topic with their case manager (use *Worksheet 8: Data Collection Worksheet for a Topic*).
- Encourage clients to review personal goals, including personal hygiene and develop a plan for addressing one or two personal goals (use *Worksheet 2* or *Worksheet 3: Goal Setting*).
- Spend time during an individual session with your client brainstorming topics of interest, which the client could later research (use *Worksheet 7: Brainstorming Worksheet for Topics of Interest*).
- Encourage clients to visit a local library and borrow or browse books of interest for mind stimulation (use *Worksheet 8: Data Collection Worksheet for a Topic*).
- Encourage clients to watch a TV show related to a discussion topic.
- In collaboration with your client, develop a list of ways to spend the day (use *Worksheet* 6: *Ways to Spend the Day*).
- Spend time during an individual therapy session with your client discussing a topic of interest or expanding on a topic discussed in the MICST group that week.
- Work with your client to monitor a goal or mental health topic discussed in the group, develop a list of coping strategies, or develop a self-care recovery plan (use *Worksheets 2*, *3*, *5*, or *10*).
- Encourage clients to tell a family member, co-resident, friend, case manager, or individual counselor about a group discussion topic.
- After a group session, encourage clients to continue discussing the topic with another group member and during the next MICST group, report back their discussion.

Chapter 5

Paper–Pencil Exercises

Mind Stimulation of Attention, Logical Thinking, Reasoning, General Knowledge, and Self-reflection

This chapter discusses the various ways that paper–pencil exercises are used to stimulate the mind and cognitive functions such as logical thinking, reasoning, attention, abstract thinking, general knowledge, and memory functioning. The paper–pencil exercises also involve self-reflection exercises whereby clients reflect on various mental health topics and respond in writing to various questions about their mental health knowledge and coping strategies. The written exercises are also used to help compensate for auditory processing difficulties that clients with schizophrenia may experience. The chapter discusses and describes the different types of paper–pencil cognitive exercises that are used in the group and how they can stimulate various mental and cognitive processes in clients. The chapter concludes with *homework recommendations* outlining ways that clients can use paper–pencil exercises to stimulate cognitive and mental functions and to enhance their overall functioning and recovery.

In the MICST model, the paper–pencil "cognitive mind stimulating" exercises are presented at various levels of difficulty, which allows all clients, independent of their educational background and cognitive functioning, to experience some degree of success, while also challenging them to a degree they can tolerate. The exercises can also be used to facilitate cognitive and mind stimulation without necessarily giving clients corrective feedback on all of their responses. Some of the paper–pencil exercises entail self-reflection exercises which enable clients to reflect on their involvement in the group and to comment on the various ways in which the group is assisting them in their functioning.

The paper–pencil cognitive exercises can also provide very valuable insight into, for example, learning deficits or difficulties that a client may have. These learning deficits and difficulties may be easily overlooked when clinicians rely too much on the traditional verbal mode of therapy whereby clients may communicate agreement with the information or "compliance," but in effect, may not have understood or may have misunderstood the information. When an awareness of a client's possible learning disability or learning deficit and loss of cognitive functioning is taken into consideration, clinicians can maximize communication by helping clients compensate for these deficits by presenting information in other modalities (i.e., written and visual modalities), or tailoring the presentation of the information to meet the client's unique learning style.

In general, clients with schizophrenia may have difficulty processing auditory information. This may be due, in part, to clients' compromised attention, concentration, and working memory, and difficulty in redirecting themselves from intrusive thoughts. In fact, research suggests that recall of verbal compared to visual information is more compromised in clients with schizophrenia (Kalkstein et al., 2010). In some of our prior work with clients with schizophrenia, we have found benefits in augmenting auditory communication modalities with visual modalities in therapy sessions (Ahmed, 1998, 2002; Ahmed et al., 1997; Ahmed & Boisvert, 2006a). The MICST paper–pencil exercises help to augment information processing capabilities for clients who may not respond as well to interventions that rely primarily on the auditory mode of communication.

Neuropsychological Functioning in Schizophrenia

Neuropsychological defects in schizophrenia have been identified extensively in the literature (Braff, 1993; Goldman et al., 1996; Heinrichs & Zakzanis, 1998; Kalkstein et al., 2010; Morice & Delahunty, 1996; Spaulding et al., 1999). Current literature on neuropsychological functions indicates that persons with schizophrenia demonstrate deficits in several areas of functioning, including attention, executive functions, inhibition, mental flexibility, processing speed, verbal memory, visuospatial memory, and working memory (Censits, Ragland, Gur, & Gur, 1997; Heinrichs & Zakzanis, 1998; Mohamed, Paulsen, O'Leary, Arndt, & Andreason, 1999; Riley et al., 2000; Saykin et al., 1994; Spindler, Sullivan, Menon, Lim, & Pfefferbaum, 1997; Stone, Gabrieli, Stebbins, & Sullivan, 1998). In some studies, verbal memory has been found to be the most impaired neuropsychological function (Censits et al., 1997; Hoff et al., 1999; Mohamed et al., 1999; Russell, Munro, Jones, Hemsley, & Murray, 1997).

Research suggests that cognitive functioning, as compared to positive and negative symptoms, is the strongest predictor of functional outcome (Green, 1996; Green et al., 2000). With increased understanding of cognitive deficits in schizophrenia, intervention programs have focused on cognitive rehabilitation strategies. Cognitive rehabilitation is designed to stimulate new learning or relearning of cognitive tasks and thus improve various domains of deficit (Hurford et al., 2011). In our original publication of the MICST model (see Ahmed & Goldman, 1994), we documented some evidence of improved cognitive functioning in a small sample using a group case-study model. Cognitive rehabilitation also focuses on using "compensatory approaches" aimed at improving patients' functioning by avoiding areas of impairment and accessing intact cognitive functions (Kern, Glynn, Horan, & Marder, 2009). This is similar to a fundamental approach in MICST; namely, assessing intact areas of functioning and avoiding "deficit" areas. Recognizing the documented evidence of cognitive deficits in schizophrenia, the U.S. National Institute of Mental Health (NIMH) has proposed guidelines for testing interventions in schizophrenia, called MATRICS (Measurement and Treatment Research to Improve Cognition in Schizophrenia). This initiative is primarily targeted at researching newer medications and adjunctive cognitive training exercises to address the cognitive deficits in schizophrenia (Geyer, 2010; Marder & Fenton, 2004).

In our MICST model, by using paper–pencil exercises for cognitive stimulation, we are addressing cognitive rehabilitation by focusing on clients relearning, or accessing their previously learned information. Moreover, the exercises are stimulating cognitive functions that are intact, but under-stimulated, which helps compensate (i.e., compensatory approaches) for clients' underlying thinking deficits. Below we provide examples of some of the cognitive functions and thinking skills, which the paper–pencil exercises are designed to stimulate and strengthen.

- *Working memory:* Group members shift from one task (synonym) to another task (antonym) or from one mathematics problem to another, being aware of the rule that governs the response to the item; or they work to solve a problem that involves holding information in mind and manipulating it.
- *Logical thinking:* Group members identify the logical connections of their associations to the concept or problem presented.
- *Cognitive fluidity:* Group members shift from one activity to another or use different rules for different exercises.
- *Group logic and validity of thinking by consensus agreement:* Group members evaluate their responses in the context of other group responses and come to accept the consensually validated response to a given problem or task.
- *Attention and concentration:* Group members, using a combination of visual and verbal prompting, attend to the specific exercise at hand and concentrate on generating the correct response to the question.
- *Accepting corrective feedback:* Through feedback on the completed exercise, group members correct or change their responses when appropriate, and in the process establish a "learner attitude" to information given by "authority" figures (group leaders) or other group members.

Goals for the Paper–Pencil Exercises

- to stimulate and utilize visual processing of information for more effective communication and increase capacity for self-reflection;
- to promote logical reasoning skills through, for example, various cognitive stimulating exercises such as analogies, synonyms, antonyms, and sequencing events based on their logical order;
- to promote abstract reasoning skills through, for example, exercises such as identifying similarities between pairs of words and grouping words based on shared characteristics;
- to promote attention and concentration on a given topic or mental exercise;
- to enable clients to practice and produce relevant verbal associations to a conversation topic;

- to enhance working memory (holding information on line to solve a given problem) through, for example, arithmetic and word-search exercises;
- to enable clients to practice long-term memory (i.e., semantic and episodic) by answering general knowledge topics and questions on mental health topics;
- to provide a structured and organized format for clients to discuss and reflect on mental health issues and personal goals;
- to maximize clients' ability to process information and share their intact cognitive functioning by using written materials, which can help compensate for auditory processing limitations;
- to learn more about clients' interests and knowledge that may not be evident in traditional verbal exchanges or interactions that rely on verbal processing capabilities;
- to access and stimulate "dormant skills" and thinking abilities that clients may not have opportunities to exercise due, in part, to preoccupation with or influence from their own "psychiatric symptoms."

We believe that actively stimulating mental and cognitive functioning and associated underlying neuropsychological processes (through, for example, using various paper–pencil exercises) is helpful and necessary for our ongoing adaptation to real-life situations. In our everyday life, most of us have opportunities to exercise these neuropsychological processes through activities such as social communication, watching TV, listening to music, engaging in hobbies or recreational activities, and reading various materials (e.g. newspapers, journals, work-related information, manuals for fixing things, and filling out written forms for different functions and activities). Many hobbies and mind stimulating games—such as crossword puzzles, word searches, Sudoku, chess, card games, and various table games such as mahjong, as well as knitting-type activities—are not only enjoyable and challenging (which makes them popular), but also provide stimulation of various neuropsychological processes underlying these cognitive activities. The MICST paper–pencil exercises provide clients with a form of mind stimulation akin to these everyday mind stimulating activities, which clients may not have the opportunity to engage in regularly.

In the MICST model, we take the position that thinking and behavior for all human beings is influenced by underlying neuropsychological processes such as attention, concentration, working memory, long-term memory (semantic and episodic), reasoning (e.g., understanding a given set of information so as to generate an adaptive response to a situation), and logical associations (e.g., correlating and connecting information that follows a common theme or set of rules).

We believe that a therapeutic environment for people with a long-term history of schizophrenia should include ongoing opportunities to engage in mind stimulation exercises, through mechanisms such as those that we propose in our MICST model. The ease with which we have found group members, many of whom have a long history of schizophrenia, engaging in these written exercises, reflects perhaps clients' ability to use already established underlying neural networks that may be otherwise dormant in their cognitive structures. Moreover, the paper–pencil exercises, in addition to providing cognitive stimulation, promote positive self-worth through, for example, affirming clients' intact thinking skills, which are reinforced through the exercises.

We believe that all of us have a reservoir of universal "adaptive" thinking processes as part of our genetic endowment. These "adaptive" thinking processes may not be dominant to the same degree in all of us. In persons with schizophrenia, "atypical" thinking processes may predominate compared to "adaptive" thinking processes for various reasons. The MICST model focuses on stimulating these "adaptive thinking processes" without necessarily challenging clients' atypical thinking, as may be done in more traditional cognitive-behavioral or metacognitive therapies.

Types of Paper–Pencil Cognitive Exercises

The cognitive exercises are often taken or adapted from educational resource materials, or have been created by various psychology student interns or externs working with the senior author (Mohiuddin Ahmed) over the years (see Appendix F for sample paper–pencil exercises). In our experience of conducting MICST, we have found that the paper–pencil cognitive exercises are uniquely able to hold clients' attention and achieve undivided task involvement in general.

Below we describe several categories of the paper–pencil exercises used during MICST groups. We describe the exercise, explain what cognitive skills the exercise is designed to address, and discuss what aspects of cognitive functioning in schizophrenia the exercise may help to stimulate. However, all the exercises share a common theme, which is stimulating the information processing that underlies our reasoning, thinking, and adaptive behavior. By using these "neutral" paper–pencil exercises, the therapist is able to structure the experience to enable clients to validate their thinking processes through a common thinking framework.

Clinicians may adapt these exercises to meet clients' different levels of functioning and interests, or use exercises from various critical thinking educational resource materials. There are also a variety of Internet resources available which provide sample cognitive exercises that clinicians can download (see *Handout 8*: *Web Sites and Educational Resources*). The list and categories of exercises, which we present, have all been used in MICST group sessions over the years.

1. Analogies and Similarities
   These exercises involve finding associations between words and concepts (analogies) and abstracting similar features between word pairs (similarities). These exercises help clients practice their logical reasoning, abstract reasoning, and thinking skills by requiring them to use a logical and common frame of reference to make correct associations between words and concepts.

2. Categorizing, Classifying, or Grouping Objects
These exercises involve placing objects in a common category, sorting objects into groups, abstracting or finding common features among a group of items, or listing objects that belong to a certain category. The exercises require clients to use logical associations as well as working memory and long-term memory. Persons with schizophrenia may have difficulty structuring their thinking, staying focused on a topic, and warding off "intrusive" associations that may not be relevant to the discussion topic. They may also engage in tangential associations not relevant to the ongoing conversation topic. These exercises help clients stay focused on a given theme, produce associations relevant to the discussion, and minimize tendencies to engage in tangential associations.

3. Composition
These exercises require individuals to compose from memory short paragraphs or respond to questions related to reading materials. These exercises are designed to stimulate free recall as well as to improve clients' ability to construct verbal thoughts and associations in meaningful and coherent sentences.

4. Comprehension
These exercises require the group members to read, comprehend, and then recall aspects of the information that was read. These exercises promote task involvement as well as working memory. Because of impaired concentration and working memory and difficulty remaining focused on tasks, persons with schizophrenia often have difficulty in remembering what is being said to them or in remembering what they have just read. Difficulty sustaining attention to verbally written materials as well as to oral communication may also be due to interference from internal stimuli. These exercises help clients practice their comprehension, reading, and recall skills to improve their overall communication skills.

5. Fact versus Opinion
These exercises involve learning the difference between fact and opinion by reviewing statements and determining whether the statement is a fact or an opinion. These exercises stimulate word associations, working memory, attention to task, and logical thinking. Additionally, the exercises are designed to stimulate reflective thinking about how ideas that are generally considered to be "true" (i.e., facts) are differentiated from ideas that may vary from person to person (i.e., opinions). We can get into conflicts in communication with others by presenting our ideas as "facts," when in actuality they represent "opinions." The exercises test clients' ability to accept "corrective feedback" and verify their thinking by consensus validation. Clients with a history of schizophrenia can have particular difficulties in communication with others. They may often think of their opinions or ideas as factual without having the ability to check for the validity of their thinking. In turn, they may have difficulty accepting "corrective feedback," due to their cognitive rigidity. These exercises can be used to generate "mental health topics" by highlighting how one can confuse facts with one's own

opinions or personalized values (e.g., atypical thinking), and how this may affect acceptance and understanding of one's mental illness and treatment options.

6. General Knowledge and Other "Neutral Topics"
   These exercises involve asking clients to remember basic facts and information covering a wide range of general knowledge topics in areas such as literature, history, science, geography, and sports. Typically, the exercises are in the form of multiple-choice questions, "fill in the blanks," or open-ended questions. These exercises are designed to stimulate long-term memory and associations as well as to stimulate the natural interest people have in wanting to test their knowledge through consensus validation. Even though personal memory or episodic memory may be impaired in clients for a variety of reasons, semantic memory or memory for factual knowledge may be somewhat more intact and accessible. By stimulating these more intact memories, clients' positive self-image is enhanced as they share their knowledge. The therapist uses the feedback session to validate clients' recall of facts (long-term memory), reinforce their memory practice, and provide corrective feedback to help clients accept new information into their knowledge base.

7. Grammar Usage
   These exercises highlight the use of grammatical skills as well as attention to appropriate oral and written communication. These exercises enhance clients' awareness of using accepted standards in oral and written language usage and stimulate their attention to their verbal and written expression.

8. Matching Objects or Persons with their Associated Place or Function
   These exercises are designed to stimulate awareness of things and activities that go together and may entail identifying roles and functions of certain occupations or the functions which different objects serve. These exercises provide memory training as well as consensual validation of one's associations and experiences. This helps clients to label and accurately identify functions of various members of society, including the functions of their treatment team members. In the process, clients can become more aware of the type of therapeutic services they are receiving and the roles of various treatment team members in contributing to their recovery.

9. Mathematics/Measurement
   These exercises involve completing various mathematical or measurement questions. Persons with schizophrenia may have lost some functional skills in using number concepts that are involved in money exchange and may exhibit deficits in working memory functions required for money management. For clients with long-term mental illness (even when educated to a high school or college level), practicing simple mathematical skills can be challenging, as well as rewarding. The rewarding aspect of the activity comes from a feeling of satisfaction of being correct and acknowledged by the therapist when right answers are given. When making mistakes, clients may be more likely to accept corrective feedback on these "emotionally neutral" exercises.

10. Sequencing Events and the Concept of Time
These exercises involve sequencing events over time so that the events follow a logical order. These exercises may involve identifying day routines and the time sequence of activities to help increase clients' attention to everyday routines and increase their appreciation for a sense of time. Often, people with schizophrenia have difficulties in remembering or paying attention to sequences of steps for a particular task. As such, their ability to do everyday tasks, including personal hygiene, or following a day routine on their own, may be compromised. These exercises help to stimulate thinking about sequential aspects of a given task.

11. Synonyms and Antonyms
These exercises involve finding similarities and opposites for various words, phrases, or concepts. These exercises help clients practice the concept of generalization and discrimination and using logic in everyday experiences. Persons with schizophrenia often have difficulties in remembering rules for the generalization and discrimination necessary for adaptive behavior and in following social rules of conduct without some degree of support and supervision. They can also be so preoccupied with their internal thoughts and ruminations that their awareness of the underlying logic in the communication process is under-stimulated or not readily accessible. These exercises promote the logical reasoning necessary to help enhance clients' adaptive thinking.

12. Visual Matching Exercises
These exercises consist of visually matching various shapes and designs with a targeted stimulus. The exercises help clients practice attention to visual details, association skills, and working memory to match relevant stimulus cues. These exercises help clients to increase their overall awareness of their physical environment and produce adaptive responses to given problem situations.

13. Word Meaning and Verbal Comprehension
These exercises involve coming up with definitions of words, and may consist of multiple-choice or open-ended questions. The exercises are designed to stimulate verbal associations, working memory, and semantic memory. The exercises also help clients to practice reality-oriented associations, while staying focused on the verbal task at hand and minimizing interference from "irrelevant" or intrusive associations.

14. Word Searches
These exercises involve finding individual words or phrases embedded in a letter grid. Often we have noted that clients readily engage in these word-search exercises, which involve focused attention and concentration, problem-solving skills, and working memory. The word search may cover a certain theme such as famous writers, musical instruments, past presidents, or coping strategies. The words in the word search can be used as a discussion topic, eliciting long-term memory and stimulating exchange of information, all of which is relevant to the recovery process.

15. Self-reflection Exercises
Self-reflection and self-assessment exercises are commonly used in psychotherapy and are often found in treatment manuals and workbooks. The MICST self-reflection and self-assessment exercises involve clients endorsing judgments and opinions about their current functioning and progress, their degree of awareness of mental health issues and coping strategies, and their mental health service needs (see Appendix B for sample self-assessment tools).

Note: Some clients may not readily participate in exercises requiring a personal assessment of their mental health status or progress. Discussing these issues may generate negative feelings and associations, which may be difficult to process once they are stimulated in clients. Discussions often have to be brief as clients with a long-term history of mental illness can easily become agitated or display a "negative attitude" when discussing mental health issues and recalling negative life experiences. Clinicians have to use their skills and sensitivity in determining how long to discuss any of these issues.

Below are examples of self-reflection exercises:

a) *Practical Skills*
These exercises involve clients reflecting on what they need to do in everyday practical situations to promote adaptive behavior. For example, clients may be asked to reflect on and list the steps involved in taking care of a pet or going shopping for food. Often, people with schizophrenia, because of their long-standing history of isolation and preoccupation with their own "thoughts" and "internal stimuli," have "lost out" in their practice and knowledge of information necessary for adapting to everyday practical situations. These exercises may help clients think about everyday practical issues and adaptive social behaviors. Clients' responses to the exercises can be used for group discussions about the "recovery process."

b) *Healthy Eating*
These exercises may involve word searches or "fill in the blanks" involving healthy diet and nutrition-related information. Persons with schizophrenia often exhibit poor health, associated with improper nutritional intake, characterized by either obesity or undernourishment. They may also display minimal awareness of the relationship between health and diet and minimal awareness of the body's needs. These exercises help to generate awareness of a "healthy diet" and a better understanding of how diet can improve the overall functioning of the body. The exercise often leads to a group discussion of diet and nutrition and the mind–body connection.

c) *Labeling Feelings*
These exercises involve identifying and labeling feelings and behaviors and helping clients connect the relationship among thinking, feeling, and behavior. The therapist may use the exercise to talk about the role of positive feelings in the recovery process and how to redirect oneself away from negative thoughts and feelings, or how to

minimize one's preoccupation with negative feelings and thoughts. The therapist may also lead a discussion on coping strategies and ways to manage negative feelings more effectively. These exercises may help clients become more aware of their thoughts, feelings, and behaviors; and more importantly, value the experience of positive feelings in controlling or displacing negative feelings and thoughts.

d) *Word Searches Involving Mental Health Issues*
This exercise involves using word-search exercises for mental-health-related, recovery-related, or medication-related words (see sample word search on mental health themes in Appendix F). The words used in the word-search exercise can be used as a springboard to discuss mental health or medication-related issues, to provide psycho-education about mental illness, or to discuss coping strategies. Discussions often have to be brief as clients with a long-term history of mental illness can easily become agitated or display a "negative attitude" when discussing personal mental health issues and negative life experiences. Clinicians have to use their skills and sensitivity to determine how far to go in discussing any particular mental health issue.

e) *Goal-setting Exercises*
These exercises involve asking clients to identify their personal goals and steps to reach their goals, as well as identifying any cognitive deficits, psychiatric symptoms, or obstacles that may have an impact on their goals. *Worksheets 2 and 3* can be used as goal-setting worksheets to engage clients more actively in goal setting and identifying the steps to reach their goals.

HOMEWORK RECOMMENDATIONS

The case manager or mental health staff participating in the group can facilitate homework and help prepare handouts if needed. The time and schedule for the exercises can be individualized based on the client's style and motivation and based on recommendations from mental health staff.

The paper–pencil exercise time, which could be scheduled into the client's day routine in the residence or hospital, can also be combined with practicing the BMR exercises (see Chapter 3).

- Paper–pencil exercises completed by clients in the group session, as well as specific materials requested by clients from previous sessions, can be put together in individualized binders for clients to review as needed.
- A set of homework assignments, consisting of paper–pencil exercises, which may be uniquely suited to a client's individual abilities and interests may be given to clients to complete in between weekly MICST sessions (see Appendix F for

sample exercises). The time and schedule can be set up in collaboration with the client's case manager or in consideration of scheduled activities at the residence or hospital if the client is an inpatient.

- In consultation with the client and mental health staff, educational resource workbooks geared to the client's level of ability and interests can be given to clients to work on during specified periods of the day.
- Paper–pencil homework assignments can be used as a de-escalation strategy when the client appears to be "unduly agitated" or experiencing psychiatric symptoms. In many such situations, reminding the client of his or her particular day routine activities, including paper–pencil cognitive exercises, may help the client to engage in a meaningful and focused activity and subsequently help the client to "take his/her mind off" current negative thoughts or feelings of agitation.
- Clients may also be given reading materials or handouts or information related to their particular interests in areas such as literature, sports, science, geography, history, or art. The client can be asked to read about the topic or comment on it by writing down their thoughts during the week (clients may use *Worksheet 8: Data Collection Worksheet for a Topic*).
- Clients may be encouraged to do journal writing. This can be best accomplished by putting together a booklet consisting of open-ended questions or "fill in the blanks," requiring the client to make brief statements about his or her thoughts, experiences, or feelings.

Chapter 6

Managing and Evaluating the Group

This chapter discusses how best to manage the group process and maximize participation from clients. We discuss ways to address various group interactions that may ensue and provide suggestions for handling different elements of the group process. We also include a section on how to start a MICST group. This section provides a sample "recruitment flyer," detailing the goals of MICST and discusses how to consider issues such as transportation, scheduling of the group, organizing group materials, and working collaboratively with clinical staff and administration. The chapter concludes with discussing ways to evaluate the group using various feedback tools and questionnaires. We also report sample outcome data from "evaluation studies" and client and staff feedback questionnaires, which we have used to evaluate MICST.

Managing the Group Process

The flexible nature of MICST allows for clinicians to adjust and adapt group activities to best meet the needs of a particular group or group session. Ideally, group sessions are conducted by a primary therapist and a co-facilitator who can assist with group activities, redirect clients to tasks, and provide individualized assistance as needed, particularly during the paper–pencil exercises.

Below we outline core management strategies to assist clinicians in effectively facilitating a MICST group.

- Assume clients can perform a certain activity or task unless they clearly demonstrate otherwise. Get all clients involved and encourage peer support.
- Operate out of a positive psychology and strengths-based model. Have clients take turns showing skills, talents, and interests. This strengthens their positive self-image, allows them to identify with "normality," and enables them to practice assertive communication. Clients may be encouraged to go in front of the "class" and use the whiteboard or blackboard to explain a concept in their own words.

- Use supportive but directive requests, such as: "We are doing this activity, come on, join us please." Not, "Would you like to join us?" since that type of request may feed into "ambivalence" and "avolition." If a client still appears to be conflicted and non-compliant, one may then say: "Maybe next time; here's something you can try for now," which may entail, for example, giving the client a paper–pencil task that has elicited his or her interest and involvement in the past. If a co-facilitator is present, he or she can work with the client to keep the client engaged in the individual exercise while the rest of the group proceeds. Indeed, one may need periodically to individualize some activities for a particular client (e.g., asking the client to do a paper–pencil task or asking a client to review part of a general knowledge book).
- Do not minimize discussions about stress, pathology, or psychiatric symptoms, as they may spontaneously come up. Give clients clarifications of medication- and symptom-related issues, in a manner that is compatible with professional and "public education" criteria. Acknowledge personal experiences, but tie these in to group themes and universal concepts that all group members can relate to. Keep mental health discussions brief and focused on common topics of coping and problem solving. Personal issues and psychiatric symptoms raised in the group sessions can be "converted" into topics for psycho-educational discussions as needed.
- Encourage clients to view the group process as akin to "learning in a classroom." Explain the issues discussed in the session (e.g., mental health, general knowledge) as one would best explain to a "teaching group," while ensuring group involvement and participation. Many clients seem to respond positively to this structure. This is consistent with conceptualizing therapy as a learning process whereby one learns or relearns coping skills to improve functioning from someone who is competent and knowledgeable to guide the learning process (i.e., the therapist). When not sure of one's own knowledge base, acknowledge it openly to the clients and indicate that you will get back to the issue or topic with more research and clarification next time.
- Operate out of a redirection and reality-based framework to keep clients focused when they appear to be preoccupied. Focus on the present and future rather than the past. As a rule, keep discussions short and be mindful of any boredom, restlessness, or inattention displayed by group members.
- Model respect for clients and allow for "unique" client behaviors and needs during the group such as stretching, needing to leave momentarily, or walking around if there is a need for movement.
- Have a variety of knowledge-based books (e.g., astronomy, general science, geography, or educational books with pictures) available for clients to browse or look at before the beginning of the group. This will help minimize restlessness or "self-occupying" thoughts for clients who are waiting for others to arrive prior to the start of the group. The books can also be used as a "cognitive stimulation activity" during the group to engage distracted clients.
- Use whiteboards, blackboards, easels, handouts, or other visual aids, whenever possible. Send spontaneously generated topics, coping strategies, mental health information, or homework sheets to a computer printer if one is available, and have a co-facilitator make copies and give these out on the spot to the group. If this is not possible, then

handouts can be prepared by the therapist after the group and passed out at the next session.

- Reinforce adhering to current treatment plan objectives and facilitate an understanding of system issues that are having an impact on clients' present life circumstances. Teach clients to self-advocate for mental health service needs with their respective mental health service providers. Members are encouraged to reflect on how their current life situation is influenced by their own actions, the perspectives of the treatment team, the community, the court system (if involved), and by other involved family members or caregivers.
- Avoid or minimize discussions of emotionally charged personal issues. Discussing "emotionally charged" issues raised by a group member is discouraged by pointing out that "atypical personal experiences" are too "person-centered" and are often "too difficult" for others to understand or validate during the group. Redirection and rephrasing strategies can be used to minimize discussions and preoccupations with emotionally charged personal issues. The therapist can encourage the client to discuss personal issues with his or her case manager outside the group session.
- Use feedback with clients to reduce "cognitive rigidity." Clients with a long-term history of schizophrenia, while appearing to be "clinically stable" and in a logical frame of mind at the moment, may have difficulty accepting "corrective feedback" to their thinking. This can lead to an "agitation experience," intensifying their psychiatric symptoms. The "feedback" experience for many of them can be associated with "negative feelings" related to personal events. This cognitive rigidity may be somewhat modified when "feedback" is used in conjunction with "neutral tasks." For example, reviewing the responses to the cognitive exercises helps to test clients' thinking according to specified rules outlined in the exercises. Reviewing the responses also helps clients to learn to accept the possibility of making mistakes and correcting mistakes by using group logic or a group-validated common thinking process. Clients tend to respond well to a systematic and organized review of the exercises whereby each group member takes a turn sharing his or her answer to a question. This orderly review helps clients to anticipate and plan their group involvement and enables them to get accustomed to an expected group routine and "rule," and in the process become more aware of social rules of communication.

The structure and sequence of a MICST session can be as outlined in Figure 6.1. The therapist usually follows the below sequence so as to address all the necessary elements of the MICST model. However, there may be times when the therapist, for example, might devote the entire middle part of the session to discussing a mental health topic (a topic usually spontaneously verbalized by a group member) that appears to hold the interest or attention of the majority of group members. Also, from time to time, we have conducted sessions entirely focused on the assessment and evaluation of the MICST group through a discussion phase.

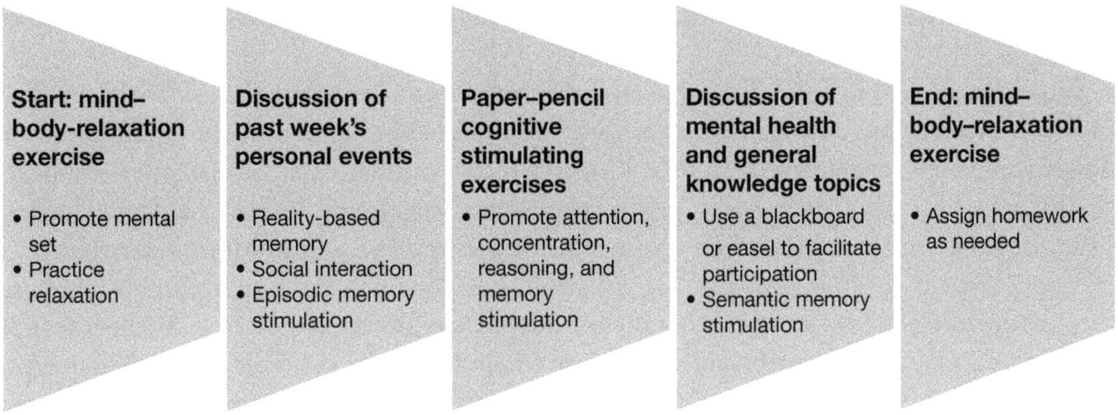

FIGURE 6.1 Structure and sequence of MICST group activities

Managing Symptom-based Presentations: Focusing on the "What" versus the "Why" of Behavior

Below we discuss scenarios for managing various potential symptom presentations during a MICST group. In working with persons with schizophrenia, we focus on *"what"* the person is doing rather than focusing on *"why"* the person is doing what they are doing. Part of the rationale for focusing on the "what" compared to the "why" of the patient's behavior comes from our clinical work and experience and some underlying theoretical assumptions. Given the often long-term history of clients' psychiatric symptoms, the question of "why" the client has particular symptoms or behavioral issues interfering with functioning may have been addressed by the client and mental health workers (e.g., therapist, psychiatrist) many times in the past, possibly without appreciable benefits. Moreover, in the process, this "line of inquiry" may have further reinforced some clients' tendencies to stay focused on the past and thus become preoccupied with or bothered by chronic symptoms. Additionally, given the complicated nature of psychiatric symptoms in schizophrenia and their dynamic interaction with various individual factors, there are many competing and alternative theories about the why of behavior (i.e., the "causes"), which are going to be difficult to address meaningfully with any particular client in a group setting.

From a recovery point of view, to promote awareness of the immediate social and physical environment and to help clients make adaptive responses to the present situation, asking "What are you doing now?" allows the client to direct attention to the present and become aware of the immediate reality of the social and physical environment. On the other hand, asking "Why are you doing that?" may lead to an open-ended discussion of various possibilities without any resolution, and in the process, may produce agitation and aggravate psychiatric symptoms. Moreover, clients may have their own established rationale for maintaining their "habits," which the clinician may not be able to confront, challenge, or change through the group process. Asking "Why are you doing that?" may just provide a vehicle for the client to express his or her views to support his or her unique thinking. This may unwittingly provide further justification to the client for a particular type of "maladaptive thinking." In this sense, "what" types of questions can help avoid this dilemma for the clinician and allow for a more productive discussion of "reality testing."

From a philosophical–existential perspective, our conscious awareness of living consists of the immediate present moment of reality, and understanding and knowing what we are doing and where we are, which in turn allows us more readily to elicit an adaptive response to the situation. In this context, redirecting ourselves to the "what" of our behavior promotes our sense of immediate awareness of the present and guides us internally to promote what is most adaptive in the situation. For persons with schizophrenia, there is often more of a need for external therapeutic supports to guide this process, as the internal guiding process may be compromised. This is where the therapist's role or the therapeutic environment's role becomes important in redirecting clients to the immediate environment by having them reflect on the "what" versus the "why" of their behavior.

Hallucinations

At times, a group member may be observed talking to him/herself and possibly experiencing overt hallucinations during the group. This group member may be having difficulty engaging in a specific group task. These behavioral episodes can be managed in various ways. One strategy is to redirect the client to a specific task, without confronting the "hallucination." Another strategy is to remind the client that his or her talking aloud will interfere with group activities, if he or she continues, and is not able to engage in group tasks. Another strategy is to ask the client to take a brief time out from the group and return in a more task-oriented manner. With some clients, we have used another strategy, which entails more directly confronting the behavior. The following actual scenario with a client highlights this strategy.

Therapist: I observe that one of the clients, Jim, who has the habit of frequently engaging in self-talking while in public, and who is usually able to limit this behavior during MICST, is engaged in self-talking and is not participating in the group activity during today's session. I decide to confront Jim by saying, "Jim, who are you talking with?"

Jim: "I am talking with my girlfriend." (Jim has alluded to having a girlfriend in the past, but there is no objective evidence of this in the clinical record, and it is not clear how much Jim's fantasy promotes this belief.)

Therapist: "But, your girlfriend is not here."

Jim: "I don't have a telephone here . . ."

Therapist: "You think you can communicate with someone who is not here, when you don't have a telephone or other means?"

Jim: "Yes, I believe so . . ." (Jim then continues talking, mentions the name of an Indian mystic, and alludes to "telepathic communication.")

The therapist then launches a discussion on telepathy, asks how many people believe in it, mentions how the nature of such beliefs is atypical, and points out that because it is "atypical," and a "personal feeling-based experience," which could not be validated by others, it will be difficult for others to understand. The therapist then gives examples of reality testing by asking clients in the room questions such as: "How many doors are there?," "How many windows are there?," and "How many pictures are hanging?" The therapist then emphasizes the need to keep this self-talking behavior private and to engage in this behavior privately, if need be; otherwise it would become disruptive to the group. Jim is then offered an activity that the therapist knows Jim likes and has expressed interest in, such as sketching on a piece of paper or drawing faces, or looking at a pictorial book entitled *How Things Are Made*.

These interventions are used to distract Jim from engaging in "self-talking," or responding to his "inner voices" (hallucinations) and to engage him in a positive mind stimulating activity, even if Jim is not following what the other group members are doing. Usually, this approach has been used successfully in redirecting clients like Jim from overt "self-talking." Jim may revert back to "self-talking" later on in the group, but is often observed to do so in a less audible manner so as not to be disruptive to the group.

There have been occasions where the therapist has discussed the topic of hallucinations by asking group members about their past and current experiences with hallucinations and how they manage these personal "atypical" experiences. This may be followed by a psycho-education discussion of research showing that areas in the brain such as Broca's area (the area responsible for speech production or talking) as well as other areas were noted, in some studies, to be active in subjects who reported auditory verbal hallucinations (i.e., experiences of hearing voices) (Hoffman, Pittman, Constable, Bhagwagar, & Hampson, 2011; McGuire, Shah, & Murray, 1993). The group may then discuss how this research supports the sub-vocal and self-talking nature of the "hearing voices" experience.

The therapist may also talk about how the intensity and frequency of hallucinatory experiences may be related to stress and agitation experiences or non-adherence to medication. The group may also discuss how the habit of hearing voices, once established, may not be completely eliminated, in spite of optimal medication management, as evidenced by many clients continuing to report these symptoms. Here the therapist may talk about managing stress and agitation experiences and its relationship to "relapse" and the recovery process; and talk about using positive redirection (*Handout 6: Redirection Strategies* provides suggestions for various strategies clients can use) and counter-conditioning techniques, such as engaging in therapeutic milieu activities to displace the habit-based hallucinatory experience.

Delusions

Delusion-based ideas by a client have often been dealt with by providing supportive listening for a brief period, then thanking the client for expressing his or her personal beliefs. The therapist then notes that it is a very personal and "atypical" belief, which is difficult for others to understand and follow. The therapist will often use a Venn diagram (see Figure 4.1 or *Handout 5*) to illustrate this point. The client is then advised to keep such thoughts to him or herself. The following scenario with the client Jim (mentioned above) may illustrate this approach:

Client: "I know how to communicate with others by telepathy even if they are not here."
Therapist: "Thanks for sharing your belief. It is a personal experience and feeling, which may be real to you, but others will not be able to understand and follow this. So let's

talk about things that everybody can follow and understand. Remember the Venn diagram we use for effective communication?"

The therapist may draw the Venn diagram on the blackboard to generate a discussion or move on to the paper–pencil exercise that the group is completing.

The communication strategy, as outlined in the scenario, aims to promote a therapeutic relationship framework within which reality-based communication can take place. The strategy is not to challenge the belief, but to point out the very personal nature of such beliefs and, more importantly, the difficulty of communicating such beliefs to others. Note that this is done within a positive psychology framework, respecting the client's right to a belief system and not challenging directly the underlying basis of the "delusional belief." Often in expressing a delusional belief, clients make tangential references to either an ongoing discussion topic or to an idea that itself can lead to a meaningful reality-based discussion (see "Clicking onto Reality-based links" in Chapter 4). The therapist may then choose to launch a discussion of the idea by soliciting input from group members.

We also do not state that the delusional belief is a part of his or her "mental illness," which may be suggested to clients in other clinical encounters. We believe that this may promote clients' continued identification with mental illness. Delusions, as well as hallucinations, can be conceptualized as entrenched behavioral habits, with supporting underlying neural networks, the expression of which may vary due to personal stress, social–environmental stimulation, or lack of active redirection.

Thought Disorder Symptoms

At times a client in the group may be observed speaking in a gibberish manner and seemingly be unable to communicate logical ideas or thoughts. This manner of communicating can often be displayed by clients with a history of disorganized schizophrenia, who exhibit varying degrees of cognitive deficits and a significant loss of both academic and social functioning. We will often use the technique of "clicking onto reality-based links" (see Chapter 4) in the client's thought processes to extract meaningful thought content or simply to redirect the client to a specific task with the goal of re-engaging the client in the group process.

In the dealing with any of the above three "symptom expressions" in the group, the clinician may also discuss the stress–diathesis model, and highlight how "perceived stress experiences" or "existential uncertainty" may trigger and intensify these symptoms. The therapist will often emphasize the positive effect of therapeutic supervision and structure, which in conjunction with medication treatment, can help clients cope with anxiety and stress and manage these symptoms better.

Atypical Behaviors

Clients with schizophrenia may experience atypical behaviors characterized by social isolation, poor attention to hygiene, aggressive verbal or physical outbursts not following social norms, and engaging in "boundary violations" (e.g., not respecting others' property, feelings, or personal space). When any of these behaviors is displayed, the therapist can positively redirect the client to a structured activity or link the behavior issue to a mental health education topic. For example, the therapist may choose to use the stress–diathesis model to explain the development of such behavioral habits and discuss ways to manage such habits in the context of milieu therapy. The therapist may also use a self-assessment questionnaire (see Appendix B) or possibly assign a homework exercise (see *Worksheets 5, 9,* and *10*) to highlight personal awareness of these behaviors and to identify coping strategies to manage these behaviors more effectively.

Examples of Managing Atypical Behaviors

Personal Hygiene A group member may comment, for example, on a particular client who is disheveled and demonstrates poor personal hygiene. The therapist may then introduce a discussion on the importance of personal hygiene, by asking various members their opinion about the importance of maintaining personal hygiene for health and social reasons, and write the answers on an easel or whiteboard. The therapist may supplement the discussion by bringing in visually presented materials about optimal body functioning, comparing the body to, for example, a "car engine model," and discussing the need for proper maintenance of the body akin to proper maintenance of a car engine. In our discussion, we have used the car engine model in different scenarios to highlight the importance of maintaining a healthy body and mind, and have found clients receptive to discussing hygiene issues in this manner. In the discussion of personal hygiene, besides, for example, discussing grooming, showering, and brushing teeth, we have talked about the importance of a proper diet and regular bowel elimination habits.

Boundary Violations These might include taking someone's possession without permission, making inappropriate "sexual comments," or touching. In the group, a client may comment, for example, about "inappropriate behavior" by another group member or by someone not in the group. The therapist may use this to introduce a discussion about various "inappropriate behaviors" that violate personal boundaries, without confronting the client against whom the comment is made. In the process, the therapist provides the group with specific guidelines of socially sanctioned behaviors and provides suggestions of strategies that may be useful by, for example, asking questions and eliciting relevant appropriate answers from group members. This avoids making a particular client a subject of discussion on matters which may make him or her "uncomfortable." The topic is addressed, thus, in the context of mental health education, social skills training, and peer teaching to promote adaptive social behavior. The therapist may also supplement the discussion by providing a questionnaire for clients to fill out, or the therapist may bring in handouts for clients to complete to help identify strategies for handling a specific problem (see *Worksheet 9: Problem-solving Worksheet*). The therapist may also emphasize what one can do in private, including engaging in personal fantasies, and what one cannot do in public without violating public standards of conduct. The therapist often recommends that further discussions of personal issues occur with the client's mental health workers outside the session to reinforce that the group format is not the best place to bring up these issues.

Anger Outbursts These can be verbal or physical. Although no actual incidents of physical aggression have been encountered in any MICST group session over a period of more than 20 years, primarily due to the selection criteria (often set by the treatment team)—requiring clinical stability and an "at risk-free" behavior status— we have had occasions whereby a group member might engage in a verbally aggressive outburst directed at another member. The therapist will actively help to de-escalate the situation by reminding the client in a calm voice about the inappropriate nature of the behavior or encouraging the client to discuss the issue with his or her counselor or case manager outside the group session. The therapist may simply change the seating arrangements to give space between the clients involved, or have the client take a "time out" and practice a relaxation exercise in or outside the group room. There have been cases where clients who were not fully stable attended the MICST group, escorted with one-to-one supervision by a mental health worker. This staff person typically assists as needed in de-escalating any challenging behavioral situations or taking the client out of the group briefly and returning when the client is ready to re-engage in the group activity.

As the above scenarios illustrate, the MICST model allows the therapist to use or improvise a wide range of options and strategies in managing different kinds of behaviors that may arise in the course of the group. Having a co-therapist or mental health clinician assisting the group is very helpful in managing the group process; it also provides staff training opportunities. If the group is to be conducted by a single clinician, which has been done by both of the authors for years, then the availability of mental health personnel near the group setting is important, as they can assist in managing some of the potentially "difficult behavior situations" that may occasionally arise.

Guidelines for Starting a MICST Group

Both in inpatient and outpatient settings, initial issues to consider in starting a MICST group often involve:

1. finding a time slot for conducting the group, which does not interfere with clients' ongoing commitment to treatment plan activities or services, milieu program-related activities, meal times, treatment team meetings, community outings, or other program activities;
2. identifying clients who could participate in the group; and
3. arranging for transportation to the group.

In the inpatient setting, the therapy room may be some distance away from the unit where the clients reside, and if the unit is a locked facility, many of the clients may not have ground privileges and thus may not be able to leave the unit on their own. For community residence clients, who are, for example, living in a supervised apartment or residential program, group or individual transportation arrangements may need to be made. Some outpatient programs may allow the group to be conducted in a residential facility whereby transportation would not be an issue. Many of the CMHC clients, who live in independent living situations, have been able to attend the MICST group at the mental health center by walking or using public transportation. In inpatient settings, there have been times when the therapist or co-therapist had to escort the clients from their residential unit to the group program. Thus, in scheduling the group meeting time on a patient's treatment plan, the therapist may need to allocate extra time in the patient's schedule to account for transportation to the group.

In planning a MICST group, it is imperative to develop a good working relationship with administrative and clinical personnel who may assist in determining times to schedule the group, clarifying the referral process, locating a group room, and working out transportation issues. Ultimately, the group referral process will need to be approved by administration and the treatment team. The standard referral process used by the facility could be used to refer clients to the MICST group. We have also used our own referral write-up to clarify the expectations and goals of the MICST group. The following is a sample referral form for a MICST group (see also *Handouts 1* and *2*, which can be disseminated to the treatment team and prospective group members to explain the nature of the group).

The Multimodal Integrative Cognitive Stimulation Therapy (MICST) Group

The MICST group (involving body movement–mindfulness–relaxation exercises, cognitive stimulation paper–pencil exercises, mental health education, and social skills training) meets once a week on ——— at ——— am/pm in the following designated place: ———————. The group is run by primary therapist ——— ——————— with a student intern/extern or a mental health worker who is involved in your care.

This group therapy is designed to address the following:

1. To stimulate memory, association, and logical reasoning to help clients process information within a "reality context."
2. To verbalize more effectively coping strategies and understanding of mental illness symptoms.
3. To increase concentration and task involvement, and increase tolerance for one hour of group interaction without "disruption."
4. To learn to practice body movement–mindfulness–relaxation exercises as a way to promote relaxation, and learn how to use positive redirection to cope with "intrusive" or "distressful" thoughts and feelings (psychiatric symptoms).
5. To improve social skills (learning to take turns in group discussions, respond to and initiate asking questions, show interest in following the conversational theme expressed in the group, and to reduce self-centered and self-occupying behaviors in the group setting.

6. To learn to relate to others through one's intact cognitive areas, recall past achievements, practice memory retrieval of personal events and knowledge of facts, and in the process, improve one's positive self-image and self-worth.
7. To learn to accept "corrective feedback" on paper–pencil exercises or check one's thinking through group feedback or objective review of factual information (obtained through Internet research or books).
8. To verbalize periodically how the group process has or has not been helpful and to participate in self-assessment of progress through completing brief questionnaires.
9. To show improved ability to process visually presented cognitive exercises or mental health education materials.

The clinician and co-therapists need to identify a set of cognitive stimulating paper– pencil exercises (e.g., mathematics, word search, general knowledge, word meaning, and comprehension) for each session, geared to the level of cognitive and educational functioning of the group. Usually, two or three exercises should be sufficient for a group session. Over the years, in active collaboration with many student interns and externs involved in co-leading MICST groups, we have developed a large number of such exercises. The exercises are patterned on or adapted from various educational resource materials. Some of the exercises (e.g., mathematics, word search, and personal assessment questionnaires) may be used again in future sessions as clients can benefit from repeated practice of these exercises. Clinicians can also readily adapt any of these exercises to best meet the needs of any particular group or client.

A specific curriculum of discussion topics is not followed, although group facilitators as well as group members may recommend discussion topics. We outline a semi-structured plan for implementing a 12-week MICST group using predetermined discussion topics and paper–pencil exercises (see Appendix D). This semi-structured plan may be helpful if you are thinking about starting a MICST group for the first time and feel more comfortable with structuring the sessions.

At times, we have made specific booklets of exercises for clients and would have clients work at their own pace in completing the exercises outside the group sessions. We observed that some clients, while waiting for the group, would display restlessness and anxiety or present a "vacant look" that seemed to signify possible preoccupation with psychiatric symptoms. Upon observing this, we might ask clients to work on paper–pencil exercises prior to the start of the group by using their individual workbook; or we might encourage them to continue on an exercise that they left from the previous session. For clients who did not appear to be interested in working on their workbook exercises during this period, we might direct them to either read or look at one of the various pictorial general knowledge books that we would bring to the session to keep clients "cognitively engaged." The idea is to teach clients the practice of mind stimulation exercises as soon as they arrive at the group and to provide practical redirection strategies to minimize ruminative thinking.

The MICST group room should be equipped with a whiteboard, blackboard, or easel. A computer printer station with an Internet connection in the therapy room or in the vicinity will be useful to research topics, validate information, and generate handouts from a particular group session. Sometimes clients might give incorrect information about a specific topic or in response to a question on a paper–pencil exercise. We have found that most clients often respond quite positively when presented with a printout of the correct information, even clients who have difficulty in accepting feedback or who may have a suspicious or "paranoid" disposition. We have also used the computer to access web sites like the "Astronomy Picture of the Day" to generate interest in astronomy and existential perspectives of life, as well as to access web sites that explore common knowledge interests of clients (e.g., baseball statistics, weather, local news).

Evaluating the MICST Group

The MICST group can be evaluated as needed through using various assessment methods. The particular assessment methods used and the frequency with which the group is evaluated will be determined by the group leader, the particular needs of a group, the group setting, the treatment team, as well as by group members' interest in participating in the evaluation process. The assessment process helps clients to reflect on their progress and functioning, and promote self-reflection. It also allows the therapist to evaluate his or her degree of success in conducting the group and stimulates new ideas and approaches to make the group more effective.

We have evaluated the MICST groups through various methods such as:

1. client questionnaires;
2. post-group reflections from group facilitators;
3. directly soliciting clients' verbal feedback;
4. reviewing changes in the quality of clients' responses on the paper–pencil exercises;
5. staff feedback questionnaires; and
6. collecting outcome data on various clinical indices.

Each of these methods will be discussed below to demonstrate how they can provide useful data.

Client Feedback Questionnaires

Over the years, group members have been asked periodically to fill out various assessment questionnaires to evaluate the effectiveness of MICST (see Appendix C for sample client feedback questionnaires). We did not use any standardized questionnaires, as our focus was not to compare group members' functioning with any standardized groups, but rather we were interested in assessing how clients perceived themselves as benefitting from the group, and learning which group elements clients felt were most helpful.

Participating in this evaluation process also helps clients increase their awareness of the various symptom control strategies they have used. Clients also use the group evaluation process to gain support and understanding of how to manage symptoms better and work toward their personal goals. The questionnaires also invite clients to identify what aspects of their cognitive and memory skills they would like to improve upon, and what aspects of the MICST model have been most helpful.

Seligman (1995) commented on a Consumer Reports Survey which assessed the effectiveness of psychotherapy; he advocated the "consumer survey technique" as a valid method of evaluating the effectiveness of psychotherapy. We feel that using client feedback questionnaires to evaluate the effectiveness of the MICST model—in conjunction with clinical observations of clients' functioning in the group, as well as reports of their functioning outside the group by staff or family members—are "valid measures" of the effectiveness of the model. Moreover, in the process of completing these questionnaires, clients are able to practice self-reflection, demonstrate that they can "internalize" and articulate the benefits of MICST, and demonstrate capacity for "insight." The following data show evidence of this.

Sample Client Feedback Questionnaire Results

Client Feedback Questionnaire 1 We designed a questionnaire (see Appendix C: Questionnaire 1) to elicit which elements of MICST clients reported benefitting from. We administered the questionnaire to 46 clients (12 inpatients and 34 outpatients) who had been attending MICST for an average of 26.9 months. As reported in our earlier publication (Ahmed & Boisvert, 2003b), all clients indicated benefitting from some features of MICST: 75% of participants noted that the body movement–mindfulness–relaxation exercise was helpful; 63% noted that feedback on paper–pencil exercises was helpful; 50% reported that discussing mental health topics was helpful; 50% reported that paper–pencil cognitive exercises were helpful; 30% felt that talking about their past week's events (an exercise stimulating episodic memory, which is often compromised in persons with schizophrenia) was helpful.

Analysis of the spontaneous comments that 27 of the 46 clients made on the questionnaire indicated that their involvement in MICST "improved their concentration," "taught them relaxation skills," "increased their knowledge by hearing about people, places, and things," and "improved their social interaction." Other comments indicated that MICST helped clients to "listen better," "improve reading and writing," "organize their thinking," and "normalize their life."

Client Feedback Questionnaire 2 We also used another questionnaire (see Appendix C: Questionnaire 2), which was administered to two different groups at two different time periods: group 1 = 15 clients (all inpatients); group 2 = 32 clients (7 inpatients and 25 outpatients). On the questionnaire, the clients were required to choose between two alternatives, one indicating "benefitting" and the other indicating "not benefitting" in 11 functional areas. Figure 6.2 presents the data, which indicate that 80–100% of the clients in group 1 reported

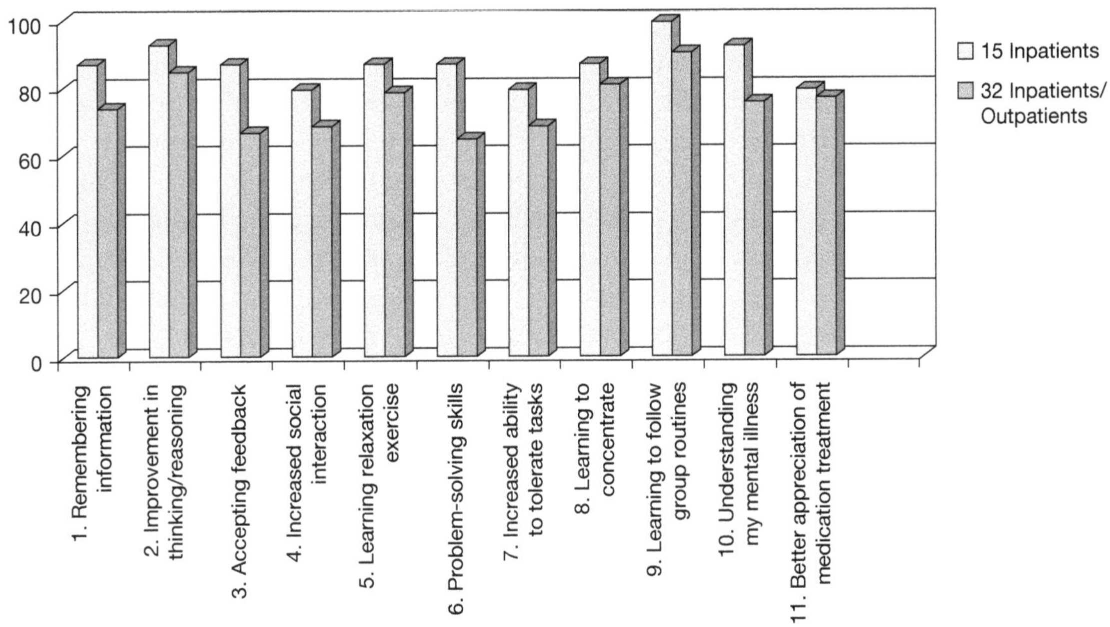

FIGURE 6.2 Percentage of clients from an inpatient group (N = 15) and clients from an inpatient (N = 7) and an outpatient (N = 25) group reporting benefitting in 11 areas of functioning highlighted in the MICST group treatment model (see Appendix C for a copy of the questionnaire)

benefitting in all 11 areas of functioning. For group 2, 65–90% of clients reported benefitting in the same 11 areas of functioning.

Client Feedback Questionnaire 3 A review of clients' responses to open-ended questions on another outcome questionnaire (see Appendix C: Questionnaire 3) is presented below and illustrates the various ways that participants reported their experiences with MICST. As noted, the vast majority of clients reported very positive benefits from the group.

Q1. How does the cognitive group (MICST) help you in the management of psychiatric symptoms in your present situation?

Examples of neutral and negative comments (11 client responses) are presented in a composite form from various participants:

"I don't know" (4); "It does not help me" (2); "Does not make me feel better about myself sometimes"; "I don't have psychiatric symptoms"; "Usual customs"; "My mind is blank from shock treatment"; "Not sure, it does."

Examples of positive comments (26 client responses): "It helps"; "I am less shy"; "Tell everybody our troubles . . . get others advice"; "It lets us [do] what we should do in case our symptom come back and give skills to help us with our sickness"; "You learn from others . . ."; "Makes me happier because it's something to do and I look forward to the next one"; "Relaxation"; "Helps me to learn of things more seriously"; "By listening . . . more attention, and knowing what the group is thinking about"; "I think looking at all the different thoughts, opinions, actions, coupled with Dr. Ahmed's [therapist] rich knowledge of information is very helpful to me"; "It comes out pretty good"; "I can't diagnose myself . . . it keeps it in order I guess"; "Helps me to talk about things"; "Help me think things through"; "Helps me to occupy my time"; "Prompt support"; "Group helps me to figure out what my voices mean"; "It helps me feel alright, because I think"; "Helps to look and consider specific mental functions, whatever thinking process . . . organize your thinking process"; "Does not benefit me personally but hear others benefitting . . . they have questions that sometimes are answered"; "Helps to learn about other people['s] illness, thus helping one to understand self"; "Morale boost to hear others talk about efforts"; "Sees the improvement"; "Release the tensions"; "So far I have not had my voices bother me while in cognitive [MICST] group"; "Helps you control your nerves."

The breadth of commentaries and insight demonstrated through these clients' statements are quite noteworthy, attesting to the effectiveness of the MICST model in stimulating various cognitive processes and assisting clients in learning various coping strategies to manage troublesome psychiatric symptoms in a better way.

Q2. What information from the group has been helpful to you in your day-to-day functioning?

Neutral and negative comments (10 client responses): "That's something I can't answer . . .": "None"; "I will catch it again next week at . . ."; "I don't think I have learned anything, I think I understood one thing but I can't remember what it is"; "I don't know" (3); "When he calls you for the group"; "Nothing."

Positive comments (27 client responses): "Daily eating habits"; "Talk about different foods I should eat to keep healthy"; "Position of different countries on the map"; "I have been more sociable"; "Helps me concentrate"; "Helps with positive"; "We are all the same, same sickness helps us deal with ourselves"; "Deep breathing exercise helps me to relax"; "It relaxes me . . ."; "It helps me [be] more focused and to be able to concentrate better"; "Paper and pencil I guess, it get[s] me through the day, it gets me more charged for the day"; "It has been a focus . . . on my daily activities . . . using my time productively"; "Keep things in order"; "Everything, I guess"; "Helps me read, helps me relax"; "Feeling the attention"; "By being towards the goodness . . ."; "Not too much, just exercises I guess"; "It helps me learn English more"; "Use exercises to relieve stress and redirection of thinking process"; "Interacting with the other people in the group"; "Think of reality helps my mental illness"; "Relaxation techniques help . . . stressful situation"; "When everybody is involved in discussion, conversation"; "The breathing exercise . . . when out of gas—asks people how their week was"; "Helped me to send a letter to someone on TV"; "Coping, when it comes to problems."

The examples of responses these clients provided illustrate how many clients are able to articulate or remember what they learned specifically from the group. The responses as a whole reflect the goals and expected benefits from MICST.

Q3. In what ways have you improved the most as a result of your participation in the group (MICST)?

Neutral and negative comments (6 client responses): "I am not sure"; "I don't know" (3); "No improvement"; "None."

Positive comments (31 client responses): "Communicating verbally and written with people"; "Healthy foods . . . I have been participating, it has been educational"; "It helped my alertness"; "Listening to Charlie [therapist] is helping me";" "Spelling"; "I am more active, I talk more, I talk about my feelings"; "Breathing exercise, we can take that home and practice"; "A little bit more open, does not bother me to talk in family group anymore"; "I smile more"; "I pick up reading better and how other people think about things"; "I feel that I can concentrate more on word thoughts"; "I have made a lot of improvements, learning more about myself . . . stress management"; "I am more charged to do right thing . . ."; "In responsibilities—I am more responsible as a result of being in group. The grounds pass that I got in fact was result of this group [MICST]"; "It makes it pretty good"; "More orderly thoughts, focus in on"; "Helps me clean my head"; "I feel better after the group"; "Reading"; "Working with the groups helps with socializing with the others"; "Yes"; "Just an idea of what to do . . . It helps your brain"; "What I learn I need time to . . . but on my mind because I was in the [hospital]"; "Concentrating better on selected topics and spontaneous thinking"; "More comfortable in talking in group setting"; "I am coordinating, thinking and not sure letting thoughts flow on their own without my guidance"; "Organize the way of thinking"; "Righting [writing] paper"; "Breathing"; "The voice don't bother me there"; "Comfortable talking in the group . . . helps with reading."

Client Feedback Questionnaire 4 We present another example of an open-ended questionnaire (see Appendix C: Questionnaire 4) with 15 clients, 11 of whom responded in two different sessions. The responses are presented below.

Q1. What do you like about the group (MICST)?

"Have a time talk"; "Talk about the brain and the universe"; "About others daily feelings"; "Learn how to cope with stress"; "Meditation help me to relax"; "Keep me at peace with my thoughts"; "Good learning like strategies"; "I like the educational values of the group with the worksheets"; "I like Dr. Ahmed's [therapist] techniques and also his expression"; "I like the writing materials . . . I learn a lot . . . I think it is fun"; "I like more in each meeting, I enjoy in participation"; "The focusing of reality and getting with the present"; "The social interaction of things that are problems with society."

Q2. What don't you like about this group?

"Paper and pencil exercises because we need pens"; "Bad vibes . . . about things [other clients' responses] that has nothing to do about this group"; "Ignorance . . . disruption"; "People are not patient or creative in this group and cause criticism to themselves, we need a longer group time"; "Nothing . . . I don't like the breathing"; "We all think and answer questions to get the right answers"; "The load of paper and pencil exercises"; "Waiting for treatment to take place"; "Too short . . ."

Q3. What kind of changes does the group need?

"A cooler . . . bigger room . . . less people"; "More talking, less writing . . . more what our psychology [therapist?] think of us": "More effort, better concentration"; "A longer time and college level teachings with essay form and books"; "Less interruptions"; "To improve myself"; "More discussion of mental health issues"; "An increase in optimistic outlook"; "To go outside and discuss our problems about why we are here."

Q4. How did this cognitive skills (MICST) group help you?

"It keeps me realizing that I am more intelligent than I thought . . . It gives a positive outlook about myself"; "It made me appreciate my freedom more"; "Learning, interacting, things, etc."; "It gave me insight and learning skills . . . and made my problems less being a part to it"; "On my concentration, learning"; "Taught me how to face daily issues with more of a positive attitude"; "It helped me a lot . . . I am correcting stress issue"; "Taught me how to face daily issues with more of a positive attitude"; "Repetition of focusing makes it easier to understand"; "It helps me relax a little"; "It has made me more aware of my problems."

Reading the responses, one can see how the basic MICST goals of providing body movement–mindfulness–relaxation exercises, paper–pencil thinking exercises, and other interventions such as using positive redirection to deal with psychiatric symptoms, are mentioned by clients as being beneficial. A number of clients reported gaining insight into and understanding of how to cope better with their symptoms, although the MICST model does not focus on this as much as other traditional therapy approaches. However, we believe our focus on incorporating the various MICST mind stimulation activities helps to raise clients' awareness and understanding of mental health and behavior issues, and facilitates their learning new coping strategies (a common goal endorsed by many other therapy approaches as well).

The ideas and issues mentioned by clients on the questionnaires can also be used to generate discussion topics about recovery. The responses we cite provide useful guidelines for what kinds of topics and issues can be highlighted, how to keep participants therapeutically engaged in a group therapy, and how to stimulate clients' self-awareness and self-reflection. To all of us clinicians, the breadth and depth of these client responses provide encouragement and hope for recovery for these challenging mental health clients. We encourage practicing clinicians as well as research clinicians to use self-assessment questionnaires increasingly as a way to assess outcomes, and at the same time provide a vehicle for clients to process their own functioning, organize in a better way their understanding of the mental health issues that affect their functioning, and increase their awareness of the benefits of therapeutic interventions.

Post-group Reflections

Another method of evaluation we have used for staff training is to discuss and share post-group reflections. We have found it important to meet with co-facilitators and student trainees to discuss impressions and observations of the group session. Ideally, at the end of each group, group facilitators share observations about the group process and outcome. This is a chance to discuss global group management issues and any particular client interactions that are deemed relevant to review. For example, nuances of certain client interactions may be important to review, and in the process, staff may discover new ways of understanding and relating to a particular client. This information can be communicated to the case manager or residential or hospital staff and used in future interactions with the client. For example, one may learn about a particular interest of a client, discover a certain learning style of a client, or find ways to improve communication and information processing with a client.

Directly Soliciting Clients' Verbal Feedback

Directly assessing clients' impressions of the different MICST group activities is important and serves to engage clients more in taking personal responsibility for their own self-care and personal goals. As is customary in measuring the impact of therapy, clinicians often solicit from clients their impressions of the benefits of therapy. In fact, self-report has been the most widely used method of assessing the impact of therapy (Hatfield & Ogles, 2004).

Clinicians can use an entire MICST session to discuss the benefits of MICST; to solicit feedback from clients about how they are benefitting from the various group activities; and to review how the individual MICST components can contribute to recovery and improve functioning.

Reviewing the Paper–Pencil Exercises

The paper–pencil exercises completed by clients over time can also provide valuable data to assess progress and possible changes in a client's level of participation. Mental health workers can develop a folder for each group participant and periodically review any progress that the client has demonstrated on the paper–pencil exercises. The changes that may be noticeable may include, for example, improvement in hand writing, improvement in organization, improvement in quality of response, or improvement in quantity of responses. Reviewing clients' paper–pencil exercises is also another "valid" way to assess clients' improvement in their thinking over time, rather than relying solely on behavioral observations.

Staff Feedback Questionnaire

We had the opportunity to administer a feedback questionnaire to 17 mental health workers who participated in MICST groups (see Appendix C: Questionnaire 5). Below we list the questions asked and the responses to these questions (we include all of the staff comments).

Q1. Do you feel that your involvement and participation in the cognitive skills (MICST) training group has been helpful to you in developing a better understanding of your clients' functioning?

"I can better see how clients process information and can see how ideas become mixed up . . . Lets me know what areas my clients need assistance with . . . I have learned useful ways to assist client[s] in functioning on tasks at hand rather [than] that client's internal world . . . Clients benefit from sharpening their cognitive skills which increases their ability to communicate . . . [C]lients gain more intense insight . . . Being able to see [the] client's intellectual functioning, I was surprised to see that our clients are higher functioning than I thought . . . I observed clients functioning better when they are asked to concentrate on a specific topic . . . It appears that the clients feel very comfortable in cognitive skills, allowing them to express their feelings."

Q2. Did you personally feel that the clients benefitted from participation in this cognitive skills training (MICST) group?

"The group appears to build self-esteem . . . They learn to listen to each other and learn discussion skills, self-esteem . . . It helps them interact with other consumers and staff, helps us to know what their needs are . . . Most clients take great pride in working on paper-and-pencil exercises . . . A community connection is made through sharing personal similarities . . . Increases socialization, increases use of thought process . . . [s]lightly."

Q3. What do you attribute the clients' motivation to attend the cognitive skills training (MICST) group to?

"Some clients really enjoy group; a few others do not like it . . . They learn to communicate and learn skills . . . They are motivated by the desire to do good work and focus on something outside themselves . . . Some of [the] clients like to have a chance to use their minds instead of just lying around all day . . . Socialization opportunities, I think some enjoy social interaction . . . I feel that the clients enjoy the group because it focuses on realistic issues . . . Clients are very comfortable with Dr. Ahmed [therapist], quick pace of the group, and the personal attention given to each client."

Q4. Are there any particular areas in which you have applied the cognitive skills training (MICST) concepts to your individual work with clients?

"Using relaxation exercise, when clients are agitated . . . Learned new ways of communicating ideas to clients by having a better idea of how they think . . . To help

> clients focus on thought, outside their illness . . . Relaxation techniques . . . having client complete a task using step-by-step instructions and thinking about what he/she is doing . . . I feel the clients can obtain good habits in the long run by giving them consistent reminders of such habits . . . Deep breathing increases communication among clients."

Analysis of ideas and thoughts expressed by these mental health workers (primarily direct-care staff who had the opportunity to observe clients' participation in the MICST group) also validates clients' perceptions of how the group has been helpful, and is remarkably consistent with our expressed goals and aspirations for MICST. These mental health workers' perceptions of the effectiveness of MICST also helps them to motivate mental health staff to reinforce MICST goals outside the group session, and helps staff develop more effective ways of interacting with clients and maximizing communication with them.

Collecting Outcome Data

Initial Outcome Evaluation

In the initial development and practice of MICST, we conducted a study with eight members, where we compared their level of functioning using a variety of intellectual and adaptive behavior measures between two time periods, one prior to their involvement in MICST, and one six months after their involvement in MICST. The results, as reported previously (Ahmed & Goldman, 1994), indicated that all participants showed improvements on some aspect of the outcome measures used—e.g., cognitive functioning as measured by the Wechsler Adult Intelligence Scale-Revised (WAIS-R), the Draw-A-Person (DAP) test, and the Multi-Function Needs Assessment (MFNA). The Multi-Function Needs Assessment was developed by the Rhode Island Department of Mental Health, Retardation and Hospitals (1986). Two of the three participants on whom complete WAIS-R pre- and post-treatment comparison data were available showed significant improvement on the Full Scale IQ, and on the DAP. All group members "displayed significant improvement in the quality of the figures by inclusion of more details, better integration of lines and parts of the body, and more realistic presentation of figures" (Ahmed & Goldman, 1994, p. 390). The MFNA scores showed "positive changes for the group members in relevant areas of functioning such as verbal communication, basic social behavior, basic social skills, and recreational and leisure activities" (Ahmed & Goldman, 1994, p. 390).

On the client feedback questionnaire, five of the six participants reported that activities helped them to think and remember better, and reported that the body movement–mindfulness–relaxation exercise and the paper–pencil exercises were most useful. On the "most improved" participant in the group, the treating psychiatrist's comment articulates the benefit of the group for this client:

> During the last five to six months, the group home staff has reported a continuing trend toward improved verbal skills and more appropriate social interactions with both staff

and other group home residents. Since there was no change in medication or staff intervention during this time, my clinical impression is that the improvement was the result of the group treatment.

(Ahmed & Goldman, 1994, p. 391)

MICST and Non-MICST Group Comparison Data

Since MICST practice was entirely supported and conducted within the routine clinical practice of the senior author (Mohiuddin Ahmed), in collaboration with a number of graduate student interns and externs, and with support from key administrative, clinical, and direct-care staff, without any external research funding, we had to use the available clinical data in the "natural" environment to compare the MICST and the non-MICST groups. In our prior publication (see Ahmed & Boisvert, 2003b, pp. 648–649), we reported the following data:

- *Comparison of program activities*: Three CMHC group homes that had participated in MICST were compared with one group home that had not participated in MICST (non-MICST Group). These two groups were compared on behavior incidents, day program attendance, and participation in evening social club activities over a three-year period. Results indicated that the MICST group compared with the non-MICST group displayed fewer behavior incidents and demonstrated more participation in daytime programs and activities as well as greater participation in evening social club events.
- *Risk factor analysis:* We also reported data that compared a MICST group of ten clients with another group of ten clients that was selected for participation in a concurrent MICST group, but this group did not materialize due to unforeseen circumstances. This presented us with a natural control group, which was not necessarily evenly matched, as in a typical experimental control group design, other than having a common diagnosis of schizophrenia and status as an outpatient Community Support Program (CSP) client in a CMHC. When compared on the "risk management ratings" that are recorded following individual sessions with clients, we noted that while the MICST group had significantly higher "risk ratings" than the non-MICST group at the baseline phase, over a course of six months, the risk rating scores for the MICST group became significantly lower than those for the non-MICST group.

We believe that the various methods of data collection that we have used, despite drawing from a limited database, highlight a potential approach to evaluating the effectiveness of a therapeutic intervention with the emerging availability of electronic clinical records and advanced computerized data collection systems. This "effectiveness study approach," using naturally occurring data, we believe, will minimize the necessity for designing a more "traditional efficacy study," and all the challenges that lie therein such as accessing a funding resource, recruiting subjects, and implementing a screening protocol based on specific selection criteria.

At various points in our data collection process, we (the authors) and the various psychology interns and externs assisting the MICST group had to rely on active support and cooperation from key administrative and clinical staff as well as direct-care personnel. We believe that the inherent appeal of the model as being "clinically effective and user-friendly" helped to generate this kind of acceptance and cooperation necessary for the data collection process. The primary clinician conducting MICST must be a team player, and while presenting the usefulness of the model to both clients and mental health workers, must be sensitive to "political professional turf issues" and avoid communicating that MICST is "superior" to or should replace other therapeutic approaches. Rather it should be presented as an adjunct therapeutic intervention in the client's service program.

In presenting our evaluation data and observations, we are presenting the notion that a psychotherapy "outcome study model" for severe and persistent mental illness, such as schizophrenia, should follow the same "design of intervention" as in chronic physical illness, such as diabetes or hypertension or as in the standard medication treatment model for schizophrenia. That is, as introduced as our position in Chapter 1, once a particular outcome has been found to be beneficial for persons with schizophrenia, it should be built into the client's therapeutic regimen on an ongoing basis ("ABB" model), without needing to demonstrate that the intervention generalizes outside the therapy sessions or that the benefits of the intervention are sustained when the treatment is withdrawn ("ABA" model). We believe that a cognitively stimulating therapeutic milieu is critical for ongoing recovery and improved outcome, and that any intervention deemed to be therapeutically beneficial needs to be routinely built into the client's therapeutic milieu or service program.

Chapter 7

Adapting MICST to Individual Therapy Sessions

This chapter focuses on applying the MICST model to individual therapy sessions with persons with schizophrenia, primarily based on the senior author's (Mohiuddin Ahmed) many years of clinical experience working in inpatient and outpatient mental health settings. The goal in individual therapy sessions is to use the core elements of MICST to stimulate and access clients' conscious "intact" memories, associations, semantic knowledge, and interests. Accessing these intact functions, in turn, leads to discussing information that is more "factual" and "reality-based." This process helps to redirect clients away from their obsessive preoccupation with "psychiatric symptoms" (e.g., delusions, hallucinations, or negative emotional feelings or thoughts). The underlying assumption is that by increasing the availability of "reality-based" themes and stimulating "intact" areas of cognitive functioning, one reduces the availability of "atypical associations" and associated negative feelings and thoughts expressed in psychiatric symptoms. At the same time, the client's natural adaptive and coping skills are enhanced by making these skills available to conscious reasoning in the therapy process. Additionally, clients are "primed" through the "mind stimulation" process to be more amenable to redirection and support from their existing therapeutic milieu and to adhere to their productive day routine, including their medication and psychosocial support services regimen. The individual therapy MICST model, involving "mind stimulation techniques," is considered to be an adjunct to ongoing medication management and other psychosocial–rehabilitation support services that clients are receiving, including case management or other forms of individual and group therapy.

The MICST model can be adapted to individual therapy sessions in various ways. In particular, we illustrate in this chapter how the MICST model can be adapted to individual therapy work by:

1. Using *computer-facilitated therapy* to engage clients more actively in the therapy process, elicit more reality-based dialogue, and facilitate clients' information processing by using visual cues and printouts from the therapy session.
2. Using the *core elements of MICST* (e.g., BMR exercises; discussion of general knowledge and personal interest topics; and paper–pencil cognitive exercises) to

structure individual therapy sessions and to individualize cognitive interventions for clients.

We use several case vignettes to illustrate how elements of the MICST model have been used in individual therapy sessions with clients with schizophrenia, as well as report on our published work on *computer-facilitated therapy*. Computer-facilitated therapy is used to enhance communication with persons with schizophrenia by, for example, using a word-processor to incorporate visual presentations of spoken words. As such it is guided by the fundamental features of the MICST model (e.g., using multimodal methods of communication) to enhance information processing in the psychotherapy dialogue.

We also discuss how clinicians can incorporate the *core elements of MICST* into individual therapy sessions. For example, we discuss how the body movement–mindfulness–relaxation exercises can be incorporated into individual sessions and how the therapy encounter can be maximized and more focused by facilitating discussions with clients drawing from their own knowledge base and personal interests. We also discuss how clinicians can use paper–pencil exercises to engage clients more actively in the therapy session by stimulating intact areas of functioning.

Computer-facilitated Therapy with Persons with Schizophrenia

Current literature suggests that working memory deficits are present in a variety of psychiatrically compromised people of all ages. In persons with schizophrenia, working memory (e.g., ability to hold information on line to follow a train of thought, solve a problem, or bring in relevant associations to sustain a conversation) is often impaired due to attention and concentration difficulties, intrusion of psychiatric symptoms, and irrelevant associations in their thought processes (Goldman-Rakic, 1994; Spindler et al., 1997). These deficits may make it particularly challenging for clients to respond successfully to traditional conversational therapy, which focuses primarily on the auditory channel of communication (hearing words and responding to spoken words). Over the years, we have published several articles demonstrating how one can use computer word-processing to conduct reality-based individual therapy sessions with persons with schizophrenia (Ahmed, 1998; Ahmed et al., 1997; Ahmed & Boisvert, 2003a, 2006a). By presenting spoken words visually via the computer word-processing screen (see Figure 7.1), communication with patients can be enhanced and become more goal-focused. Figure 7.1 illustrates the layout of the work station in conducting computer-facilitated therapy with clients.

The fundamental features of computer-facilitated therapy include the following:

- The therapist does the typing of the therapist's questions and the client's responses, which the client can view, correct, or clarify to make sure he or she understands what is being typed.
- The therapist's questions, clarifications, and statements can be put in parentheses to differentiate these from the client's verbalizations.

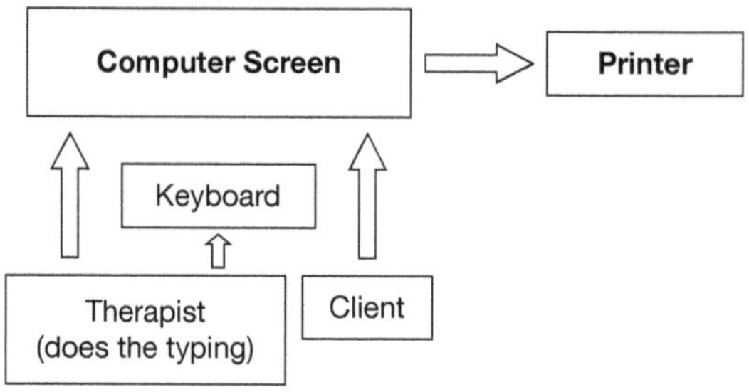

FIGURE 7.1 Layout of the workstation for computer-facilitated therapy with persons with schizophrenia

- The therapist can type verbatim responses to questions or type selected aspects of the client's responses during the conversation. The therapist can also use any other abbreviated form as long as the client consents to what is being typed.
- Printouts from the session can be shared with the treatment team as long as the client consents.
- The printouts given to clients can act as a reminder of the issues discussed in the session and can aid the client in rehearsing and practicing coping strategies in between sessions.
- The printouts can be placed in the clinical record and shared with the treatment team to support the client's recovery process, as well as to give the treatment team knowledge and information about areas discussed in the individual sessions that can be addressed later in follow-up sessions with the client.

Using visual representation of spoken words via computer technology is consistent with the widespread use of various forms of visual media and typewritten forms of communication such as handouts, PowerPoint presentations, and texting devices, all of which are routinely used today in a wide variety of educational, business, and social environments. While in many forms of therapy, including dialectical behavior therapy or other variants of cognitive-behavioral therapy, written materials may be used, computer-facilitated therapy deliberately uses written materials and visual representations of spoken words to compensate for clients' auditory processing deficits. These other therapy approaches may not acknowledge this in their rationale for using written materials.

Computer-facilitated therapy is a variant of the multimodal aspect of the MICST model in that it enhances and stimulates thinking processes during the therapy interaction by providing a multimodal communication format. Combining visual and auditory modes in the therapy interaction helps to stimulate clients' mental functioning and enhance attention and concentration while clients are engaged in the therapy dialogue. This multimodal approach also helps to compensate for clients' working memory deficits by providing visual cues and prompts related to what the client is conversing about. This helps clients to stay focused in a reality-based conversation, in part by providing immediate feedback, via the computer screen, to the clients' verbalizations.

Computer-facilitated therapy also assists clients in long-term memory practice or rehearsing issues discussed in the session by providing clients with printouts immediately following the therapy session. This helps to generalize the positive effects of the therapy session (remembering issues and ideas discussed) by giving the client an opportunity to review what was discussed in the session. Even when clients are experiencing chronic active psychiatric symptoms and have been unresponsive to medication or other interventions, we find that through the computer-facilitated dialogue process, many clients are able to express their thoughts more clearly and often in an insightful manner.

We provide five examples of how computer-facilitated therapy can be used in individual work with clients. Computer-facilitated therapy can be used:

1. to facilitate information processing and reality-based conversations;
2. to facilitate the client's reporting of his or her psychiatric history and gaining insight into "psychodynamic issues";
3. to generate cognitive-behavioral statements or coping strategies;
4. to provide computer-generated printouts summarizing themes and issues discussed during the more traditional verbal-type therapy dialogue in a session; and
5. to organize the client's history, issues, and goals by using a computer "text box" style of writing.

Each example is followed by vignettes extracted from actual therapy sessions with clients who present with varied degrees of "cognitive deficits" and "regression" as a result of their long-term history of schizophrenia. We have excluded any identifying information or clinical material that would jeopardize anonymity or confidentiality.

Example 1: Using Computer-facilitated Therapy to Facilitate Information Processing and Reality-based Conversations

Vignette 1

This client consistently exhibits inappropriate laughter and often talks to himself. The client's clinical symptoms are generally unresponsive to medication or other traditional milieu or therapeutic interventions. The client was involved in brief sessions of psychotherapy involving computer-facilitated communication. The therapist's questions are in parentheses.

> (Q. *"What makes you laugh?"*) "I don't want to get too high or too low . . . I want to stay in the middle, it makes me feel good, I am not depressed when I laugh . . . It is not right for people to laugh too much . . . It is not normal." (Q. *"Does medication help you?"*) "Does not do anything, once in a while it helps." (Q. *"Do you want to stop laughing?"*) "Yes, but I don't want to get depressed . . . When I am not laughing, I get depressed . . . I don't want that, I want to get party feel like everyone else . . ."
>
> *(Ahmed, 1998, p. 401)*

In another session, the same client commented on the benefit of computer-facilitated therapy by stating: "It helps . . . I can remember by seeing the words on the screen in my head" (Ahmed, 1998, p. 402).

This patient was able to talk coherently about issues, including his educational history and drug use, and refrained from laughing inappropriately while reading the essence of our dialogue on the computer screen. The client's ability to organize his thought processes and minimize "inappropriate verbalizations" during the computer-aided therapy dialogue was quite notable. We believe that providing the opportunity for the client to review his spoken language on the computer screen actively interfered with his psychotic thought processes and associated behaviors (e.g., laughing inappropriately to inner voices or communication), and promoted awareness and more self-control over his psychiatric symptoms.

Vignette 2

This client expresses delusions of grandeur in routine conversations, while showing considerable insight and understanding of coping strategies, a good memory for issues discussed in session (in part, because of computer printouts from the sessions), and articulates well the positive benefits derived from medication to control psychotic symptoms. Several sessions are combined here.

> (Q. *"Can you tell me the important things we have discussed so far in various sessions?"*) "We talked about psychological processes of the brain, we just scanned over it, nothing deep . . . we were talking about trauma and injury . . . and we were discussing how brain and our mind reacts to injury . . . When brain is functioning properly, we don't have hallucinations . . . we don't have nightmares . . . we don't have fears . . . we stop medications, we have fears, hallucinations . . . it is necessary to stay on medications . . . Would you believe, when we complain about side effects they decrease medication . . . We talked about the importance of medication, hallucinations, sleeping well . . . proper diet . . . and keeping busy . . . I am not having hallucinations now . . ." (Q. *"What do you mean by hallucinations?"*) "Hallucinations are frightening nightmares that we feel really happening to us and we cannot separate them from reality . . . it takes over our lives, and we live in the fear of dying or someone close to us being murdered, for instances." (Q. *"How do you know when such an experience is real or not real?"*) "When you are ill, you cannot tell when it is real or not real, in the past when I was very ill, I would be punching at nobody or in the air, I could not tell the difference . . . if a person makes sense to the doctors or others around him, then he is not mentally ill, but if a person does not make sense and he is babbling, then he is ill."
>
> (Q. *"How does this kind of work with the computer help?"*) "I can reflect on what I said. I can see the train of my thought . . . I can see how my brain processes are functioning . . . everything is in unison . . . and it is a step-by-step process . . . and we are not jumping around . . . before when I was talking, I would find that my brain was not in unison with my words. I would be talking, but my brain was not functioning . . . I could not say the words . . . (now) when I have to discuss my thoughts, I have to keep at even keel and discuss things that other people can corroborate with me."
>
> *(Ahmed, 1998, pp. 401–402)*

The above excerpts highlight the client's improved reality-based conversational skills and evidence of insight into psychiatric symptoms when the therapeutic conversation is aided with visual representation of spoken words. It would have been difficult to conduct a meaningful therapeutic dialogue using only traditional conversational therapy with this client who continues to exhibit active psychotic thought processes in spite of complying with medications and psychosocial treatment. For this client, the therapy process needs to address creatively how to "recruit" the client's "intact" cognitive skills, which may not be readily apparent, to facilitate information processing and coping.

Example 2: Using Computer-facilitated Therapy to Facilitate the Client's Reporting of His or Her Psychiatric History and Gaining Insight into "Psychodynamic Issues"

Vignette

This client reportedly has a very high IQ (substantiated by the client's education history and verbal skills) with a long history of psychiatric problems and varied psychiatric diagnoses, including schizoaffective disorder. The following session excerpts demonstrate how the client was able to verbalize and articulate his psychiatric history and symptoms and inner psychological turmoil through the computer-facilitated dialogue. In addition, notice how the client expressed insight into the dynamics of his symptoms through the computer-facilitated cognitive stimulation techniques. In the following examples of the dialogue between the therapist and client, please note that when the therapist offered a question, a (Q) is displayed in the text below, and often without the actual question written. This was done for brevity of computer recording, which enabled the therapist to concentrate more on typing what the client was saying. Material in parentheses represents clarification or summary by the therapist.

Commenting on using the computer-facilitated dialogue process in the initial therapy session: "It is like writing my journal . . . I feel I have complete control of my day of everything I do, including going to the bathroom, taking a shower, getting dressed, doing errands, chores, working (three days a week), and studying . . . I write down the start time and end time. I have three journals, one pocket size, one medium size, and one large, a very complicated system of keeping. I want to be more efficient." (Q.) . . . At age 13 or 14, in Junior High, my behavior became noticeable, my parents took me to see a psychiatrist and a social worker, it did not help . . . I was worse by the time I got to the High School . . . I was nearly incapacitated . . . I was first hospitalized in my Senior Year . . ." (Q.) . . . "Things got badly, after my discharge from (hospital). I lived in my own apartment that (hospital) tried to set up and I was told that I tried to ingest (some household cleaning material) . . ., but I don't have recall . . . I was given ECTs (not sure how it benefitted) . . . I started college . . . lived in a dorm, but I was thrown out . . . my political views were very conservative and it disturbed my roommate . . ." (Q.) . . . "I was there only one week, but I was afraid that I would be contaminated if I share the bathroom . . . the Dean said I should seek psychiatric help . . . I was not expelled . . ." (Q.) . . . "Finally (following several unsuccessful placements and expression of suicidal thoughts about not being able to take care of personal hygiene out of fear of sharing bathrooms) I returned to my parent's house . . . I have moved out now and then to attend colleges . . ." (Q.) . . . "I have a terrible anger problem. I express my violent thoughts to my counselor and therapist, but I don't act on them, but because of my expression, they have a duty to warn—both suicidal and homicidal thoughts. I end up going to hospital . . . I have been in clinical treatment for longtime, and I confess my thoughts . . ."

This client's reporting of the details of his psychiatric history is consistent with his medical record. Using the computer-facilitated technique allowed the client to present his life story in a focused and reality-based conversational manner, which may not have been possible using only the traditional verbal mode of therapy.

The following session excerpts reveal the level of insight and understanding the client has of his psychiatric symptoms, yet also illustrate the ongoing difficulty the client has in being preoccupied with his psychiatric symptoms, which interferes with his everyday functioning. We believe that using visual prompts and inviting the client to actively edit what was typed or written from the dialogue, strengthened the client's understanding and communication of the inner psychodynamic process behind his symptoms.

Client commenting on analysis of depression: In response to the therapist's question: "*What's your understanding of the depression episodes that you mentioned you had gone through?*", the client stated the following: (1st stage) "rapid de-compensation with high level of agitation . . . triggered by an incident that was frightening . . ."; (2nd stage) "Lasted two days but within that stage of feeling, there was a stage of angry outburst . . ."; (3rd stage) "Anger led to reconstitution of the self, got back energy and clarity back." (Q.) . . . "Yes, emptiness stage is most difficult to tolerate; anger outburst helps to get out of 'emptiness.'"

Client commenting on skills training needs to achieve his professional goal: (Q.) . . . "I have a high level of emotional arousal in social situations . . . tendency to over-disclose personal information . . . poor awareness of how the recipient of communication might respond . . ." (Q.) . . . "Yes, that's how I inadvertently drive people away . . . have serious time management problems . . . My compulsive record keeping of everything I do takes time away from my substantive work. My obsession in trying to master all different fields of study makes me less efficient in my daily life . . ."

Client commenting on the benefit of computer-facilitated therapy dialogue: "Yes it does help in my own way . . . I have been making adjustments to my thoughts, feelings, and actions so that I will be more efficient . . . there are many more external demands on my system so I don't have the luxury to be totally thorough in everything I do . . . I used to be punished for lack of thoroughness, now I am being punished for lack of efficiency . . ." (Q.) ("*Who is punishing you?*") "Providence and the Chief . . . Providence is God and Chief is my personal boss, he is not a part of me, he is a discrete supernatural entity" (Q.) . . . "Freud would call the Chief a very overdeveloped and punitive Superego . . ."

This client demonstrates a high level of education, introspection, and "buried insights." Given the framework of visually presenting his spoken words, the client was able to express deep-seated personal thoughts and insights. We believe that this level of communication, using the computer-aided technology, engages the client more in the therapy process, which may eventually contribute to improved cognitive functioning and awareness. Many insightful statements that the client made were aided by the therapist's exploratory questions and the client's opportunity to see his thoughts on the computer screen. This allowed the client to organize his thoughts more logically and coherently. This level of organized thought expression, revealing his insights and understanding, may not have been possible to such a degree in an auditory-based conversational mode. We believe that this level of communication and mind stimulation technique, using computer-aided technology, engages the client more actively in the therapy process.

Example 3: Using Computer-facilitated Therapy to Generate Cognitive-behavioral Statements or Coping Strategies

The following examples demonstrate how computer word-processing can be used to generate cognitive-behavioral statements, specific suggestions, or coping strategies for clients. Because of the client's active involvement in developing these coping strategies and "self-statements," the client develops a "sense of ownership" for generating these statements. The statements are specifically tailor-made to the client's unique condition and level of verbalization, and thus potentially have a more positive influence in guiding the client's behavior and thoughts.

One can use this collaborative process of developing client self-statements and coping strategies to address any specific psychological difficulties such as depression, anxiety, anger, or persistent preoccupation with "negative thoughts" (all potential issues that one may address in traditional psychotherapy sessions). This can be done in a manner that minimizes negative affect, which can often accompany discussions of personal problems, by "objectifying" the discussion process through using the visual modality—a process analogous to writing in a journal.

Vignette 1

This client, with a history of schizophrenia, often engages in inappropriate teasing or verbalizing anger in social situations. This has caused problems for the client and has been a management challenge for staff. The following statements were generated in collaboration with the client and printed out so that the client could use these self-statements outside the therapy sessions to guide his thinking and behavior.

Staying Out of a Verbal or Physical Fight

"A lot of times, I often get into difficulty with others for teasing other clients or staff inappropriately. I don't check myself to see what I should or should not be saying or think about how others may react to me in ways that will cause trouble for me. By making other people angry by what I say to them in the long run gets me into all kinds of trouble in different situations."

"Sometimes when I am upset or want to get attention, I tend to say or do things without thinking whether other people are going to get mad at me. Sometimes seeing other people get worked up or mad by what I say or do is "exciting" and "enjoyable" to me, although it is kind of a "bad attention." I need to change my ways and not try to get "bad attention" that way."

Avoiding Teasing

"I always had difficulties in checking my thoughts before saying them to people. Whenever I feel like saying something, I need to say to myself: 'What do I want to say to the person? What will the person most likely think, say or do if I say what I want to say?' I also need to think whether I will get into trouble or not if I say or do something that my mind tells me to do. By checking my thoughts and actions this way, I will be able to avoid making inappropriate teasing comments that causes trouble for me in the long run."

Following Social Rules of Communication

"Talking to people is like a game. There are some rules that one has to learn to follow. If I don't follow the rules, people get upset with me. One of the rules of talking is that you don't say or tease somebody because that makes the person as well as other important people get upset with me. Then I am breaking the rules of the game of talking with people. I cannot say whatever comes to my mind at the moment just because it might be fun or amusing to me. I have to think that what I say will also be in some ways pleasing to others, and the important people in my life will also be happy knowing what I said or did. By thinking this way, I can check my inappropriate teasing behaviors many times in different social situations."

Effective Listening

"I need to listen to people and use eye contact. I need to not just hear their words and listen to what they are saying while I am looking away at something else or thinking about something else in my mind. By not looking at the person or persons with whom I am talking or who are talking with me, I am missing a lot of information about how people are thinking, feeling, and reacting to what I am saying or doing. I need to change this kind of habit and remind myself to look at the person or persons with whom I am talking."

The therapist, in formulating these statements, did active paraphrasing on behalf of the client, and clarified the meaning of each statement before finalizing the statements, all the while getting acknowledgment from the client that he understood and completely agreed with the statements. One can formulate other cognitive statements and coping strategies tailored to a particular client's self-control training needs, to help a client cope with a specific symptom or problem, or to help a client work toward specific treatment plan goals.

Vignette 2

Here the session provides specific prescriptive behavioral guidelines developed in active collaboration with the client. The ability to formulate therapeutic statements relevant to a given client's situation will depend on the clinician's individual skills and experience, but independent of the clinician's experience, the clinician should be able to formulate some meaningful statements for the client to practice, based on what was discussed in the therapy session.

Behavioral Prescription

1. *Remember the importance of being aware of your schedule of activities and learning to remind yourself about what you are doing on a given day.*
   Knowing what you are supposed to be doing on a given day, helps you direct your thoughts and energies to positive activities and feelings, which will help prevent you from getting overly agitated and depressed. It also helps you to function in a positive manner, providing you with a sense of accomplishment when you do what you are supposed to do. This helps you develop social skills that are necessary for your continued improvement in functioning.

2. *The following guidelines will be helpful to you as you remind yourself everyday of what you are supposed to be doing at different times of the day.*
   This will help you not to dwell on thoughts and feelings that make you angry, and agitated, or depressed, such as thinking about things and events that happened in the past that might bring up unhappy feelings and thoughts in your mind. You have to learn to let go of your past, and redirect yourself to the immediate present, and the future ahead of you, by focusing on what you have to do for the day, and reminding yourself of the schedule for the day. Your case manager or mental health counselor will help you develop a day routine, following your individual treatment plan goals. Your day routine could include the following:
   a. You should develop your schedule of activities in consultation with your caseworker and other involved people in your life (see *Worksheet 11: Day Routine Weekly Schedule* template).
   b. Carry a simple list of your schedule of activities for every day of the week.

c. The day schedule should include all activities, including your personal hygiene, daily chores, recreational activities, and different program activities that you currently attend.
d. If you do not like any particular aspect of your daily chores, you should still do what you are supposed to do until you have a chance to change your schedule in consultation with your supervisor or case manager. What is important is that we do what we have agreed to do or what we are supposed to do.
e. Follow your personal hygiene routine.
f. Practice smiling and saying hello to people.
g. Think that people are friendly and supportive of you.

Example 4: Using Computer-generated Printouts to Summarize Themes and Issues Discussed during the More Traditional Verbal-type Therapy Dialogue in a Session

The following examples show how toward the end of a more traditional conversational psychotherapy session, one can use computer-aided technology to summarize the main points and issues discussed in the session in active collaboration with the client. The client participates in editing what is being typed on the computer screen, and receives the printouts to review after the session. This process can enhance the "generalization" of the therapy experience and help clients remember better, rehearse, and practice coping strategies in between sessions.

Vignette 1

Below is a summary of the issues discussed with the client in the initial session. The client actively participated in the write-up:

1. Reviewed psychiatric and substance abuse history.
2. Acknowledged heavy drinking since age 19 and started drinking more following family death.
3. Able to hold jobs for a long time, but due to "hearing voices" as well as "drinking more," lost jobs and became involved in mental health services on a consistent basis.
4. Married briefly and worked part-time jobs while continuing to drink and take psychiatric medications.
5. Stopped taking psychiatric meds and drinking; wanted to be like anybody else.
6. During this non-compliance phase with psychiatric medications, the client experienced more intense psychiatric symptoms, and was involved in an assault incident for which charges were filed. The client claimed to be "out of his mind" during this phase of living independently.

7. The client states that he is doing well in his current placement, looking forward to doing some part-time work, enjoys participating in various groups and other programs, and acknowledges that in spite of bothersome medication side effects (which in the past led the client to discontinue medications), he is currently medication compliant for fear of relapse. The client also reported being sober at present.
8. The client also states that he enjoys social stimulation and interactions, which he was avoiding, and agrees that this may have contributed to his psychiatric difficulties.
9. The client is willing to maintain current gains and accomplishments, and would work toward a supervised apartment placement in the future.
10. The client was encouraged to write a diary on his thoughts and feelings, as he is reportedly doing now, and may consider writing them on a computer (as the client is computer-literate), and save the writings on a disc for printouts if need be.
11. The client agreed to meet in therapy to gain support and understanding of coping strategies and to participate in cognitive stimulation exercises to promote further recovery.

The traditional verbal conversational mode of therapy would not typically allow for or provide such a summarization of session themes in the form of a printout, which the client can use in between sessions to review. Recognizing the client's long history of authority conflicts and lack of response to more traditional verbal therapy modalities, the client appeared to be much more involved in the therapeutic dialogue process and agreed to follow up suggestions and ideas generated in the session. As for all of us in our daily life, written commitment compared to verbal commitment can have a stronger impact on motivating us. We believe that this technique of using written materials has the potential to engage clients more effectively in the therapy process, increase their awareness of their psychological functioning, and motivate them to reflect on and implement more consistently the behavioral strategies discussed in the sessions.

Vignette 2

Here a summary is provided of the main issues and themes discussed during a course of therapy.

1. Existential preoccupations: The client reports having thoughts that "bad things" might happen and he cannot seem to get rid of the thoughts, which in turn, may immobilize him from any action. This may be associated with feelings of uncertainty, what one may experience in one's day-to-day existence.
2. The client acknowledges that mental illness may have something to do with it. We talked about the universal nature of such feelings, and that the difference between people who appear to be functioning well and people who have mental illness is whether one is able to push out these thoughts and pay attention to one's daily activities. It is the ability of "redirection" that helps people to deal with these troubling and existential thoughts that may occur on a daily basis.

3. The client is dealing with "losses" and "illnesses" in the family. This is also something that we all go through, which the client finds difficult to cope with.
4. We talked about using the "body movement–mindfulness–relaxation exercises" (see Chapter 3) on a daily basis from time to time, to break up the monotony of daily life, and more importantly, to generate "blood flow" in the body, as well as to take the mind off any "obsessive troubling thoughts."
5. The client acknowledges that he has not had the opportunity to discuss these kinds of personal and existential questions and issues before with anybody, and he feels okay to discuss them now.
6. We talked about the effect of energy depletion, which may happen after one has been feeling good for a prolonged time, and doing a lot of things and activities without knowing the build-up of stress, and then "crashing." We talked about monitoring one's build-up of stress, learning to take "breaks," or doing different things, including resting, talking with people about things that are bothering you, watching TV, going for a walk, watching the surroundings as one passes through, and listening to music.

This session illustrates some of the underlying core symptoms that many persons with schizophrenia experience, such as dealing with uncertainties of daily living, being immobilized by "ambivalence," obsessive preoccupation with negative thoughts, and lacking motivation for everyday activities. The session also touches on the issue of relapse resulting from a breakdown of "stress regulation." This can be triggered either by "positive" events (engagement in seemingly too many productive activities) or "negative" events (family stressors, substance use, physical illness), making some persons with schizophrenia prone to relapse, which has been a puzzling issue for many caregivers, in spite of the client's seeming adherence to treatment interventions.

The therapist needs to use words and language in a way that is understandable to the client. This can be achieved by the client actively collaborating in generating the content that will be typed in the session summaries. By using computer-aided mind stimulation technology, the therapist can maximize more traditional conversational psychodynamic or cognitive-behavioral therapy discussions with clients by enhancing the client's information processing, and subsequently his or her ability to understand and to "tolerate" more easily explorations of "psychological dynamics and issues." Furthermore, the printouts allow the client to remember or rehearse issues discussed without relying on his or her subjective memory of the session. Relying on subjective memory will allow us only to partially recapture the core issues and themes of a session. This is due, in part, to the inherent limits of our short-term and working memory (Baddeley, 2007; Cowan, 2001), which make it difficult for most people to remember the details of a lengthy conversation such as the conversations that often ensue during traditional verbal therapy.

Vignette 3

Here the therapy summary highlights specific topics, daily activities, interests, and treatment team issues for a client with a long-term history of schizophrenia, substance abuse, and a mild learning disability. The therapy focus was more direct in generating suggestions and coping strategies within a supportive relationship framework, as the client has a history of non-adherence to any prescribed treatment regimen and has associated "authority" conflicts.

1. Personal hygiene: The client states that he has been washing his face, brushing his teeth, and taking a shower on a daily basis. The client thinks that he has been doing this more consistently in the past year or so (coinciding with the beginning of therapy). We talked about the importance of maintaining good personal hygiene habits to remain healthy.
2. Current activities:
   a) Gardening: The client is helping out with gardening at his program residence. He described in detail what vegetables have been planted; how with another client, under staff supervision, they weed and maintain the garden. We talked about how gardening is a type of work, and that working with one's hands on projects is good for mental health and making oneself feel better (i.e., it can increase one's positive self-image and worth).
   b) Fishing: The client missed out on the fishing trip last week due to not feeling well, but enjoys going fishing, as he used to do in the past, whenever there was an opportunity.
   c) Picnic and other activities: The client enjoys going out with the group.
   d) Girlfriend: The client talks with his "girlfriend" regularly.
   e) Family contact: The client enjoys meeting with his sister once a month . . . Talked about how the client's sister looked up to the client when they were younger and grew up in a difficult family situation (the client previously in a session has shared a traumatic experience in childhood when the parents were separated) . . . Encouraged client to maintain active contact with family.
3. Multidisciplinary Team Meeting (MDT) and relapse issue: The client reported not attending the last MDT meeting as he was not wanting to think about the "relapse" issue (related to over-the-counter substance abuse) that was to be brought up in the meeting. We talked about the functions of the MDT meetings in highlighting positive accomplishments and gains, and that it is always good to know how one is doing from others' perspectives, especially when a family member is also present at the meeting. The client stated that "relapse" will not happen as he is being closely monitored by staff, and in some ways the client has become used to and accepting of this monitoring.
4. Appearance and mood: The client acknowledged, when pointed out, that he looks more contented and happier with his present life situation than before, showing less discontent and ambivalence about medication or supervision.

The above session note reflects suggestions about daily living skills, while noting the client's complicated history of childhood trauma, learning disability and school failures, authority conflicts, poor attention to personal hygiene, and self-medication to relieve psychic pain either through over-the-counter medication or alcohol abuse. Again, the client's participation in the write-up process and receiving handouts maximizes the possibility of remembering and thus practicing what was discussed in the session.

Example 5: Organizing the Client's History, Issues, and Goals by Using a Computer Text-box Style of Writing

The examples below illustrate how using a text-box style of writing on the computer screen can help clients actively collaborate in discussing their personal history, treatment, and issues affecting their functioning. Additionally, the organizational structure of the visual prompts enhances the client's ability to reflect on personal goals and aspirations, and to identify realistic steps to achieve these goals. The process allows both the clinician and client to contribute ideas, keeping in mind that the final written version reflects the client's full agreement and understanding of the issues discussed (see Figure 7.2 below).

Scenario 1

Issues important in understanding a client's life and development.

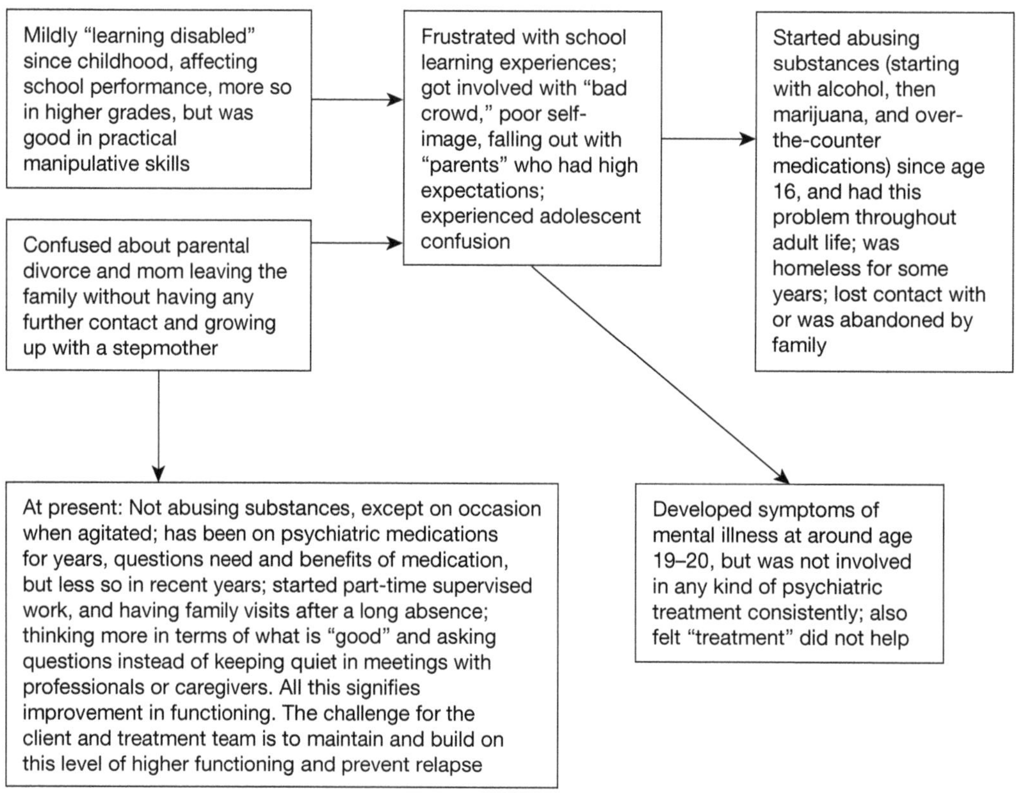

FIGURE 7.2 Life history recordings

The lines extending from the boxes help connect ideas and events by highlighting contributing factors from the client's developmental history. This "organizing visual" helps provide some "dynamic interpretation" of symptoms and behaviors in a concrete manner that the client can understand. Through this understanding, the client can more clearly discuss treatment issues and specify goals. This written text-box recording, a copy of which the client will receive, allows both the client and clinician to revisit these issues more systematically in future sessions. Furthermore, these computer-generated recordings serve to document more objectively the client's active involvement and collaboration in the therapy.

Scenario 2

Important issues in understanding a client's recent "relapse" and personal goals (see Figure 7.3 below).

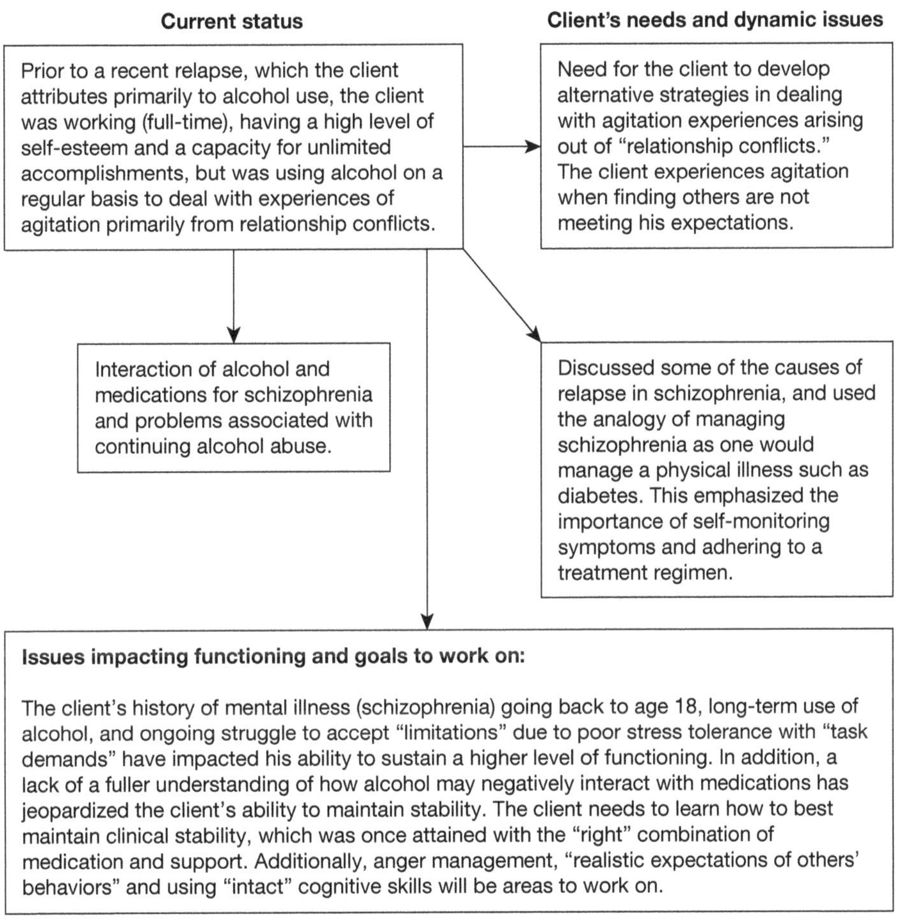

FIGURE 7.3 Relapse events and goals

Scenario 3

In this example, the text-box format is used to record a summary of a client's goals. The client actively collaborated in the process despite the client's limitations in routine verbal conversation (e.g., being underproductive and often only verbalizing "Yes" or "No" answers to questions). The client's own statements are captured in quotes in response to the therapist's questions, supportive prompts, and occasional paraphrasing.

Current activities and goals: things and activities the client likes to do or would like to accomplish this year. *(Please note that the parenthetic statements and phrases reflect the therapist's clarification of the client's thoughts and expressions.)*

1. "Catch a big fish when I go fishing"
2. "Do better in bowling"
3. "Record some music on cassette"
4. "Maybe move out . . ." *(supervised apartment)*
5. "Try to stay out of drugs"
6. "Read or look at some magazines . . ."
7. "Do homework" *(paper–pencil cognitive stimulating exercise)*
8. "Practice regularly exercises" *(relaxation exercise taught)*
9. "Continue to take medications so that I am not agitated . . . hearing voices . . ."
10. "Talk with staff . . . take PRN when agitated . . ."
11. "Work with staff *(treatment team)* about my goals . . ."
12. "Meet with family and keep in touch by phone."

Areas client has made progress in. These are stated in the client's own words or paraphrased by the therapist while getting the client's full agreement with the statements:

"My hygiene . . . eating better . . . a lot of progress in staying away from 'drugs' . . . Taking PRN's make me calmer . . . thinking about what is possible now for me . . . I am now more accepting of my mental illness and substance abuse and accepting of treatment suggestions [therapist paraphrasing for the client] . . . I see progress in me . . . feel better about myself, and keep the progress going."

Using the Core Elements of MICST to Structure Individual Therapy Sessions

Vignette 1

This case presents a client with a diagnosis of "disorganized schizophrenia," mimicking Kraepelin's (1883) original conceptualization of schizophrenia as "dementia praecox." This client has been exhibiting severe cognitive deficits (he had one year of college education), social anxiety, and isolation, and has been continually hospitalized for many years. The client talks to himself in jargon, does not participate in any structured activities, but follows a simple day routine, including medication adherence but needs assertive prompting. One of the mental health workers who initiated the referral noticed that at times the client talked about baseball games, mentioning some of the famous baseball players from a particular team and seemed to know most of their jersey numbers.

After an initial assessment, involving a review of the clinical record and an interview, the therapist designed a therapy protocol which involved two elements of the MICST model:

1. *sensorimotor activities*; and
2. *paper–pencil mind stimulating exercises.*

A deliberate decision was made not to focus on any traditional conversation therapy themes such as exploring "personal issues or dynamic interpretations," or giving suggestions for coping strategies. When initial efforts were made to do this, the client seemed to get confused and "agitated," and would frequently make "incoherent" and "illogical" statements.

The first part of the therapy involved *sensorimotor activities* requiring the client to follow and initiate simple movement exercises. In this phase of the therapy, the client was asked to play an "exercise game," where he was asked to do a series of exercises with requests such as, "Stand up," "Sit down," "Take five steps," "Face the wall until I call your name and ask you to turn around," and "Catch the ball." The client was also required to initiate the same requests for the therapist to follow.

These roles that the client played in the exercises were designed to give him practice in initiating requests for others to follow and to follow others' requests. It was hoped that this would help promote a greater degree of adherence to requests or prompts made by others, such as staff requesting that the client attend certain day program activities. In the process of playing either role during these exercises, the client also had the experience of "breaking away" from his preoccupation with internal thoughts and achieving a greater sense of contact with the immediate social environment. This phase of the therapy also entailed simple deep breathing exercises to a count of ten to teach the client how to take a relaxed posture on request, develop greater self-control, and minimize future episodes of agitation.

The second part of the therapy involved giving the client a series of *paper–pencil mind stimulating exercises* as the initial assessment indicated that, in spite of his "mental confusion" expressed in verbal conversation, the client was able to sit down and write responses to written tasks. Various exercises were used such as analogies, identifying antonyms and synonyms, arithmetic word problems, practical knowledge questions, personal body self-awareness, problem-solving skills, as well as personal memory exercises. Given the client's ongoing confused mental status and "agitation experience," which worsened with any kind of negative feedback to his thinking process, it was decided simply to have the client engage repeatedly in the same set of exercises without correcting or reviewing his responses. This gave the client the opportunity to practice and self-correct his own thinking and, it was hoped, in the process generate "improvement." The paper–pencil exercises provided the client with the opportunity to practice semantic memory recall, personal memory recall, practical reasoning, working memory, and following rules and instructions, even without the benefit of any corrective feedback to which he was resistant.

This client was involved in 26 sessions over two years. He showed significant improvement engaging in the sensorimotor exercises, which once learned, remained stable, and were performed consistently. The client demonstrated some improvement in participating in structured activities (including outings to local restaurants and ordering his meals), and showed a degree of plateau in his level of performance. The consistent training in responding to task requests through sensorimotor exercises, we believe, contributed to the client's improved level of functioning in being more receptive to milieu therapy such as participating in community trips, adhering more consistently to the program routine, and displaying fewer "behavioral issues."

On the paper–pencil mind stimulating exercises, the client showed some notable isolated knowledge and memory, as well as various areas of intact cognitive functioning. However, like many clients who have a history of schizophrenia and a continuous prolonged period of hospitalization, he showed variable functioning in performing tasks such as completing the same set of thinking and reasoning skills exercises. The client, for example, often showed good money exchange skills, as a practical survival skill, but showed inconsistency in performing this skill. This suggests variable motivation and inconsistency in the client's ability to remember skills that had been mastered without receiving occasional cues and prompts. This type of "inconsistent performance of a task," we believe, makes it a challenge for many persons with schizophrenia to benefit from the more "sequential" cognitive skills training curricula or programs. Moreover, it suggests the need for building "prompts" and "cues" into the environment to enable clients to practice the skills that they may already have in their repertoire.

The MICST exercises can serve as a "template" for clinicians to use in working with severely regressed persons with schizophrenia, who are often excluded from any kind of psychotherapy service. The MICST approach and exercises can provide the treatment team with information and ideas on how to structure the client's day routine in a better way, and build into the client's therapeutic milieu various kinds of mind stimulation exercises, prompts, and supports.

Overall improvement was noted in the client's production of appropriate associations in later sessions compared to earlier sessions, which suggested benefits from continued cognitive stimulation exercises. However, the client's episodic memory problems and delusion-based thought processes continued to be expressed at the same level, showing resistance to change. While showing isolated memory for specific knowledge and events, the client did not show any improvement over time in acquiring new information, indicating "cognitive rigidity." However, practicing various cognitive tasks allowed the client to demonstrate more intact reasoning and thinking, which he had not had the opportunity to demonstrate or practice before.

Vignette 2

The following case involves using computer-facilitated communication, paper–pencil cognitive exercises, and using reading on certain topics of interest (e.g., geography, astronomy, science, or history book materials) to stimulate thinking, memory, and logical associations.

The specific issues discussed via computer-facilitated collaborative conversation were:

1. the client's childhood upbringing;
2. failures in college, in spite of having high SAT scores, due to the onset of schizophrenia and the client's perception of the effect of substance use in precipitating mental illness;
3. feelings of abandonment when his parents passed away;
4. the client's mental confusion and agitation experience with the onset of schizophrenia and subsequent repeated hospitalizations;
5. current behavior issues and concerns affecting the client's functioning; and
6. the importance of a productive day routine, including involvement in cognitive stimulating paper–pencil exercises and reading science-related material, in which the client expressed a strong interest.

The therapy discussion focused on active involvement in a day routine, adherence to a personal hygiene routine, improved social communication, and effective management of anger–frustration experiences on a daily basis. Active redirection strategies were often discussed as strategies that the client could use to manage restlessness and to redirect himself from engaging in incoherent or tangential statements that he would often make in interpersonal communication. This client also showed an active interest in doing paper–pencil exercises, specifically mathematics, analogies, and word-search problems. He demonstrated intact cognitive skills that otherwise were not obvious during routine interactions, was able to sit down for a prolonged time, and was amenable to discussing personal issues in between paper–pencil exercises. The therapist also had him read particular sections of geology and astronomy books and summarize briefly what he had read to stimulate logical thinking, association, task involvement, and reality checking. The therapy also highlighted using mindfulness training and raising the client's awareness of the immediate environment to promote more adaptive responses.

This client readily engaged in the above activities during individual therapy sessions and often would complete paper–pencil exercises as homework. This type of client, because of a strong tendency to bring in "tangential associations" in conversation with staff or other clients, which is often a common characteristic of many clients with schizophrenia, is often excluded from individual psychotherapy. However, using the MICST model structure, this client could actively participate in individual psychotherapy sessions and demonstrated degrees of improvement in overall functioning and adjustment to community living. The client demonstrated less anxiety-associated hyperactivity and a reduction in tangential or "idiosyncratic" associations in conversations.

Summary

The MICST exercises discussed in these various clinical vignettes of individual therapy sessions can be used by clinicians in their work with persons with schizophrenia, by adapting, modifying, or creatively adding similar cognitive and body movement–mindfulness–relaxation exercises to fit a client's particular needs. This flexibility is possible because the MICST model is not a manualized treatment approach, nor based on a curriculum of sequential skill attainment, and does not aim for the retention of skills without any external prompt or support. Once a client appears to respond positively to a set of therapeutic MICST activities, the client's demonstration of this improved functioning during MICST therapy sessions alone could justify building routine cognitive stimulating activities and exercises into the client's therapeutic milieu and treatment plan.

We believe that using the core features of MICST (i.e., paper–pencil exercises, discussions of semantic knowledge or neutral topics of interest, and mind–body exercises) primes clients to participate more readily in discussing issues that may be more routinely explored in traditional conversation psychotherapy sessions.

Independent of a client's educational attainment, we have found almost all clients to be receptive to simple arithmetic exercises and word-search exercises. These exercises, in particular, are effective in engaging clients in more focused information processing and logical thinking. Using paper–pencil exercises also helps to identify clients' information processing difficulties, such as not understanding directions, having difficulty holding information in mind to solve a given problem (e.g., an addition or a subtraction problem), or giving an inappropriate association in a word problem. Once primed with the various MICST mind stimulation exercises, clients may be more easily engaged in other tasks or discussions requiring their attention, concentration, and working memory (e.g., clients may be able to engage more readily in discussions related to their current functioning, personal history, and goals). Also, clients are generally receptive to engaging in simple body movement–mindfulness–relaxation exercises (as outlined in Chapter 3), and practicing these exercises as a positive redirection coping strategy.

Chapter 8

Expanding the MICST Model to Substance Abuse Clients

This chapter discusses the application of the MICST model to dually diagnosed substance abuse clients. We provide several case studies demonstrating how the various facets of MICST can be used with this patient population. We also present results from feedback questionnaires to illustrate the impact of MICST in facilitating reality-based discussions, engaging clients in mind stimulating activities, and helping clients learn more effective coping strategies.

Variants of the MICST model have been used by the senior author (Mohiuddin Ahmed) with dual-diagnosed psychiatric inpatients and with clients in a residential program of a community mental health center. The MICST model, as applied to substance abuse populations, is different from other traditional substance abuse counseling models. The MICST model does not focus on or emphasize substance abuse knowledge and information, or self-evaluation and assessment in relation to one's substance abuse history. Also, unlike traditional counseling or peer support group models, the MICST model focuses more on stimulating clients' intact reasoning skills, and exploring and activating "available" psychological resources for recovery. Activities or discussions that may provoke negative self-evaluations are avoided, such as asking clients to report in detail the difficulties they experienced in the past with substance abuse. A persistent focus on these problem areas, which sometimes may occur in traditional counseling approaches, may reinforce the client's identification with a negative self-image and may not necessarily generate enthusiasm or motivation for behavior change. We believe that a therapeutic modality of the MICST nature, when provided in conjunction with other supportive rehabilitation and clinical services, will help to enhance a client's overall functioning and recovery.

The specific components of MICST as applied to substance abuse groups are in many ways similar to the MICST group structure that we used with persons with schizophrenia. The following structure has been used:

1. relaxation/deep breathing exercise at the beginning and end of the sessions;
2. talking about the past week's events;

3. paper–pencil cognitive training exercises;
4. feedback on paper–pencil exercises;
5. discussion of issues related to mental health and substance abuse;
6. paper–pencil self-evaluation exercises.

In our initial application of the MICST model to an inpatient dual-diagnosed group (i.e., persons with schizophrenia and substance abuse), we focused primarily on the body movement–mindfulness–relaxation (BMR) exercises, assessment of substance abuse history through a structured questionnaire, and using clients' responses to generate discussion of substance abuse issues. We used a blackboard or easel to write down clients' responses to specific discussion questions.

Substance Abuse Questionnaire

Below we report results from a questionnaire asking clients to provide their insights into substance use and its impact on their functioning. The following results are a composite of responses provided by six clients over three group sessions. Some of the responses below are the paraphrased statements provided by the therapist when the client's response needed to be clarified.

1. **Why do people drink/do drugs?** The categories in bold type listed below (e.g., loneliness, boredom) reflect the themes extracted from the clients' responses.

   General Responses:
   "To relax"; "socially accepted"; "like the taste"; "to get high"; "feel good"; "forget about responsibilities"; "hide . . . escape reality"; "cheaper to drink (readily available)"; "because of addiction."

   Loneliness:
   "No one to sleep with"; "crying days"; "alienated from people"; "drinking alone"; "despair"; "not being accepted by people"; "alone in a crowd."

   Boredom:
   "Dull feelings"; " nothing to do"; "same as loneliness"; "feeling like I am wasting time"; "decreased values"; "no place to go"; "nothing to do"; "too much time on my hand[s]"; "lack of knowledge"; "depression."

   Day to Day Problems:
   "Do not have any concerns about other people's whereabouts"; "wondering about future plans"; "in and out of sickness (frequent relapse)"; "feeling like I am wasting time away"; "dealing with hate from patients and staff"; "dealing with loss of parents (disconnection from family)"; "dealing with my mental illness and medication effects (side effects)"; "I don't care, I want to get out . . . feeling cooped up"; "having anxiety and worry . . . not getting anywhere."

2. **Conflict, what do we mean?**
   "Fighting with each other"; "choosing between situations—making right decision"; "whether to take drugs or alcohol or stay clean/sober"; "negative versus positive feelings"; "fighting voices"; "what is real v[ersu]s what is not real"; "struggle within self."

   Resolving conflicts, what do we mean?
   "Working things out peacefully"; "desire to use better attitude"; "being aware of the consequences"; "courage to change"; "accept challenges"; "take risks."

3. **Why am I at this (psychiatric inpatient) facility?**
   "I am mentally ill"; "no place to go"; "wandering in the streets, depression"; "messing around with drugs"; "arrested for drinking, disorderly behavior"; "because of developing illness"; "court placed me"; "volunteered"; "no place to stay."

4. **What are my problems?**
   "Afraid to communicate"; "afraid to think what is right"; "difficulty in getting along with people"; "paranoid about it"; "drinking and using drugs"; "myself"; "financial"; "accepting mental illness, not talking about it"; "personal . . ."; "chronic use of alcohol"; "hearing voices."

5. **What do I have to do to get out of this (psychiatric inpatient) facility?**
   "Believing in people trying to help me"; "dealing with the past"; "behave myself"; "respect others"; "prove to the court"; "go along with programs I don't need to be in . . . meds I don't need"; "work to get better"; "take my meds, work with staff, needs supervision"; "I don't need this program . . . I don't have a problem"; "go to groups, team mandate."

As one can see, each of the responses can lead to a further discussion to promote understanding and insight into the dynamics of substance abuse. The breadth and range of issues highlighted by group members in three sessions is quite impressive. This particular group was terminated as the therapist's assignment was changed, but nevertheless, the experience provided some initial data on using MICST with a substance abuse group.

In using the MICST model with subsequent substance abuse groups, we thus purposely underemphasized substance abuse topics and issues, recognizing that many clients already have sufficient knowledge and understanding of the "negative" effects of substance abuse. We chose rather to focus on cognitive stimulation through paper–pencil exercises, body movement–mindfulness–relaxation exercises, discussions of general knowledge topics, and self-assessment.

Subsequently, two groups were conducted following the basic outline of MICST in two residential substance abuse programs in a community mental health center. We reported the findings at the 23rd Cape Cod Symposium on Addictive Disorders (Ahmed & Boisvert, 2010). The studies that we reported were conducted in the context of actual clinical practice, and the therapy provided was viewed as an adjunct to other rehabilitation and counseling services provided to clients in the group home setting.

Group A comprised 22 male clients who attended 4–6 sessions, and Group B comprised 7 females and 16 males, who attended 4–6 group sessions. Clients in both groups all had long-standing problems with substance abuse, often dating back to childhood and adolescence, significant involvement with the criminal justice system, and a significant history of receiving mental health services.

MICST Components Questionnaire

Various questionnaires were used to evaluate the effectiveness of the MICST model with these two groups. One questionnaire asked clients to comment on whether they felt they benefitted from the relaxation and mindfulness exercises and to indicate whether they were able to develop more self-control and use redirection strategies to manage negative "preoccupations" more effectively. We present a summary of the data in Figures 8.1 and 8.2.

The data support the view that clients had positive impressions of the BMR exercises, which were often accompanied by a discussion of mindfulness. Given the characteristics of both groups, whereby many of the clients have had many "ups and downs" in their recovery process, and are usually quite vocal and open with their opinions, and given that group participation was voluntary without any "privilege granting" authority by the clinician, who was an outside consultant, this pattern of responding provides evidence for the positive benefits of the MICST model for these clients.

Substance abuse clients often have doubts about their "self-control," and may have frequent relapse episodes, in spite of the fact that they may have gone through many rehabilitation and recovery programs in the past. Even though sessions were of brief duration, the vast majority of the clients indicated they learned ways to practice some degree of "self-control" and redirection strategies.

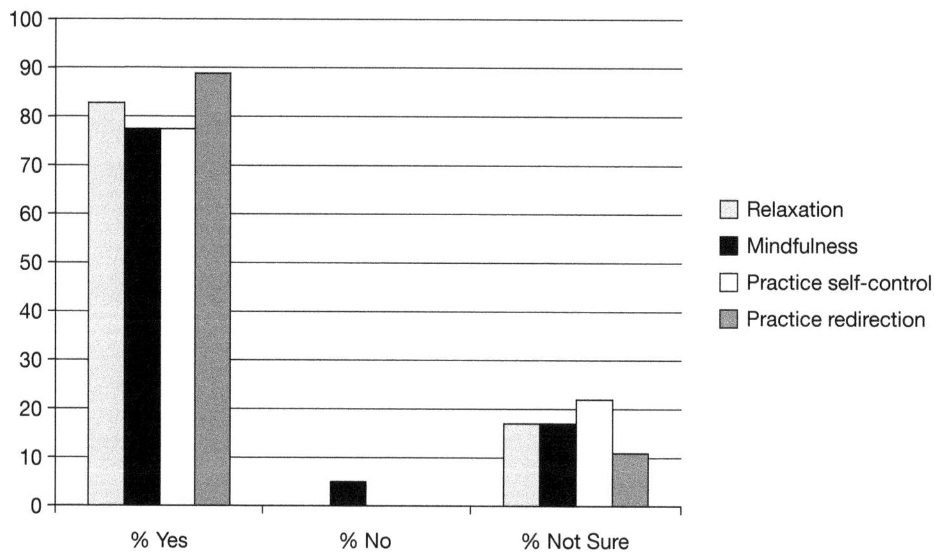

FIGURE 8.1 Substance Abuse Group A (18 males): Results from a self-assessment questionnaire showing percentages of clients endorsing benefits of relaxation and mindfulness exercises and acknowledging learning to practice self-control and positive redirection

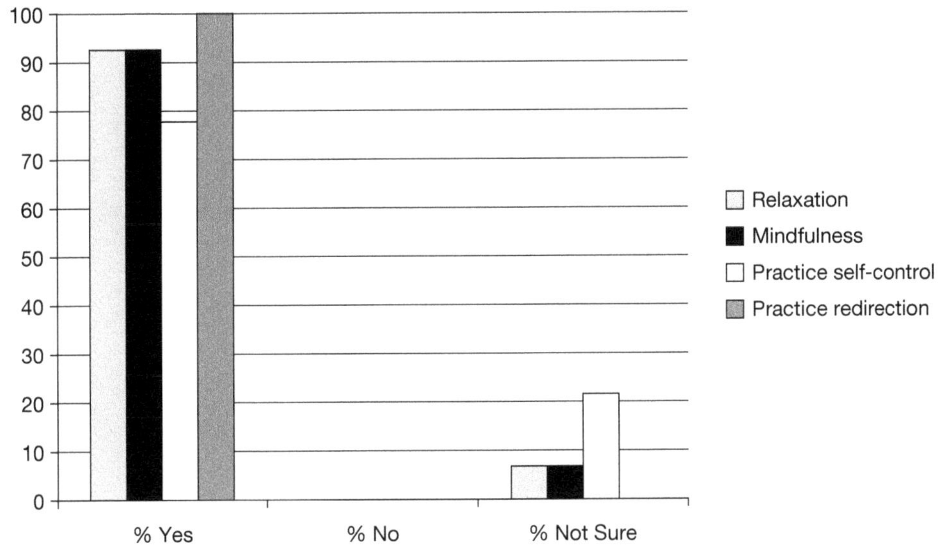

FIGURE 8.2 Substance Abuse Group B (12 males and 6 females): Results from a self-assessment questionnaire showing percentages of clients endorsing benefits of relaxation and mindfulness exercises and acknowledging learning to practice self-control and positive redirection

Personal Recovery Goals Questionnaire

Clients were asked to identify their personal goals for recovery, barriers to achieving their goals, and steps they needed to take to reach their goals. Some of the client composite responses are presented below; counselors can use these as part of the therapy dialogue process, as the issues raised by clients are likely to apply to many clients with substance abuse problems.

Present Life Circumstances

"I'm trying to plug back into the program, fixing my relationship my family . . . learning to stay clean, drug free . . . trying to get better . . . follow my treatment plan, pay attention to teachers, follow rule[s], achieve more concentration and self-control . . . trying to beat this addiction problem . . . to better myself and life in the future . . . involved in court probation, not involved with my family . . . anger outbursts, panic attacks, lack of concentration, self-esteem . . . feeling despondent . . . going to NA and AA on a daily basis, working on a better relationship with God . . . I had substance abuse in past, now I'm in treatment . . ."

Goal

In Six Months

"I will have my life back . . . Staying clean . . . To be teaching again . . . I am in step one to achieve my goals . . . decent job . . . sober living . . . job, car . . . continue recovery, safe living . . . stay clean.

One Year

"I will be the happiest man . . . have my license back . . . car, money, bank . . . custody of my children, back to school . . . college degree . . . have a motor cycle . . . be clean . . . own place . . . have family for support . . . own apartment."

Five Years

"Associate degree in business and law . . . receive the miracle the program has to offer, have a sponsor . . . healthy relationship, reunited with family . . . home and family . . . to be a US citizen . . . own painting business . . . sponsoring men, have a dream home . . ."

Goals and Behavioral Issues that Put Barriers to Achieving your Goals

Goals

"Controlling my temper, not out at people . . . must complete this program to move on to something else . . . need to get back to my life, take directions from my sponsor (AA) and other positive members in recovery . . . be productive in my treatment progress . . . [as] court ordered . . . want to change my life . . . to better myself . . . need help . . . to get my life back in order . . . "

Barriers

"Resorting to alcohol and drugs . . . drug use . . . negative attitude, compulsive behavior . . . substance abuse . . . resentment issues . . . because my life was unmanageable . . . have a crack and cocaine problem . . ."

Steps that I Need to Take to Reach My Above Goals

"Stay clean, go to meetings, keep in touch with sponsor, get psychotherapy and be open minded and willing to surrender to a higher power . . . need to have a constant conscience of my disease, pray[er] meetings, continue to stay clean, sober day by day . . . stay connected, be honest, work hard . . . must go to meetings, 12 steps (AA), go to school, get a job . . . graduate from the program, teach again . . . go to NA, AA, take road test, get a van for painting . . . get new sponsor, join group, plug back into the program . . . go to meetings, pray, have faith, be open-minded, stay focused, release self-doubt, open up with people win recovery . . . learn grounding techniques when anxious, take medication to concentrate, learn anger management and self-esteem tips . . . start looking for jobs, stay clean, stay spiritual in my life and recovery . . ."

As we can see from these responses, clients were well able to articulate their personal problems, goals, values, and insights, which they appear to have internalized. This was not necessarily a product of their involvement in MICST, but through their MICST participation, these insights and thoughts may have become more conscious and pronounced. This illustrates that many substance abuse clients may already have a reasonable understanding of their recovery goals and steps to reach their goals. However, despite their often long-standing history of treatment, their insight and knowledge do not necessarily get translated easily into sustained behavior change as is evidenced by clients' frequent relapse experiences. This calls into question the traditional therapy emphasis on promoting knowledge and insight into substance abuse by focusing on past problems with substance use. We believe that the MICST model's emphasis on cognitive stimulation, redirection strategies, and strengths and capabilities might be a useful adjunctive therapy in the recovery process for these clients. We encourage further research and investigation in this area.

Self-assessment Questionnaire

From time to time, clients were given self-assessment questionnaires to reflect on their understanding of what they liked or learned in a particular MICST group session. These exercises were designed to promote self-understanding, assessment of recovery goals, and benefits perceived from participating in MICST. Filling out a questionnaire of this nature, as we have commented before, provides an opportunity for self-reflection and awareness, which is consistent with any general psychotherapy goal. However, it also provides the opportunity for clinicians and clients to assess more "objectively" the effectiveness of the MICST model for a given session. The following is a sample of composite responses by clients over several sessions (see Appendix B: Self-assessment Tool 1)

1. **What issues and activities were interesting or helpful to you today?**
   "All of them . . . the breathing exercise (multiple responses), word search (multiple responses), behavior, feeling, thought exercise, human needs worksheet, being able to change the way we think . . . none . . . meditation (multiple responses) . . . awareness (multiple responses) . . . math . . . thinking skills (multiple responses) . . ."

2. **What issues or activity would you have liked to discuss more in the group?**
   "N/A . . . brain cells . . . dealing with anger . . . more breathing and meditation skills (multiple responses) . . . depression of the mind and how not to think and think all the time . . . feelings/thoughts . . . positive thinking . . . mental illness/ mental health . . . thinking activities . . . logical thought process . . . not sure . . . mental illness"

3. **What activity or discussion topic would you like to see included in the group for the next week or in the future?**
   "Redirecting self to talk to positive issues . . . anxiety (multiple responses) . . . more math exercises (multiple responses) . . . more meditation skills . . . about the brain (brain–behavior relationship) . . . more about depression (multiple responses) and about (underlying) thought

process . . . meditation (multiple responses) . . . sleep . . . more word searches . . . thinking activities, positive thinking . . . not sure (multiple responses) . . ."

4. **How would you rate your degree of involvement in the group today on a scale of 1–5 (1 = least involved; 5 = most involved)? (N = 28)**
   1 = 7%   2 = 3%   3 = 32%   4 = 29%   5 = 29%

5. **How do you rate your mood today on a scale of 1–5 (1 = very unhappy or depressed; 5 = very happy, generally contented or not depressed at all)? (N = 27)**
   1 = 18%   2 = 30%   3 = 26%   4 = 19%   5 = 7%

6. **Do you feel that you are making progress toward recovery and gaining self-control? (1= not at all; 5 = very much so)? (N = 28)**
   1 = 0%   2 = 4%   3 = 46%   4 = 25%   5 = 25%

7. **What are the most productive activities you have been involved in during the past week?**
   "Talking to the Doctor . . . expressing my feelings . . . self-help . . . working in the kitchen (client run), groups and meetings, coming to treatment (MICST group) . . . Meetings . . . thinking activities . . . getting into the residency program . . . recovery meetings, NA, AA (multiple responses), played basketball . . . self-help groups . . . recovery . . . working out (exercise) . . . being clean . . . reading, doing pushups . . . writing in a journal . . . working on Step 1 (AA Recovery, multiple responses) . . . meeting with case manager . . . connect to people . . . coming here (to MICST group) today (multiple responses)."

8. **Are you practicing deep breathing and other mindfulness strategies? (N = 25)**
   Yes = 56%   No = 36%   Not Sure = 8%

9. **List the positive activities that you are using to divert your attention away from preoccupations with "negative thoughts or feelings":**
   "Reading, watching movies, writing, word searches . . . working on homework assignments, spending time with peers, listening to music, watching TV, reading . . . NA/AA meetings, recovery groups, working out . . . reading, writing out . . . writing music (multiple responses) . . . praying, talking about music . . . working on anger by breathing activities . . . coming to treatment . . . prayer (multiple responses) . . . positive actions and thoughts . . . helping others, healthy manners . . . staying focused on the groups and my recovery . . . paying attention during groups . . . sleeping . . . stay focused and positive . . . NA/AA (multiple responses) . . . family . . . paying attention, doing groups . . . positive actions by acting on thoughts . . . coming to treatment . . . talking with others . . ."

The responses provide evidence of the effectiveness of the MICST model for substance abuse clients. The open-ended nature of the questionnaire required self-reflection and assessment and the ability to reflect on one's mood and progress toward recovery goals. It can also be considered to be a thinking and memory exercise. Many clients were able to participate meaningfully in this type of questionnaire, and the majority of the clients' responses suggested that they benefitted from various MICST group activities.

Clients' Spontaneous Comments about their Participation in MICST

We also invited clients to write any spontaneous thoughts or ideas about their group experience. Nineteen clients responded with short comments about the group. Overall, in conducting the MICST group with substance abuse clients, we found the group members to be very responsive to the body movement–mindfulness–relaxation (BMR) exercises, word-search and mathematics exercises, and the personal self-reflection exercises. A composite presentation of their responses, to protect anonymity and confidentiality, is presented below:

- *"I would recommend (this) class (MICST group) to anyone who finds themselves out of balance, spirit, soul and body . . ."*
- *"I think this class should be done in a lake or pond, where there is a peaceful surrounding where man can become one with nature . . ."*
- *"The breathing exercises are especially good for relieving stress . . . This class is of value to recovery . . . since most forget . . . what skill they have to combat their addiction . . ."*
- *"This class . . . reinforces skills such as breathing, think (thinking), and modification (behavior) in an addict . . . once again this should continue emphasis on the personal and mental health issue . . ."*
- *"I see I have learned a few things in a short time that I have been in this program . . ."*
- *"I feel it (the group) has been helpful in relieving stress and seeing one's eyes to new ways of thinking . . ."*
- *"My opinion is that this group is very important in our recovery, because of the physical exercise and mental concentration . . ."*
- *"The group was helpful for different reasons. It helps break the ice with speaking in groups; it helps realize the importance of using the mind skills and planning, small goals or just having questions that dig up ideas . . . from memory that may have forgotten . . ."*
- *"They (counselors) were very helpful in making to understand my thought process and to change them to be positive and taught breathing exercise to relieve stress and anxiety . . . done a good job in showing and reminding us about the other things in life that can help us to recover . . ."*
- *"Mindful breathing is good to calm your nerves, the word searches made me keep focus on one thing . . ."*
- *"The therapists have done a good job . . . this group is very informative. I enjoy the breathing exercise and doing the worksheets stimulates the mind . . ."*

The clients' responses on the various questionnaires and their active engagement in the various MICST activities suggest that clients can become actively engaged in meaningful group activities and in discussing relevant treatment goals through the MICST model. The MICST model's emphasis on information processing requires clients to reflect on how their processing of information influences their thoughts, feelings, and behaviors in a given social and physical environment. MICST tries to raise clients' awareness of their "sense of connection" to the world at large, the social, and the cosmic world. As such, the clinician should be comfortable in addressing existential and spiritual perspectives in the group. Also, to promote social connectedness and information sharing, the clinician encourages discussions of general topics such as geography, history, anthropology, science, religion, and astronomy.

We believe a positive psychology approach, which underlies the MICST model, stimulates the intact and positive skills in clients' repertoire, helping clients to redirect themselves away from their preoccupations with "negative" and "problematic" thoughts and behaviors associated with substance abuse. We hope that substance abuse counselors and recovery-oriented programs will be encouraged to incorporate some of the elements of the MICST approach in their treatment programs and clinical work with clients.

Chapter 9

Expanding the MICST Model to Geriatric Clients and Populations with Physical Disabilities

Elements of the MICST model have been used by the senior author (Mohiuddin Ahmed) in individual therapy work with geriatric adult clients with physical disabilities in nursing home settings. This chapter discusses the application of the MICST model to these client populations. Several case studies are discussed, which illustrate the various ways that the MICST model has been applied in individual work with these clients. We conclude with guidelines for implementing MICST in individual sessions with nursing home clients.

The MICST goals for these client populations in nursing home settings can be conceptualized as follows:

- Reduce personal feelings of "distress," regardless of the client's age or physical illness associated with his or her level of disability.
- Assess cognitive or learning deficit-like issues that are affecting clients' communication processes and explore how best to relate to clients through accessing their "intact skills" and functioning within a positive psychology framework.
- Practice body movement–mindfulness–relaxation (BMR) exercises to promote relaxation, to make clients aware of being "alive," and to redirect clients from preoccupations with negative feelings and thoughts.
- Stimulate clients' episodic memory (personal events) and semantic memory (knowledge of facts and information). The episodic memory exploration does not typically focus on painful memories from the past, as is usually done in traditional therapy, except in some initial assessment sessions (if deemed appropriate), or for a cathartic (unburdening) effect for clients who have not had opportunities to share such experiences and who volunteer to talk about such experiences without active probing by the therapist. Otherwise, the focus of the exploration is on recalling positive recent and remote memories and recognizing that the agitation experience associated with painful memories may be heightened by actively exploring past negative memories.
- Provide cognitive stimulation through discussing general knowledge topics or using paper–pencil exercises involving, for example, mathematics, word searches, reasoning skills, analogies, and general knowledge questions.

- Provide relationship support to reduce feelings of loneliness, and help direct clients to thoughts and activities that can enhance adjustment to the present living situation and reduce personal "distress."
- Provide an "existential perspective" in dealing with the uncertainties of living, the perception of which may become more pronounced with the aging process, supporting clients' religious faith, and at the same time provide science-based knowledge about human existence and our relationship to the universe.
- Facilitate clients' adjustment to the nursing home placement and adherence to the nursing care and routine. Often clients' adjustment to and "compliance" with the nursing home care can cause distress and agitation and subsequently can present as a management challenge to the nursing home staff.
- Provide effective client consultation to nursing home staff, based on knowledge of the cognitive and behavioral functioning of the client gained through the therapy process.
- Provide consultation to the psychiatric medication service provider, drawing from the therapeutic involvement with the client and behavioral functioning data, to ensure appropriate medication management of clinical and behavioral symptoms and to reduce the risk of over-medication, which has been a national concern in the United States.

There has been emerging research that has shown how "cognitive stimulation therapy" can enhance specific cognitive functions in dementia patients, enhance their quality of life, and retard the rate of dementia (Matsuda, 2007; Spector & Orrell, 2006; Spector, Orrell, & Woods, 2010; Woods, Thorgrimsen, Spector, Royan, & Orrell, 2006). Moreover, the importance of cognitive stimulation is being recognized by the general public—several Internet sites have been developed such as PositScience.com, Lumosity.com, and TheBCAT.com, all of which recognize the benefits of cognitive stimulation in everyday life. These programs as well as various other mental exercises such as crossword puzzles, Sudoku, and brain-teaser-type exercises are being marketed to the general public as "brain training" exercises designed to sharpen and improve mental functioning.

The following case scenarios illustrate how elements of the MICST model were used in individual therapy with nursing home clients, all of whom have some form of physical and cognitive impairment or age-associated disabilities. Fictitious names are used to protect the anonymity of the clients.

Clinical Vignette: James

James was referred for persistent anxiety and occasional mood instability symptoms. James is generally compliant with the nursing care routine. He shows some shakiness due to a combination of medication side effects and a history of a stroke affecting his walking. In the initial assessment and in subsequent therapy sessions, James related well to the therapist. He showed an active interest in doing paper–pencil cognitive exercises, such as simple arithmetic, word association tasks, and learning to practice a simple body movement exercise for relaxation and mindfulness. The therapist explained to the client how these activities can be used to redirect him from negative thoughts or agitation experiences. Through the process of reviewing his responses to the exercises, James acknowledged that he had learning difficulties in school. He indicated that he did not receive any remedial education and had a poor self-image associated with school failures.

James also shared some very personal "painful experiences" of his childhood and adult life, characterized by "abandonment" by parents and spouse, and how he developed alcohol abuse while maintaining competitive employment all his life. He stated that he had not shared this part of his life experience with anyone before. He seemed to agree with the therapist's assertion that this sharing process may have helped him unburden himself of these deep-seated feelings and memories. He was subsequently given specific coping strategies to help him "leave the past behind" and focus on the present. The coping strategies entailed engaging in a productive day routine by following the activity schedule of the nursing home, doing paper–pencil cognitive stimulating homework exercises (e.g., simple mathematics geared to his ability level and word association tasks), and practicing a simple body movement exercise for relaxation and mindfulness.

Below we describe the MICST strategies that were used with James. These strategies could be used with other clients with similar characteristics:

BMR Exercises

These exercises consisted of the following, which could be done sitting or lying down:

1. Lift one hand at a time up and down slowly, without stopping, keep the movement continuous, with elbow going down first, and watch the hand movement going up and down, and do this to a count of ten (due to this client's heart condition, only very slow breathing was instructed; the breathing exercises can be omitted for other clients with "breathing difficulties").
2. Repeat the exercise with the other hand.
3. Do a "slow clapping movement" with both hands extended and coming together, but do not fully clasp the hands, and then withdraw, all in a slow motion. Concentrate on the hand movement.
4. With the heels grounded, lift the toes ten times slowly, one foot at a time, and mentally focus on the toes moving up and down.

The client was instructed to practice these exercises three times a day—morning, noon, and evening—as well as any other time when he felt anxious or agitated. The client quickly learned these exercises, reported practicing them diligently, and found them to be an effective coping strategy not only to induce relaxation, but to ward off anxious and negative thoughts and feelings.

Paper–Pencil Exercises

One of the striking features in working with James was his eagerness to engage in paper–pencil exercises, primarily involving simple mathematics, word association, reasoning, and general knowledge questions. The exercises seemed to stimulate his latent thirst for learning basic educational skills, which he admitted he missed in his early school years due to learning difficulties. Going over the exercises, James showed a variable fund of general knowledge. He answered many questions correctly, but was not able to provide correct answers to some questions that most people would have learned in school, such as "How many states does the United States have?" Below is a sample of the exercises used along with whether the client provided the correct answer:

Who is Cassius Marcellus Clay?	Correct answer
Who invented the light bulb?	Correct answer
What does the word magnify mean?	Correct answer
What is the Vatican?	Correct answer
How many states does the United States have?	No answer
In what continent is the United States?	No answer
Name 3 spring activities	No answer
If you walk 4 miles per day for 12 days, what is the total miles walked at the end of the 10th day?	Correct answer
How much is 15% of 200,000?	No answer
If you buy a coat on sale for $150.00, and the cost is 25% off its regular price, how much did it cost before?	No answer

James did quite well on analogy and reasoning-type questions, which required him to select the correct answers from among the alternatives or to supply the answer on his own. A sample of the exercises is as follows:

A pear is to fruit as spinach is to: Correct answer
Lemon Tomato Vegetable

Hamburger is to eat as coat is to: Correct answer
Shoe Wear Weather

James provided correct answers on the additions and subtraction problems, including five digit addition and subtraction, showing excellent working memory involving carry-over problems as below:

83214	92134	31284
−37605	−82476	+14163

However, with multiplication tasks, James was not able to do any carry-over problems consistently, which may have reflected an undiagnosed learning disability contributing to his school difficulties. His difficulty in performing these exercises did not appear to be secondary to his loss of cognitive functions due to a stroke, as he indicated that in school he never could learn how to do carry-over problems.

The above examples demonstrate how using cognitive stimulating paper–pencil exercises helped this client access and stimulate thinking, reasoning, working memory, and concentration; and in the process, helped counter the client's persistent preoccupation with ruminating anxiety and negative memories. Moreover, the feedback process promoted cognitive flexibility and openness to accepting new information. The exercises also provided the therapist with insight into the client's learning difficulties and associated anxiety or mental confusion related to his lack of understanding or inability to perform certain tasks. This in turn helped the therapist learn how best to support the client's adaptive thinking processes to enhance his coping with his present life circumstances.

James showed a high degree of involvement in the therapy process through his completion of various paper–pencil exercises, his willingness to accept corrective feedback, his active listening, affirmation of suggestions and ideas shared by the therapist, and his consistent practice of the body movement–mindfulness–relaxation exercises. Within six months, he showed fewer anxiety symptoms, had a mild downward adjustment of his psychiatric medication, and was more productive during the day by accepting volunteer responsibilities, even though his medication regimen remained essentially unchanged. Two weeks before James passed away from medical illness, he reported to the therapist that he was still practicing the BMR exercises, did not have anxious feelings, and was not bothered by thoughts about his past ("It is not bothering me anymore. I am not anxious anymore."). The two-year involvement in using MICST interventions, we believe, contributed to a sense of tranquility and improved functional outcome that the client was able to experience before his death.

Clinical Vignette: Gary

When Gary was first interviewed, he was lying in bed (he uses a wheelchair or walker for mobility, depending on mood and energy), and was expressing agitation symptoms and "aggressive thoughts" in reaction to his feeling discomfort with his bed. In the initial interview with the therapist, the client immediately complained of his "bed condition" and expressed anger: "I am going to jump through this window, if they do not change my bed . . ." The therapist was able to engage him in the assessment interview by promising to bring his concerns about his bed to the staff, which the therapist did. During the assessment, the therapist noted that Gary did very well in reasoning and with the factual information portion of the standard assessment protocol for the agency. Gary's performance contradicted a notation in the clinical record of "questionable mental retardation," an impression which may have been influenced by the agitated mood he displayed during his initial assessment in the nursing home.

To further explore his fund of knowledge and to engage him in a mind stimulating activity, the therapist then asked Gary questions about his geographical knowledge, such as "What is the capital of New Mexico?" and "What is the capital of Greece?" As it turned out, Gary knew practically all the capital cities of the U.S. states as well as capitals of many other countries. The therapist then proceeded to explore his knowledge of history, by asking where the ancient kingdom of Assyria was and at what time period it existed, to which Gary gave nearly correct answers: Iraq, and it existed somewhere around 3,000 BC. The therapist then introduced some of the BMR exercise components that Gary could practice while he was lying down. The client responded positively to the practice, and was advised to use the hand movement, leg movement, and simple breathing exercises for a specified number of times (i.e., ten) to promote relaxation and to use the counting method as a goal-setting and goal accomplishment experience. He was advised to use these exercises as a coping strategy to deal with anger–agitation experiences, which he agreed to do.

In subsequent sessions, based on Gary's receptivity and ability to engage in high-level discussions, the therapist engaged him in discussing various general knowledge topics, as well as philosophical and existential issues. The therapist also reinforced practicing the BMR exercises. As the therapeutic alliance was strengthened, Gary reported his educational, psychiatric, and family history in more detail. Gary's mood stabilized over time. He often greeted the therapist enthusiastically, even though he was lying in bed with discomfort, giving the impression of looking forward to engaging in intellectual discussions with the therapist. Over time, he began to socialize more, began to use his walker more often, and went out to the dining room to eat rather than eating in his room.

The case illustrates the effectiveness of using "intellectual discourse" which promotes adaptive thinking and behavior. Since this aspect of Gary's life was dormant, and was activated during the therapy process, it may have had a positive effect on his functioning. Additionally, he was able to use the BMR exercises as a coping strategy for relaxation and affirmation of being alive by noticing his body movement, in spite of being severely limited in his ability to move his arms and legs freely, a condition which afflicts many nursing home clients. This type of experience provided him with positive redirection from his agitation and stress experiences. We also believe that through teaching Gary the BMR exercises and engaging him in intellectual and philosophical discussions, a stronger therapeutic alliance was established, allowing him to divulge personal painful memories from the past, and in the process, experience some "cathartic release" of emotional burdens and tension.

Clinical Vignette: Joan

Joan is wheelchair-bound, needing assistance with personal care and exhibits frequent behavior outbursts and paranoid ideation. A variety of MICST interventions were used to engage her more productively in the therapy process. She learned to practice the BMR exercises, while sitting down in a wheelchair or lying down in bed. The exercises were practiced by a slow and non-stop movement of each of the limbs, and counting to ten, while breathing in a relaxed manner, inhaling with the mouth closed, exhaling with the mouth open, and concentrating on the movement of the particular limb involved. She was instructed to perform the exercises 3–4 times a day.

In addition, Joan was given a set of paper–pencil cognitive exercises. During the paper–pencil exercises, she did well with analogies, word associations, and word-search exercises, at which she seemed to excel. However, possibly due to a "stroke-related" loss of functioning, she did exhibit some mental confusion, word-finding difficulties, and difficulties with carry-over multiplication problems. She was highly engaged in receiving corrective feedback on the exercises, and showed high motivation for learning. Through the MICST exercises, the therapist was able to establish a therapeutic alliance to address anger and stress-management issues, as well as provide behavioral consultation to the nursing home staff. The therapist also helped her develop a day routine structure using an activity log (see Figure 9.1 below), along with specific reminders for ways to cope with anger–depression experiences. As a de-escalation strategy, staff members were advised to use the written routine posted in her room for positive redirection, rather than confronting the client about any negative behavioral incident.

Clinical Vignette: Ralph

Ralph is in reasonably good health, has had a productive work history and active family involvement, but for some years, due to persistent complaints of "hearing voices," and age-associated disabilities, was deemed by the family as not being able to live independently in the community. Ralph is divorced, and all his children are grown up with their own family responsibilities. Ralph has not responded significantly to medication interventions or adjustments. He is ambulatory, does regular walking, and engages in light physical exercises to keep his movement and agility intact, in spite of some weaknesses with the aging process. He was able to relate well to the therapist by talking about personal events from his past and various childhood experiences. Over the course of therapy, the therapist developed a genogram of Ralph's family, and frequently used this to engage him in a personal memory exercise as a way to counter

Daily Activity Log for _________________________________

7–9	9–10	10–11	11–12	12–1	1–3	3–9
Personal Hygiene and Breakfast	1. Body-Movement-Mindfulness Exercise* 2. Look outside and enjoy the scenery 3. Watch TV news programs	1. Squeeze "Stress Ball" and transfer ball from one hand to another 2. Attend activity program	Lunch	Nap	Paper–pencil exercises (e.g., word search, arithmetic, word puzzles), watch TV, or attend routine activities	Milieu program, afternoon snacks, and any other structured or non-structured activities
*Body Movement Exercise	1. Breathe in through your nose with closed mouth, and breathe out through open mouth slowly following the inhale and exhale process, and counting 5–10 times. 2. Work with each hand, moving slowly, as if feeling the air, and looking at the movement of the arm, and feeling good about being alive (5–10 times). 3. Do the same with two hands moving to each other and touching slowly, while watching (5–10 times). Do the same with each leg, feeling the energy flow (5–10 times).					
Positive Redirection	Direct your mind actively to "positive" memories and thoughts or "structured activities" to divert your mind.					
Consult with Staff	Talk with staff or bring attention to staff around health issues. You are a good advocate for services for yourself, continue doing that.					
Family Visit	Focus on asking your family how they are doing, find out what is going on in their lives, and consult with them around health issues if needed.					
General Strategies	Practice catching yourself engaging in "unhappy memories" and actively *redirect yourself to the present moment.* Accept your limitations with the aging process as well as those of other residents around you. They all need services as you do, and they all want to manage their disabilities in the best possible way. Don't ask questions that human beings cannot answer, or get angry or upset about things you cannot change, such as *your past or certain circumstances of your present life*. Work with staff and your family to make the best of your present life.					

FIGURE 9.1 Sample activity log outlining specific day activities and MICST coping strategies

his mentioning of hearing voices, which often dominated prior sessions with mental health workers.

Over time, Ralph was increasingly able to engage in talking about his past life experiences, family relationships, work history, painful memories of his past, and family conflicts. He demonstrated an intact memory and good conversational skills in narrating these events and in the process did not mention hearing voices. The therapist consulted with nursing staff and the prescribing physician and recommended focusing on ensuring adequate sleep and dealing effectively with his stomach distress, and not focusing on exploring or assessing his "hearing voices." The therapist explained that the client's "hearing voices" might reflect a long-standing habit associated with "agitation states," and might not be amenable to any new medication adjustments, as indicated by his long involvement in psychiatric medication treatment.

Clinical Vignette: Elisa

Elisa has age-associated disabilities, and is frequently depressed secondary to feelings of intense anger for loss of functioning and being placed in a nursing home. Elisa has a history of psychiatric treatment and repeatedly talks about depressive ideation with staff and family members. She exhibits a high level of verbal and cognitive skills and related well to the therapist. The therapist emphasized practicing the BMR exercises for relaxation and mindfulness, and developed handouts of cognitive-behavioral statements that she agreed with and could practice as a way of coping with negative feelings of depression.

A sample handout (like Elisa's) is presented below, which clinicians are free to modify or adapt to their specific client situations and circumstances.

Personal Goals and Coping Strategies for ____________

I can take care of my mind and body by:

- maintaining personal hygiene, healthy eating, activity, rest, and sleep;
- working with staff in addressing my personal care and medication needs;
- communicating my personal needs to a staff member.

I will discuss my health issues only at certain times and with certain caregivers; at other times I will think positively, visit happy memories, and do things that I can do to keep focused on the present, and enjoy the moments of everyday living. I will work with what I have and not think so much about what I do not have. I will practice the following:

- Body movement exercises for relaxation—the ones Dr. Ahmed [therapist] taught me: breathing, moving arms, legs, with counting up to 5, and then move up to 10 or 15. It also gives me a sense of goal achievement.
- To help with sleep, I will practice breathing with counting up to 100; repeat as necessary or use any other technique that helps. I won't let my mind think about unpleasant memories before sleeping.
- Journal writing.
- Pay attention to things around me with appreciation and enjoyment.
- Take charge of my feelings, as they are mine, and steer them in the direction of feeling happy, no matter what situation I am in.
- Feel good that I am breathing, seeing things, and am alive and that we all live with existential uncertainties, and have to use our personal faith, beliefs, and understanding to help us cope.
- Not deplete my psychic energy by getting angry and upset about things and life events that I cannot change.
- Be aware of built-up stress and depletion of "energy" when engaging in seemingly pleasant and enjoyable activities. I may experience "physical exhaustion" due to my low stress tolerance and aging process, and I may mistakenly associate this with "depressed feelings."

I will keep track of my day and time and follow through with specific activities for the day such as:

- Watching TV, reading, listening to music, having family visits, doing word searches, and math exercise or any structured activities that I am involved in.
- During family visits, I will talk about how my family is doing, what is happening in their lives, and try not talk about my personal problems (depression), as I have done in the past.

We believe that the flexibility of the MICST model allows clinicians to adapt specific strategies to address the unique functioning and needs of clients in a nursing home setting. We hope that the ideas we shared will give clinicians a sense of competency in conducting MICST psychotherapy sessions with nursing home populations. Ongoing consultation and collaboration with the nursing home staff are important to help reinforce clients' practice of MICST coping strategies. In using the MICST model with clients in individual therapy, the clinician should possess certain skills and characteristics as outlined below:

MICST THERAPIST CHARACTERISTICS

- Basic elements of respect, specificity, genuineness, self-disclosure, confrontation, immediacy, concreteness, empathy, unconditional positive regard, and congruence (Truax & Carkhuff, 1967; Rogers, 1951). To this we add: using mind stimulating exercises, which allow clients to access their intact cognitive processes. The dialogue process involving this kind of positive interaction, directed away from focusing on "symptom" assessment and exploration, provides a base for developing a therapeutic alliance, which later on in sessions can be used to address painful memories or emotions that some clients may need to express spontaneously in the course of the therapy process.
- Basic counseling techniques to help clients resolve feelings from the past and develop coping strategies in dealing with psychiatric symptoms, including using cognitive-behavioral statements.
- Broad-based knowledge of geography, history, science, and astronomy.
- Practice in meditation, including appreciation of religious faiths and prayers/mindfulness practice, and Tai Chi-type exercises involving slow body movement without stopping to promote maximal attention and concentration to one's movement.
- Many clients with advanced age, as in nursing home settings, also have more intense awareness of uncertainties with living and dying. The therapist should be comfortable in addressing these issues by supporting clients' individual religious faiths and practice.
- An understanding and appreciation of learning disabilities and learning deficits in identifying appropriate cognitive stimulating paper–pencil exercises.
- Good interpersonal skills in not only developing a therapeutic alliance with clients, but also in developing a collaborative alliance with other caregivers in the nursing home setting.
- Sound knowledge of medication treatment interventions for psychiatric symptoms and behavioral consultation skills, specifically in designing, in collaboration with nursing staff, behavior data collection methods to address optimal adjustment of psychiatric medications. In view of the increased national concern in the United States about over-medication, this role may become more important in the coming years.
- In case of a therapist's lack of skills or training in any of the specific areas listed above, availability of a consulting psychologist in the service system may be necessary to adopt the MICST model interventions fully in individual therapy work.

We conclude below with some general guidelines for implementing MICST in therapy sessions with nursing home clients.

Guidelines for Implementing MICST in Therapy Sessions with Nursing Home Clients

1. Use simple relaxation, deep breathing, and stretching and postural exercises to promote mind–body awareness, a feeling of connection to the physical world and surroundings, and to help with focusing and attention to one's body and the immediate environment. This type of exercise can be used as a positive redirection strategy to divert attention away from "distressing" thoughts and feelings, often associated with disability or other psychological conditions.
2. Highlight the concept of goal attainment by using the counting method in the relaxation exercises, and emphasize a positive self-image.
3. Use simple mathematics exercises (e.g., addition, subtraction, multiplication, division) to improve alertness and working memory. The exercises should be geared to the client's skill level. It is not important whether the person does the exercise correctly or not; it is more important to focus on giving the client the opportunity to practice and stimulate working memory.
4. Use word-search exercises to promote working memory, attention, and concentration, but also logical associations that may be compromised. Word-search exercises may involve personal memory and semantic memory types of content.
5. Use a genogram to stimulate memory and associations of family relationships.
6. Use various paper–pencil exercises or verbal responses to visually presented questions relating to personal events (autobiographical memory) as well as questions related to general knowledge (semantic memory) to elicit more productive associations and recall of facts and information.
7. Use goal charting, identifying clients' personal goals, and then prioritize each goal selected. Identify steps and barriers and markers for progress. Use written materials or computer word-processing to help clients participate collaboratively with the clinician in discussing goals and therapeutic issues.
8. Support discussions of the client's preferred religious faith and bring in science-based knowledge from, for example, astronomy, as needed to imply that as human beings we all have to deal with the uncertainty of life, independent of our unique life circumstances. This type of discussion may help to promote a sense of contentment and connection to all human beings, independent of disability or changes in one's life circumstances associated with the aging process.

Chapter 10

Concluding Thoughts

We believe that the MICST model has applicability to a wide range of clinical populations such as persons with schizophrenia, clients with a long-term history of substance abuse, and psychiatrically and physically compromised clients in nursing homes. Clinicians may find that in working with these challenging clinical populations, they have limited interventions that have been clinically validated and as such, may have limited expectations for these clients. Clinicians may also have difficulty "connecting" with these clients through traditional interventions that rely heavily on verbal–auditory processing.

The MICST model is aimed at expanding clinicians' repertoire of intervention strategies to engage clients who historically are difficult to engage through traditional therapy interventions. By providing structured multimodal activities and interventions, we hope that the MICST strategies will increase clinicians' confidence in their ability to engage these "clinically challenging clients" more actively in the therapy process and stimulate clients' intact areas of cognitive functioning that are often under-utilized or possibly unrecognized during routine clinical or social interactions.

As discussed throughout the book, we believe that information processing deficits are at the core of clients' difficulties in adjusting to the social world and developing effective coping strategies. We believe that adaptation to the physical and social environment depends on how we process information, which may be influenced by a variety of factors such as age, illness, social conditions, temperament, culture, and individual stress tolerance. The challenge for any therapist or counselor, or a therapeutic milieu team using a psychosocial rehabilitation approach, is to help clients overcome behavior deficits, reduce stress, and improve coping. Clients will need to learn new coping strategies and find new ways of processing information in their social and physical interactions that will lead to more "adaptive" behaviors. In the MICST model, "mind stimulation" plays an important role in the therapeutic process, in conjunction with medication management and therapeutic milieu interventions.

Information processing deficits can contribute to social norm violations, withdrawal, and "disconnection" from others and the world at large. This in turn can lead to increased "stress experiences" in clients which may reinforce isolation and atypical behavioral habits.

Engaging in psychotherapy is one of the many ways that one can make changes to one's thinking and information processing capabilities by learning more effective ways to adapt to the environment. This can be achieved, in part, by enhancing "positive behaviors" that are valued by the person as well as by others, and in the process, reduce "negative behaviors" and personal distress. The MICST model stimulates "positive behaviors" through a positive psychology framework aimed at increasing clients' connections to others, stimulating positive traits and skills, accessing areas of "intact functioning," and helping the client displace atypical and negative behavioral habits by using redirection and mindfulness strategies.

As is evidenced in the theoretical underpinnings of MICST, our active use of positive redirection and mindfulness and "under-emphasis" on exploring negative emotions and memories is analogous to "cauterizing the personal wounds" and stimulating the surrounding "intact areas" to promote positive mental health and recovery; as opposed to "bleeding the wound" for the purpose of "healing the psyche" as may be done in some more traditional psychotherapy approaches. For some people, exploring and gaining knowledge of past "experiences" is helpful to the degree that it provides the person with insight, which they can then use to manage their present symptoms more effectively. For some clients, it may produce a therapeutic cathartic and desensitization experience with their "negative" past so as to make them feel "healthier" and release them from the habit of preoccupation with negative events from their past.

However, we believe that for people who have persistent and severe mental illness, such as schizophrenia or other long-term psychiatrically disabling conditions, focusing on "probing negative memories" to promote "understanding" and healing may not be therapeutically productive for reasons cited earlier in the book. Rather, we emphasize helping clients focus on the "what" of their behavior rather than the "why" of their behavior. The aim is to raise clients' awareness of what they can do differently to adapt better to the environment and to learn ways to cope more effectively. Moreover, having "insight" into one's difficulties, which many clients with schizophrenia and long-term substance abuse demonstrated during the therapy sessions, does not necessarily translate into behavior changes in real-life situations for clients. We feel that many of these clients have difficulty in generalizing their insights into specific behavioral change and need active prompts and supports built into their therapeutic and social milieu for the continued maintenance of "therapeutic gains."

We have suggested that psychiatric symptoms may best be conceptualized not simply as "biochemical brain dysfunctions," but also as reflecting long-standing entrenched behavioral habits reinforced through overusing and over-relying on the underlying neural pathways that support them. We emphasize that one cannot use the straightforward application of the "medical-disease-treatment model" of intervention to psychological conditions. That is, having the knowledge of a "causative factor" contributing to a mental health condition or behavioral difficulty will not necessarily lead to an understanding of how to eliminate the causative factor and achieve symptom reduction. For example, if one arrives at the conclusion that a client's past "trauma experiences" combined with biological vulnerability to psychosis contributed to the onset of psychiatric symptoms, this will not necessarily determine how best to "treat" the client. The client's feelings and "behavioral symptom presentation" may become part of the client's habit repertoire. Limited success is likely to be achieved if, for example, one relies primarily on medication interventions without any concomitant behavioral strategies to help manage the symptoms or to teach the client or the client's therapeutic support team how to displace the negative behaviors and symptoms with "positively valued" behaviors.

Through this book, reflecting our many years of clinical work, we propose to make a case for an "adjunctive treatment approach," which conceptualizes therapeutic interventions for persons with schizophrenia as combining traditional medication and psychosocial support services with interventions that address clients' intact areas of functioning and promote the development of clients' capabilities, interests, and prosocial behaviors that have been under-stimulated and under-utilized. We believe that the MICST model will serve to complement more traditional therapeutic interventions, and we advocate for routinely building in elements of the MICST model to clients' treatment programs and therapeutic milieu as a way to provide clients with ongoing mind stimulation activities.

In our clinical experience, one of the most striking features attesting to the "effectiveness" of the model is the evidence of clients' active involvement in various MICST elements in spite of their long-term history of schizophrenia and "active psychotic thought processes." Many clients demonstrated a high degree of attention, concentration, and task involvement on paper–pencil cognitive stimulating exercises and were able to participate actively according to their own ability in the group activities. For example, a client diagnosed with "catatonic schizophrenia" with extremely limited verbalizations and thought blocking, who communicated very little intelligibly, participated in MICST paper–pencil cognitive exercises and body movement exercise from the very beginning with prompts and supports. In his early years of attendance, this client rarely initiated conversation, but eventually showed notable improvement. After attending MICST for more than ten years, the client became increasingly animated in conversation, initiated comments readily, and often made a point of thanking the therapist repeatedly before leaving the group, showing a sense of positive connection to the group process. The client attended the group by walking quite a distance, without transportation support, indicating a high degree of motivation. The MICST group was the only therapy program that the client attended, outside the milieu program. Often many of these clients considered "unsuited" for traditional conversational psychotherapy are primarily receiving medication management and psychosocial milieu services to maintain their "risk free" status of functioning, and may be considered "clinically stable," needing no further mind stimulating interventions, which we believe is a disservice to these clients.

We were often impressed with the depth of knowledge and information that many clients displayed on a variety of subjects, including issues related to mental health and substance abuse. Their individual and collective knowledge was remarkable considering their interrupted education and long-term history of mental illness. Many clients demonstrated a remarkable capacity for reflective thinking and capacity for revealing their "wisdom" when provided with appropriate mind stimulation activities.

The MICST model provides a format of various mind stimulation techniques to enable clinicians to explore the "hidden" wisdom, knowledge, and talents that many clients possess. For example, a client with a diagnosis of paranoid schizophrenia, who enjoyed doing the paper–pencil cognitive exercises and would frequently ask for homework or additional work during the group, dropped out of the MICST group after several years of attendance and discontinued mental health services. On a chance encounter with the therapist some years later in the community, the client approached the therapist and commented something to the effect: *"Dr. Ahmed, you remember me? I used to be in your group, and we did a lot of thinking exercises . . . it opened my mind and made me think for myself. It made me realize that I can take care of myself . . . I am keeping busy, living at home (with parents), and I am not taking any medication."* Another client with active psychotic manifestations, such as "talking to himself" in public, with a long-term history of paranoid schizophrenia, who had difficulty in responding to the structure of group routine, when properly engaged and prompted, could recite lyrics of many songs, including reciting lengthy paragraphs from Edgar Allen Poe's "The Raven." Another client in a nursing home setting, who had a long history of paranoid schizophrenia, and was physically impaired and wheelchair-bound due to a stroke, reveled in demonstrating his knowledge of "greetings" in different languages. In the course of therapy, he often shared his appreciation of the arts, specifically El Greco's paintings. In one of the therapy sessions, the therapist brought up the topic of fingerprinting, and shared his family history—that the therapist's maternal grandfather, Azizul Haque (see Wikipedia) was involved in the invention of the fingerprint method—to which the client replied: "No, no, he did not invent, he only discovered, only God invents, and man discovers . . ." The therapist was then able to engage with him in a philosophical discussion of Plato's Theory of Forms. The client showed a remarkable capacity to participate and contribute to this level of intellectual discussion with only a high-school level of education, no work history, and a lifelong history of schizophrenia.

The case we want to make is that clinicians should not underestimate clients' abilities and capabilities by being "deceived" by clients' physical appearance, behavioral mannerisms, long-term history of mental illness, and their often long history of "unresponsiveness" to various treatment strategies that have been tried or that are in place.

We have also noticed that staff members, such as nursing staff, direct-care mental health staff, and psychiatrists, who were at times present or happened to observe the MICST sessions, often remarked on clients' increased involvement in various tasks and activities. We also had similar positive comments expressed by experienced counselors and psychologists, who were involved in conducting MICST late in their professional careers. For example, one mental health counselor commented that in his 30 years as a psychologist–mental health counselor, conducting the MICST group was the most rewarding experience for him. Another clinical forensic psychologist volunteered to conduct MICST outside his routine job functions for two years upon the retirement of the senior author (Mohiuddin Ahmed). We encountered similar acceptance of MICST when the model was first presented to psychology interns and externs, indicating its user-friendly nature and "intuitive appeal."

We believe that psychotherapy services provided by various mental health disciplines such as clinical and counseling psychology, mental health counseling, social work, nursing, and psychiatry (above and beyond medication management that some psychiatrists do in private care), have legitimate roles and functions in serving the client populations that we describe. Each discipline can make its own unique specialized contributions in designing and implementing psychotherapy services and interventions. However, in the public sector, specifically for clients with schizophrenia and long-term substance abuse, *psychotherapy services* provided by, for example, clinical and counseling psychologists and psychiatrists are not routinely built into clinical service programs. Such services, however, are available to clients in the private sector, thus creating a dual standard of services for these clients, one for the private sector and one for the public sector. For example, in the public sector, the role of clinical psychologists has become narrowed to providing primarily psychological and forensic evaluations and often not providing any direct clinical services to clients. Moreover, many community mental health centers may not have any clinical or counseling psychologists on the staff to serve the "clinical and behaviorally disordered populations" who are receiving services. The role of psychiatrists has also become relegated to providing medication management services, even though they may be trained to provide effective psychotherapy for these clients; and often they do not have any time allotted for collaboration around behavior functioning assessment or psychotherapy service implementation.

In addition, in the field of psychotherapy and mental health, there is no universally accepted objective evaluation system using, for example, functional behavior analysis data, to assess the effectiveness of clinical interventions (e.g., psychotherapy, medication, milieu therapy). This lack of a more objective evaluation system to assess, for example, medication effectiveness or psychotherapy effectiveness, coupled with the frequent non-availability of clinical–behavioral consultation and collaboration, we believe, have led to consistent overuse of more traditional interventions beyond their efficacy value. For example, some would argue that there has been an overuse or over-reliance on medication interventions across institutional and community settings for persons with schizophrenia. This has possibly contributed to some iatrogenic health-associated illnesses and increased "cost," and has limited the potential for further improvement in the quality of life for some of these clients. In this same vein, we hope that psychotherapy provided by any discipline will have some objective criteria or guidelines, as some forms of psychotherapy may likewise have "negative consequences" or limited effectiveness for some clients. These guidelines need to be developed by both provider agencies and funding agencies, including the insurance providers.

Because of our own professional training and identification with clinical and counseling psychology, and the fact that MICST was developed in the context of our own clinical experience, we believe that clinical psychology and counseling psychology have a special role in providing psychotherapy to “information-processing compromised clients” across a broad spectrum of clinical populations, specifically schizophrenia and related psychiatric disorders, and other persistent clinical conditions. These psychologists’ training in bio-behavioral issues, behavior–learning theory, and evaluation and assessment, uniquely suits them to collaborate with mental health clinicians who provide psychotherapy and social support services as well as with medication-prescribing clinicians (e.g., psychiatrists and nurse practitioners) around optimal management of medication services. We hope that clinical and counseling psychologists entering the practice field will find working with this population very rewarding, as they will have the opportunity to apply their specialized knowledge and training in the service of these clients. Correspondingly, teaching universities need to incorporate more focused training of clinical psychologists to serve this population and work in tandem with state and national mental health service organizations and provider agencies to ensure funding for specialized psychology services for these “challenging mental health populations” in the public sector.

We hope that clinicians from various professional disciplines such as psychiatry, psychology, mental health counseling, social work, nursing, rehabilitation, and occupational therapy, and any other allied healthcare disciplines, will find the MICST model user-friendly and readily adaptable to their clinical work with clients. MICST can also be used as a training model for new clinicians entering the field who have not had experience working with clients with schizophrenia. We hope the book will inspire clinicians to adopt elements of MICST in their ongoing clinical work and give them an enhanced sense of competence and “comfort” in working with challenging clinical populations. We also sincerely hope this book will promote more research and investigation into identifying more effective therapeutic strategies in dealing with clients with schizophrenia and other similar “challenging clinical populations.”

Handouts

PHOTOCOPIABLE RESOURCE

Handout 1: MICST Group Components

1. Body Movement–Mindfulness–Relaxation Exercises (BMR) (5 minutes)

The group starts and ends with a 2–3 minute relaxation exercise. Group members stand and count aloud ten breaths. While taking these breaths, they are instructed to move their arms up while breathing in and down while breathing out. Members are taught to take turns leading the exercise to experience the feeling of being a leader and the value of adhering to a group structure. There are other variations of the BMR exercises: The group facilitator can ask members to stand erect in a stretched position and engage in the breathing exercise, or ask them to watch one hand moving up and down slowly without stopping as in Tai Chi. The BMR exercises are used to help members learn to develop mental control and concentration by paying attention to subtle body movements and the breathing process. The exercises teach clients to use deep breathing to promote relaxation and to redirect themselves away from "troubling" thoughts and feelings. Lastly, the exercises promote alertness to the immediate social environment, a skill needed for successful adaptation to everyday experiences.

2. Group Discussion Exercises: Mind Stimulation Discussions of the Past Week's Activities, Personal History, General Knowledge and Mental Health Topics (20–25 minutes)

Group members take turns talking about an activity they did during the past week, and may at times discuss what they are doing for the day or what they have planned for the upcoming week. The discussion is framed in a short-term past–present–future orientation to facilitate recall of current and recent past memories. These exercises are designed to promote the group sharing process, using current activities and goals to exercise memory functions and to facilitate clients' verbal production and social dialogue using a reality-based and "here and now" framework. Group discussions also focus on general knowledge topics and mental health topics as they are spontaneously brought up in the group session.

3. Paper–Pencil Exercises: Mind Stimulation of Attention, Logical Thinking, Reasoning, and Self-Reflection (25–30 minutes)

Group members complete paper–pencil exercises using mostly "neutral" cognitive exercises and topics (e.g., factual information, logical reasoning, word associations, comprehension, antonyms and synonyms) that promote associative reasoning, comprehension, logical reasoning, memory stimulation, as well as task attention and concentration. The "neutral topics" help to focus concentration and attention and minimize symptom-related behaviors that can surface in conversations or activities that are more emotionally laden. Using visually presented information such as written exercises helps to compensate for difficulties clients may have in processing verbal information.

PHOTOCOPIABLE RESOURCE

Handout 2: MICST Fundamental Features and Core Goals

Fundamental Features

- Information processing is seen as the core to successful adaptation
- Underemphasis of a "deficit-focused" approach
- Positive redirection to factual and reality-based information
- Sensory motor stimulation and mindfulness training
- Cognitive and memory stimulation
- Incorporating verbal and visual communication modalities
- Using feedback to reduce "cognitive rigidity"
- Incorporating an existential perspective to facilitate discussions of spiritual issues and dealing with life's uncertainties.

Core Goals

- **Stimulate memory, association, logical reasoning,** so as to help clients process information and communicate such information within "a reality-based framework"
- **Maximize benefits from therapeutic interactions,** mental health education, and milieu treatment available in the hospital or community setting
- **Teach clients to verbalize strategies for coping** and understanding symptoms affecting behavior
- **Increase concentration and task involvement** and increase toleration of one hour of group interactions without disruption
- **Promote deep breathing exercises** as a way to relax, promote attention to one's breathing process, divert one's mind away from "intrusive" psychiatric symptoms and "negative thoughts," and become more aware of the "here and now" reality
- **Improve social skills:** learn to take turns, ask questions of other group members, show interest in following conversations in group, and reduce self-centered and self-pre-occupying behaviors in the group setting
- **Teach clients to relate to others through stimulating intact areas of cognitive functioning:** talk about events or recall past accomplishments or achievements, practice memory retrieval of factual information, relate to others through talking about "accomplishments," share information, and get feedback
- **Teach client to accept corrective feedback** on paper–pencil cognitive exercises, and through this process, reduce "cognitive rigidity" or agitation associated with "correcting" one's thinking, and in the process improve self-image
- **Help clients to verbalize specific areas in which the group has been helpful** and in the process become mindful and aware of activities necessary for further recovery and for maintaining clinical stability
- **Improve clients' ability to process visually presented cognitive exercises and mental health education materials** to improve their ability to engage in reality-based discussions.

PHOTOCOPIABLE RESOURCE

Handout 3: What is Mind Stimulation?

Mind Stimulation is similar to physical exercise. Just like we need to exercise our body to stay healthy, we need to exercise our mind to stay healthy.

Mind Stimulation refers to stimulating or "exercising" various brain functions and skills such as our memory, attention, concentration, problem solving, logical thinking, and communication skills.

By stimulating these different brain functions, we improve our memory and concentration and can focus better on what we need to accomplish for the day.

By participating in different activities during the day and setting goals, we strengthen our mind. As we strengthen our mind, we can function better in the environment, work toward our goals, accomplish our tasks, and feel more productive and positive.

Examples of Mind Stimulation Activities

- Reading a book, magazine, or newspaper
- Completing exercises and activities such as word searches, crossword puzzles, Sudoku puzzles, chess, checkers, knitting, or playing cards
- Watching a movie or TV show and discussing it with a friend
- Talking about a favorite topic
- Practicing a hobby or starting a new hobby
- Working on a project such as woodworking
- Playing computer games or video games
- Learning a new skill or playing a sport
- Researching a topic on the Internet.

PHOTOCOPIABLE RESOURCE

Handout 4: BMR Exercise Instructions For Clients

PERFORM THE BREATHING EXERCISE TEN TIMES BY COUNTING TO TEN. STAND UP. WHILE STANDING UP, SLIGHTLY BEND YOUR KNEES TO FEEL THE WEIGHT OF YOUR BODY GROUNDED TO THE EARTH. YOUR STANCE SHOULD BE SIMILAR TO SOMEONE IN A SKIING POSITION (see figure).

MOVE BOTH OF YOUR HANDS WITH YOUR PALMS UP AS YOU BREATHE IN THROUGH YOUR NOSE, AND MOVE BOTH OF YOUR HANDS, WITH YOUR PALMS DOWN AS YOU BREATHE OUT THROUGH YOUR MOUTH. THE MOVEMENT OF YOUR HANDS SHOULD ALWAYS BE CONTINUOUS (see figure).

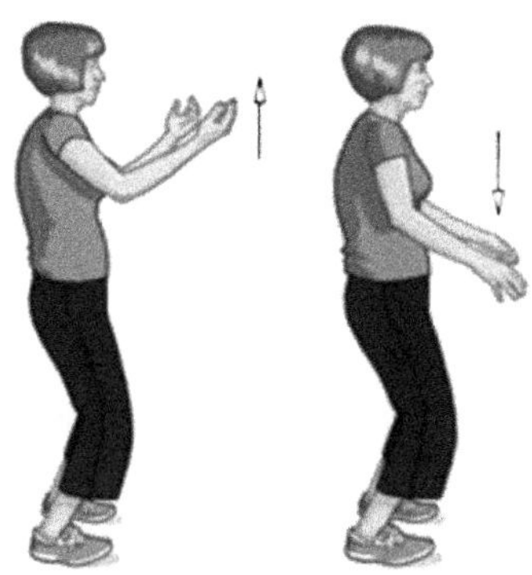

COUNT EACH COMPLETE REPETITION UNTIL YOU REACH TEN. REMEMBER AS YOU BREATHE IN WITH YOUR MOUTH CLOSED, RAISE YOUR HANDS. AS YOU BREATHE OUT WITH YOUR MOUTH SLIGHTLY OPENED, LOWER YOUR HANDS. AFTER YOU HAVE REACHED A COUNT OF TEN, SIT QUIETLY FOR ONE MINUTE AND NOTICE YOUR SURROUNDINGS.

Note:

BY FOCUSING ON THIS ACTIVITY AND PRACTICING YOUR BREATHING EXERCISE, YOU ARE PAYING ATTENTION TO YOUR BODY AND THE PRESENT. YOU ARE NOT PAYING ATTENTION TO NEGATIVE THOUGHTS OR FEELINGS THAT SOMETIMES BOTHER YOU. YOU ARE FEELING GOOD THAT YOU ARE ALIVE AND CAN NOTICE YOUR BODY WORKING AND MOVING.

PHOTOCOPIABLE RESOURCE

Handout 5: Venn Diagram of Communication Rules

Common Frame of Reference in Interpersonal Communication

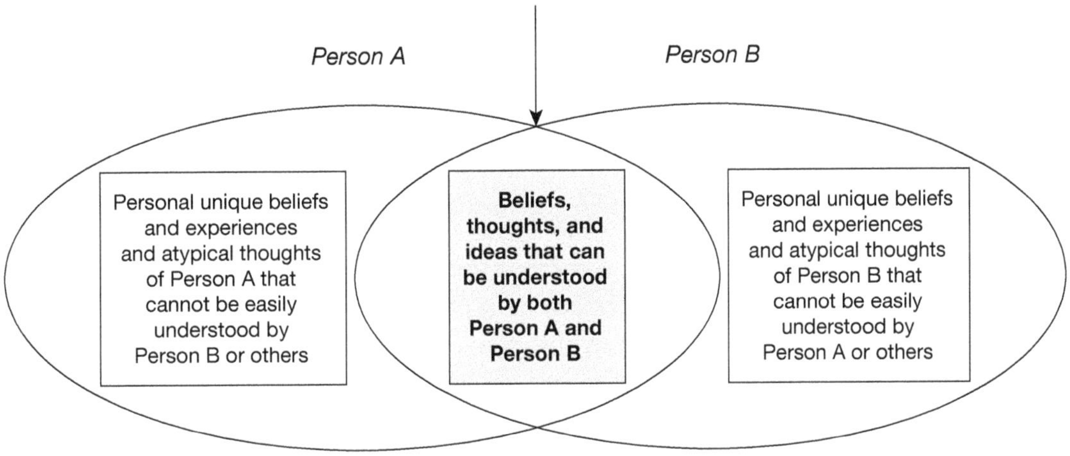

Atypical and unique personal thoughts are difficult to communicate effectively to others. However, thoughts that are logical, goal-directed, and that can be consensually validated can be communicated more effectively to others. To engage in reality-based discussions, we need to find a common frame of reference and discuss thoughts and ideas that can be validated and understood by others.

Common Frame of Reference

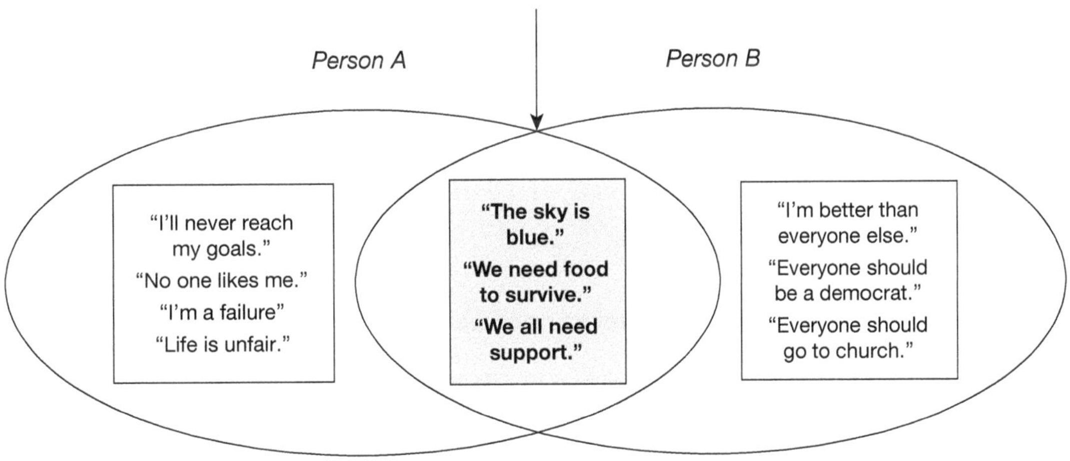

Note: This handout can be given to clients to help reinforce rules of communication and to reinforce the goal of engaging in reality-based discussions. Clients can bring the handout to the group to use as a frame of reference during group discussions

PHOTOCOPIABLE RESOURCE

Handout 6: Redirection Strategies

Attending to the present moment is considered to be a skill and also an intervention. You can teach yourself to *redirect* your attention to the immediate circumstance or moment and as a result be less bothered by distractions and worries. You can practice focusing on your breathing to help train your mind to focus on the present. As you are focusing on the present moment, you will be less distracted by internal preoccupations or worries, and you will be able to focus your attention more on the current task or immediate moment.

Ruminating or worrying can remove you from the present and contribute to stress and anxiety. Redirection strategies can interfere with preoccupations with negative thoughts and help redirect your attention to "neutral topics".

Redirection strategies can help you access intact areas of functioning while "stepping aside" from disorganized, idiosyncratic, or symptom-based thinking. There are various things you can do to redirect yourself from troublesome thoughts and feelings. Below are several examples.

Examples of Redirection Strategies

- Focus on something in the room
- Practice a mind stimulation activity such as a crossword puzzle, paper–pencil cognitive exercise, or a computer game
- Practice the BMR exercises
- Engage in a physical movement or exercise
- Write something down such as a "to do list," or shopping list
- Talk to a friend, relative, or family member
- Read a newspaper or book
- Listen to your favorite radio station or music
- Go to the computer and look up a favorite topic
- Write out a plan for the rest of the day.

Handout 7: Positive and Negative Memories of Life Events

PHOTOCOPIABLE RESOURCE

Our personal memories consist of both "positive" (pleasant and happy) and "negative" (unpleasant and unhappy) memories. Awareness of our "negative memories" can sometimes help us resolve personal conflicts or re-energize us toward self-improvement. However, if we focus too much on "negative memories," we may become "fixed" on these memories and they can develop into "habits of thinking." These negative thinking habits can increase stress, depression, or anxiety and negatively affect our daily functioning.

Focusing on our more "positive memories" can be therapeutically helpful in alleviating distress and helping to "disconnect" us from any preoccupations with negative memories. We can improve our mood and mental status by practicing redirection to positive memories such as memories about ourselves or about a person who has affected our life in a positive way.

We cannot "delete" negative events that may have happened in our life by thinking repeatedly about them or by going over them again and again. However, we can replace "negative memories" about the events by thinking about positive memories or doing activities on a daily basis to keep ourselves busy and engaged in the present.

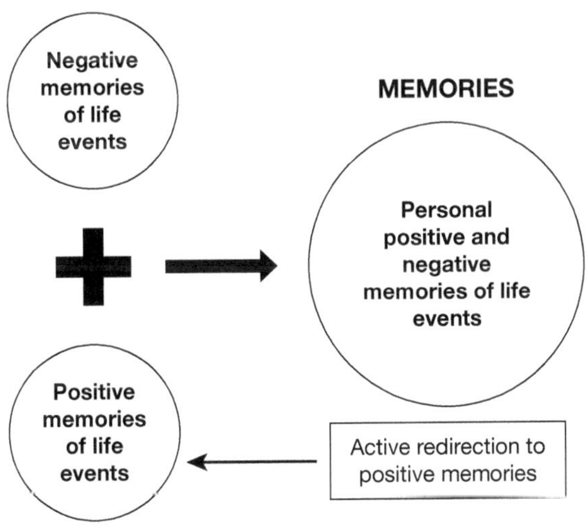

PHOTOCOPIABLE RESOURCE

Handout 8: Web Sites and Educational Resources

- **Mind Stimulation Computer Exercises:**
  - http://www.braingym.com
  - http://www.lumosity.com
  - http://www.PositScience.com
  - http://www.TheBCAT.com

- **Mind Stimulation Paper–Pencil Worksheets and Exercises:**
  - http://www.education.com/worksheets
  - http://www.teach-nology.com
  - http://www.worksheetplace.com
  - http://www.math.com
  - http://www.wordsearch.com
  - http://www.armoredpenguin.com/wordsearch/

- **Psycho-education—US National Institute of Mental Health:**
  - http://www.nimh.nih.gov/health/educational-resources/index.shtml

- **Critical Thinking Skills Workbooks:**
  - http://www.criticalthinking.com/searchBykeyword.do?code=c&catalog=c&searchKey=new+products
  - http://www.prufrock.com/Logic-and-Reasoning-C1109.aspx
  - http://www.teacherstorehouse.com
  - http://www.thefind.com/family/info-critical-thinking-workbook

- **Meditation Site:**
  - www.greatday.com

All sites accessed February 26 2013.

Worksheets

Worksheet 1: BMR Charting Record

PHOTOCOPIABLE RESOURCE

Name: ______________________ Date: ______________

Record your degree of concentration (1 = "very distracted by unwanted thoughts"; 10 = "not distracted at all by unwanted thoughts and able to focus on the exercise")

Record your degree of relaxation (1 = "very tense"; 10 = "completely relaxed and comfortable")

Day	Practice Session	Concentration (mind) 1——10	Relaxation (body) 1——10
Monday	1		
	2		
Tuesday	1		
	2		
Wednesday	1		
	2		
Thursday	1		
	2		
Friday	1		
	2		
Saturday	1		
	2		
Sunday	1		
	2		
Number of sessions practiced for the week:			

PHOTOCOPIABLE RESOURCE

Worksheet 2: Goal Setting Worksheet–A

Name: ______________________________ Date: __________________

Goal to achieve this week:

Steps to reach this goal:

1. ______________________________
2. ______________________________
3. ______________________________

Goal to achieve this month:

Steps to reach this goal:

1. ______________________________
2. ______________________________
3. ______________________________

Goal to achieve in six months:

Steps to reach this goal:

1. ______________________________
2. ______________________________
3. ______________________________

Ongoing goal:

Steps to reach this goal:

1. ______________________________
2. ______________________________
3. ______________________________

PHOTOCOPIABLE RESOURCE

Worksheet 3: Goal Setting Worksheet–B

Goals are desirable projections into the future about things we would like to accomplish or achieve. Goals need to be stated in ways that are agreed upon by the treatment team to validate their objectivity and possibility of accomplishment.

In order to achieve our stated goals, the following need to take place: We need to identify a) where we are right now in relation to our goals; b) what steps we need to take to achieve our stated goals; c) what others need to do, or what events need to happen so that we can accomplish our goals; and d) what barriers we need to overcome to achieve our goals.

What am I doing now?

My goals for the next

1 week:

1 month:

6 months:

→

Steps I need to take to reach my goals:

1.

2.

3.

↓

The things that others need to do or the events that need to happen so that I can accomplish my goals are:

The barriers that may prevent me from reaching these goals are:

PHOTOCOPIABLE RESOURCE

Worksheet 4: Weekly Schedule

Name: ______________________________

Dates:

	Monday	Tuesday	Wednesday	Thursday	Friday	Saturday	Sunday
8–9 am							
9–10 am							
10–11 am							
11 am–12 pm							
12–1 pm							
1–2 pm							
2–3 pm							
3–4 pm							
4–5 pm							
5–6 pm							
6–7 pm							
7–8 pm							

Worksheet 5: Early Warning Signs and Coping Strategies

PHOTOCOPIABLE RESOURCE

Name: ______________________________ Date: ____________________

STRESS ZONE

Things that cause me stress:	Warning signs that I am getting worse:
______________________	______________________
______________________	______________________
______________________	______________________
______________________	______________________
______________________	______________________
______________________	______________________
______________________	______________________

RELAXATION ZONE

Things that relax me:	Ways to cope with warning signs:
______________________	______________________
______________________	______________________
______________________	______________________
______________________	______________________
______________________	______________________
______________________	______________________
______________________	______________________

PHOTOCOPIABLE RESOURCE

Worksheet 6: Ways to Spend the Day

Name: ______________________________ Date: ____________________

Things I could do today:	One thing I will plan to do today:
______________________	[ ]
______________________	
______________________	
______________________	
______________________	

Things I could do this week:	One thing I will plan to do this week:
______________________	[ ]
______________________	
______________________	
______________________	
______________________	

Things I could do this month:	Two things I will plan to do this month:
______________________	[ ]
______________________	[ ]
______________________	
______________________	
______________________	

Worksheet 7: Brainstorming Worksheet for Topics of Interest

PHOTOCOPIABLE RESOURCE

Name: ______________________ Date: ______________

My favorite subjects in school:

____

____

____

My favorite topics to talk about:

____

____

____

Topics that my friends and family enjoy talking about:

____

____

____

Topics that I am interested in learning more about:

____

____

____

One topic from the list that I would like to start gathering more information on:

____

PHOTOCOPIABLE RESOURCE

Worksheet 8: Data Collection Worksheet for a Topic

Name: ______________________________ Date: ____________________

Where I looked for the information (e.g., books, Internet, talked to others, library):

____

____

____

____

What I learned about the topic:

____

____

____

____

What I found most interesting about the topic:

____

____

____

One thing I would like to tell the group about the topic:

____

PHOTOCOPIABLE RESOURCE

Worksheet 9: Problem-solving Worksheet

Name: ______________________________ Date: ____________________

The current problem is:

I know this is a problem because (list negative consequences of the problem):

Possible *solutions* to this problem are:

1. ____

2. ____

3. ____

People who can help me resolve this problem:

One thing I can do today to help resolve this problem:

PHOTOCOPIABLE RESOURCE

Worksheet 10: Self-care Recovery Plan

Name: ______________________________ Date: ____________________

Self-improvement Goal:

- Two steps I can take to help me reach this goal:
  1. ______________________________
  2. ______________________________

- Two ways my family or friends can help me:
  1. ______________________________
  2. ______________________________

- Two ways my treatment team can help me:
  1. ______________________________
  2. ______________________________

- Two things that may prevent me from reaching my goal:
  1. ______________________________
  2. ______________________________

- Two things I will notice that will be a sign that I am reaching my goal:
  1. ______________________________
  2. ______________________________

Worksheet 11: Day Routine Weekly Schedule: Recording Form

PHOTOCOPIABLE RESOURCE

Complete the Day Routine using codes for specific activities and rating on a scale of 1–3 for completion data (**Note: the schedule should be completed in consultation with staff**)

	8–10	10–12	12–2	2–4	4–6	6–8	8–10	10–12	12–8
Monday									Sleep
Tuesday									Sleep
Wednesday									Sleep
Thursday									Sleep
Friday									Sleep
Saturday									Sleep
Sunday									Sleep

Codes for activities: A: Personal hygiene; **B:** Breakfast/lunch/dinner/snack; **C:** House chores; **D:** Day program or community outings (bowling, shopping, eating out); **E:** Individual counseling; **F:** Doctor's appointment or other medical appointment; **G:** Family visits; **H:** Recreational activities (e.g., TV, music, exercise, reading); **I:** Practice of relaxation exercise; **J:** Any other activity, specify (e.g., paper–pencil MICST exercises)

Rating of compliance: 1 = non-performance; 2 = partial performance; 3 = satisfactory performance. For example, satisfactory performance for personal hygiene would be coded in the chart as **A** (3).

Expected level of performance for each activity will be reasonable compliance with the task. The client will not be negatively confronted for non-compliance, but positively encouraged through relationship support and counseling to increase his/her level of compliance. The client's non-compliance will be processed in individual counseling sessions or in family meetings.

Appendices

Appendix A

MICST Mental Health Discussion Topics

PHOTOCOPIABLE RESOURCE

MICST Mental Health Discussion Topics

- Anxiety—what it means and how to manage it
- Brain behavior functioning
- Causes of emotional stress and ways to effectively manage stress
- Concrete steps in problem solving
- Different medications that members are taking, classes of psychiatric medications, side effects versus benefits of medication, use of PRN medication
- Does heredity play a part in mental illness?
- How are thoughts, feelings, and behaviors interconnected?
- How different components of cognitive skills are stimulated by the MICST model: understanding the importance of following directions, use of attention and concentration, working memory, and long-term memory in adaptive behaviors
- How involvement in a productive day routine and cognitive stimulation can disrupt preoccupation with negative thoughts and reduce agitation
- How medications and psychosocial rehabilitation help in recovery and coping
- How psychiatric history may affect cognitive functioning in terms of logical associations, reasoning, memory, attention to tasks, following directions, and use of working memory
- How we set up realistic personal goals and identify steps to achieve these goals: differentiating realistic from wishful fantasy
- Importance of accepting corrective feedback (primarily using neutral paper–pencil exercises)
- Importance of making the best of the present and letting go of the past
- Importance of monitoring one's internal stress in order to prevent relapse while achieving or striving to achieve goals or expectations
- Importance of work in recovery
- Key elements of relapse prevention
- Physical and emotional manifestations of mental illness
- Rationale for social interaction in the group when group members ask each other about the past week's events
- The need to work collaboratively with "significant" others for the recovery process
- The role of family and a network of friends and support in the recovery process
- The role of food, exercise, and other healthy habits
- Types of memory: semantic (knowledge of facts) and episodic (autobiographical) and how personal memory can be disrupted or confused in psychiatric conditions; how long-term memory and recall of factual information (general knowledge) are intact in many clients
- Understanding symptoms of schizophrenia: paranoia, delusions, and hallucinations

PHOTOCOPIABLE RESOURCE

- Ways to develop social skills and goal setting
- Ways to manage anger effectively
- What do we mean by the stigma of mental illness?
- What does it mean to be happy?
- What does it mean to be "discharge ready"?
- Who can we turn to in the treatment of mental illness?

Appendix B

MICST Self-assessment Tools

PHOTOCOPIABLE RESOURCE

Self-assessment Tool 1

Name: ________________________________ Date: ____________________

1. What issues and activities were interesting or helpful to you today?

2. What issues or activities would you have liked to discuss more in the group?

3. What activity or discussion topic would you like to see included in the group for the next week or in the future?

4. How would you rate your degree of involvement in the group today on a scale of 1–5 (1 = least involved; 5 = most involved)? Explain your number rating.

   ☐

5. How do you rate your mood today on a scale of 1–5 (1 = very unhappy or depressed; 5 = very happy, not depressed at all)? Explain your number rating.

   ☐

6. Do you feel that you are making progress toward recovery and gaining self-control? (1 = not at all; 5 = very much so)? Explain your number rating.

   ☐

7. What are the most productive activities you have been involved in this past week?

8. Are you practicing deep breathing and other mindfulness strategies?

9. List the positive activities that you are using to divert your attention away from preoccupations with "negative thoughts or feelings."

PHOTOCOPIABLE RESOURCE

Self-assessment Tool 2

Name: ______________________________ Date: __________________

MY OWN SELF-ASSESSMENT

Skills and positive behaviors that I have and that I display now:

I need to work on or improve myself in the following areas:

Skills that I used to have but I don't seem to have now:

My desire to be (where do I want to be, where do I want to go, how do I get there?):

Self-assessment Tool 3

PHOTOCOPIABLE RESOURCE

Concentration Skills

Name: ______________________________ Date: ____________________

1. How do you rate your ability to concentrate on a scale from 1 to 4? (please circle)

Very good	Good	Some problems	A lot of problems
1	2	3	4

2. Would you like to see improvement in your ability to concentrate? (circle your response)

   Yes   **No**   **Not sure**

3. What will help you improve your concentration? (circle all that apply)
   a. Thinking about what I need to do when I am doing something
   b. Not paying attention to what others around me are doing
   c. Listening to instructions given to me, so I understand what I have to do
   d. Trying to remember what I am supposed to do as I am doing the task, and not letting my mind wander away
   e. Talking to myself silently to maintain my concentration on the task at hand
   f. Thinking about how to finish the task when I am in the middle of doing it
   g. Any other thoughts you may have.

4. When you concentrate and finish a task, how do you feel?

   I feel good   **I don't have any feelings**   **I don't care**

5. What do concentration skills help you with? (circle all that apply)
   a. Social conversation
   b. Talking with staff
   c. Explaining my thoughts and feelings to others more clearly
   d. Learning not to be bothered by my psychiatric symptoms while I am talking or doing something
   e. Following instructions in my day routine or in a job situation
   f. Paying attention to my day schedule and following through with activities that I am supposed to be doing
   g. Remembering activities that I need to do on a daily basis
   h. Any other thoughts or ideas you may have.

6. In your own words, can you state some of the reasons why you have difficulties with maintaining concentration or what you think might interfere with your ability to concentrate on a given task. ______________________________

   ____

PHOTOCOPIABLE RESOURCE

Self-assessment Tool 4

Assessing Areas of Functioning

Name: ______________________________ Date: __________________

We would like to know the areas of your functioning that you think need improvement. This will help us to talk about issues that are important to you and other members in the group. We know you are working with your treatment team in these areas.

<u>Personal hygiene:</u> Please circle the appropriate response category

Needs improvement *No improvement needed* *No opinion*

If you circled "needs improvement," please state what specific areas need improvement:

<u>Behavior control:</u> Please circle the appropriate response category

Needs improvement *No improvement needed* *No opinion*

If you circled "needs improvement," please state what specific behaviors need improvement:

<u>Hearing voices:</u> (Please check off all that apply)

____ I have a problem, but I can think about something else or do something else and not let it bother me.
____ I have no problems in this area.
____ I am working to control "hearing voices" with the help of my doctor and treatment team.
____ I have a problem in this area, but only when I am agitated or upset.

<u>Preoccupations:</u> I find myself spending a lot of time thinking about my problems or thinking about "negative experiences" from my past:

Yes *No* *Sometimes* *No opinion*

<u>Areas I need to work on with my treatment team are:</u> (please circle all that apply)

Anger management	Finding a job	Excessive anxiety
Volunteering	Daily activity schedule	"Thinking" skills
Medication compliance	Attention/concentration	Memory skills
Stress management	Communication skills	Social isolation

Appendix C

MICST Feedback Questionnaires

PHOTOCOPIABLE RESOURCE

Cognitive Skills Training (MICST): Questionnaire 1

Name: ________________________________ Date: ____________________

All responses should be "verbatim." Preferably the questionnaire should be explained to each client by his/her case manager or someone not affiliated with the group.

1) How long have you been attending the cognitive skills training group?

2) What do you do in the group?

3) How does a specific activity such as deep breathing exercises, talking about the past week's events, paper–pencil exercises, and discussion of issues that are brought out spontaneously help you?

   a) Relaxation:

   b) Talking about the past week's events:

   c) Paper–pencil exercises:

   d) Discussion of other issues and topics:

   e) Going over the exercises (feedback session):

4) How does the group help you in the management of your psychiatric symptoms?

5) What information from the group has helped you the most with your functioning?

6) What would you like to add to the group format to make it more effective?

Cognitive Skills Training (MICST): Questionnaire 2

Name: ________________________________ **Date:** ____________________

Please respond to the following items by choosing between the two alternatives, "Yes," or "No" for each item listed. This questionnaire is designed to get your feedback as to the benefit you perceive you have gained as a result of your participation in cognitive skills group treatment.

Please give your opinion of "Yes" or "No" to each of the following items by checking off in the appropriate box next to the item.

Areas of Functioning	"**No**, the Cognitive Skills Group does not help me in this area."	"**Yes**, the Cognitive Skills Group does help me in this area."
a. Remembering information		
b. Improving my thinking and reasoning skills		
c. Accepting feedback to my answers or learning to change my answers when necessary		
d. Increasing social interaction		
e. Learning relaxation exercises		
f. Learning to concentrate on tasks		
g. Problem solving (e.g., keeping information in my mind while working to solve a problem)		
h. Tolerating a task over a longer period of time		
i. Learning to follow a group routine		
j. Understanding my mental illness symptoms		
k. Getting a better appreciation of medication treatment		

PHOTOCOPIABLE RESOURCE

Cognitive Skills Training (MICST): Questionnaire 3

Name: ______________________________ Date: ____________________

Q1. How does the cognitive group (MICST) help you in the management of psychiatric symptoms in your present situation?

____

____

____

____

____

____

Q2. What information from the group has been helpful to you in your day-to-day functioning?

____

____

____

____

____

____

Q3. In what ways have you improved the most as a result of your participation in the group (MICST)?

____

____

____

____

____

____

PHOTOCOPIABLE RESOURCE

Cognitive Skills Training (MICST): Questionnaire 4

Name: ______________________________ Date: __________________

Q1. What do you like about the MICST group?

____

____

____

____

____

Q2. What don't you like about this group?

____

____

____

____

____

Q3. What kind of changes does the group need?

____

____

____

____

____

Q4. How did this cognitive skills (MICST) group help you?

____

____

____

____

____

Cognitive Skills Training (MICST): Questionnaire 5

PHOTOCOPIABLE RESOURCE

Staff Feedback Questionnaire

Q1. Do you feel that your involvement and participation in the cognitive skills (MICST) training group has been helpful to you in developing a better understanding of your clients' functioning?

____

____

____

____

Q2. Did you personally feel that the clients benefitted from participation in this cognitive skills training (MICST) group?

____

____

____

____

Q3. What do you attribute the clients' motivation to attend the cognitive skills training (MICST) group to?

____

____

____

____

Q4. Are there any particular areas in which you have applied the cognitive skills training (MICST) concepts to your individual work with clients?

____

____

____

____

Appendix D

Semi-structured Plan for a 12-week MICST Group

Semi-structured Plan for a 12-week MICST Group

PHOTOCOPIABLE RESOURCE

Week 1

- Start with: BMR exercises
- Review the past week's events
- Group discussion topic: *Ways to spend the day*
- Paper–pencil exercise: *Word search on activities*
- End with: BMR exercises

Week 2

- Start with: BMR exercises
- Review the past week's events
- Group discussion topic: *Pros and cons of medication*
- Paper–pencil exercise: *Analogies/similarities*
- End with: BMR exercises

Week 3

- Start with: BMR exercises
- Review the past week's events
- Group discussion topic: *Famous discoveries/famous presidents*
- Paper–pencil exercise: *General knowledge questions*
- End with: BMR exercises

Week 4

- Start with: BMR exercises
- Review the past week's events
- Group discussion topic: *Stress management and coping skills*
- Paper–pencil exercise: *Math/Word search on mental health*
- End with: BMR exercises

Week 5

- Start with: BMR exercises
- Review the past week's events
- Group discussion topic: *Famous writers and books read*
- Paper–pencil exercise: *Visual matching/grouping*
- End with: BMR exercises

Week 6

- Start with: BMR exercises
- Review the past week's events
- Group discussion topic: *Creation and religions*
- Paper–pencil exercise: *Identifying facts versus opinions*
- End with: BMR exercises

PHOTOCOPIABLE RESOURCE

Week 7

- Start with: BMR exercises
- Review the past week's events
- Group discussion topic: *Jobs held and types of jobs*
- Paper–pencil exercise: *Composition/Matching profession with tool*
- End with: BMR exercises

Week 8

- Start with: BMR exercises
- Review the past week's events
- Group discussion topic: *Family of origin and family supports*
- Paper–pencil exercise: *Self-evaluation of accomplishments and goals*
- End with: BMR exercises

Week 9

- Start with: BMR exercises
- Review the past week's events
- Group discussion topic: *Sports played, types of exercise*
- Paper–pencil exercise: *Listing members in a group/Sequencing events*
- End with: BMR Exercises

Week 10

- Start with: BMR exercises
- Review the past week's events
- Group discussion topic: *Geography*
- Paper–pencil exercise: *States and capitals/Word meanings*
- End with: BMR exercises

Week 11

- Start with: BMR exercises
- Review the past week's events
- Group discussion topic: *Brain functioning*
- Paper–pencil exercise: *General knowledge questions*
- End with: BMR exercises

Week 12

- Start with: BMR exercises
- Review the past week's events
- Group discussion topic: *Cognitive stimulation and MICST exercises*
- Paper–pencil exercise: *Self-evaluation of benefits from MICST activities*
- End with: BMR exercises

Appendix E

Clinician Instruction Sheets

PHOTOCOPIABLE RESOURCE

CLINICIAN INSTRUCTIONS—BMR EXERCISES

The group leader briefly explains the rationale for the exercises by stating or paraphrasing the following:

"WE WILL BEGIN WITH A DEEP BREATHING EXERCISE TO HELP US RELAX AND BECOME AWARE OF OUR BREATHING AS WELL AS OUR BODY MOVEMENTS. THIS EXERCISE REMINDS US THAT WE ARE ALIVE AND ARE CONNECTED TO THE EARTH. WE WANT TO PRACTICE BEING AWARE OF OUR BREATHING, OUR BODY MOVEMENT, AND THE IMMEDIATE PRESENT MOMENT. IN THE PROCESS, WE BECOME MORE ALERT, THINK MORE CLEARLY, AND LEARN TO RELAX AND NOT FEEL STRESSED."

The group leader then describes the exercises:

"WE WILL PERFORM THE BREATHING EXERCISE TEN TIMES BY COUNTING OUT LOUD TO TEN. COUNTING PROVIDES US WITH THE STEPS NEEDED TO REACH OUR GOAL OF TEN REPETITIONS."

"PLEASE STAND UP. WHILE STANDING UP, SLIGHTLY BEND YOUR KNEES TO FEEL THE WEIGHT OF YOUR BODY GROUNDED TO THE EARTH. YOUR STANCE SHOULD BE SIMILAR TO SOMEONE IN A SKIING POSITION."

(*The leader demonstrates the posture:* see figure below.)

"WITH YOUR KNEES SLIGHTLY BENT, BREATHE IN THROUGH YOUR NOSE WITH YOUR MOUTH CLOSED, AND THEN BREATHE OUT THROUGH YOUR MOUTH KEEPING YOUR MOUTH SLIGHTLY OPENED."

"AS YOU FOCUS ON YOUR BREATHING, NOTICE WHAT YOU ARE DOING AND HOW YOU ARE WORKING TOWARD YOUR GOAL OF TEN REPETITIONS."

"LET'S PRACTICE THE BREATHING AND COUNTING. WE WILL COUNT OUT LOUD EACH COMPLETE REPETITION UNTIL WE REACH TEN . . . READY . . . GO."

"NOW, WE ARE GOING TO DO IT SLIGHLY DIFFERENTLY. THIS TIME YOU WILL ALSO MOVE BOTH OF YOUR HANDS PALMS UP AS YOU BREATHE IN THROUGH YOUR NOSE, AND MOVE YOUR HANDS PALMS DOWN WITH BOTH ELBOWS POINTED DOWN AS YOU BREATHE OUT THROUGH YOUR MOUTH. THE MOVEMENT OF YOUR HANDS SHOULD ALWAYS BE CONTINUOUS."

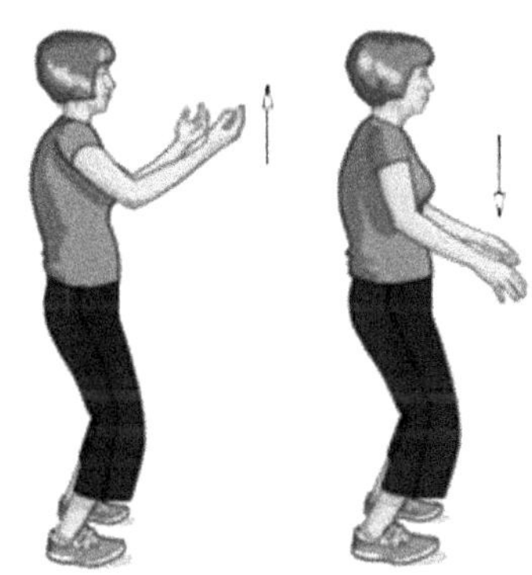

(The leader demonstrates the movement: see figure.)

PHOTOCOPIABLE RESOURCE

"LET'S DO THE FULL EXERCISE NOW. WE WILL COUNT OUT LOUD EACH COMPLETE REPETITION UNTIL WE REACH TEN. REMEMBER AS YOU BREATHE IN WITH YOUR MOUTH CLOSED, RAISE YOUR HANDS. AS YOU BREATHE OUT WITH YOUR MOUTH SLIGHTLY OPENED, LOWER YOUR HANDS. READY . . . GO."

Note: *The group leader can add this alternative "one hand" arm movement version as needed. When asking members to stand with knees in a slightly bent position, instruct them to move only one hand during the arm movements, but always maintaining focus on the moving hand (the group leader may need to demonstrate). Again, have the members do the exercise for a count of ten breathing repetitions.*

Optional: *Additional comment to be added if using the "one hand" version:*

"THIS EXERCISE HELPS US TO FOCUS ON OUR BODY MOVEMENT MORE DEEPLY, TO FEEL GOOD TO SEE HOW OUR HAND IS MOVING UP AND DOWN, AND FEEL GOOD TO BE ALIVE IN THIS WORLD. WE ARE HAVING AN EXPERIENCE OF TOTAL CONCENTRATION DURING THIS EXERCISE, AND WHILE WE ARE DOING THIS, WE ARE NOT THINKING ABOUT ANYTHING ELSE. WE ARE LEARNING TO TAKE A BREAK AWAY FROM OUR TROUBLESOME THOUGHTS. IT IS TEACHING US HOW TO LEARN TO PUSH AWAY NEGATIVE THOUGHTS AND CONCENTRATE ON SOMETHING POSITIVE. THIS IS HOW WE PRACTICE DOING DIFFERENT THINGS ON A DAILY BASIS, PUSHING OUR ANXIOUS AND TROUBLING THOUGHTS AWAY AND FOCUSING ON SOMETHING THAT MAKES US FEEL GOOD."

Optional: *The leader can reiterate the following before or after the BMR exercises:*

"BY FOCUSING ON THIS ACTIVITY AND PRACTICING OUR BREATHING, WE ARE PAYING ATTENTION TO OUR BODY AND THE PRESENT MOMENT. WE ARE NOT PAYING ATTENTION TO NEGATIVE THOUGHTS OR FEELINGS THAT SOMETIMES BOTHER US. WE ARE FEELING GOOD THAT WE ARE ALIVE AND CAN NOTICE OUR BODY WORKING AND MOVING. AS WE LOOK UP WHEN WE INHALE AND EXHALE, WE FORGET ABOUT OUR PERSONAL PROBLEMS AND SEE OURSELVES CONNECTED TO THE UNIVERSE AROUND US."

"WE ARE LEARNING TO PRACTICE A RELAXED AND ASSERTIVE BODY POSTURE, STANDING TALL AND ERECT, AND TO FEEL COMFORTABLE IN THE CURRENT SOCIAL ENVIRONMENT. WE ARE ALL PRACTICING THIS AS A GROUP AND WORKING TOGETHER."

"WE ARE ALSO LEARNING HOW TO PRACTICE REACHING A GOAL THAT WE SET UP. THAT IS WHY WE DO THIS EXERCISE TEN TIMES, AND COUNT EVERY TIME WE DO IT. THIS IS SIMILAR TO STEPS WE HAVE TO TAKE TO REACH A GOAL AND BEING ABLE TO FEEL GOOD WHEN WE REACH THE GOAL WE SET OUT TO DO."

Note: *Group members may rotate in leading the BMR exercises for each group session. When a client leads the BMR exercise, it is best to eliminate any visual imagery and have the client focus rather on just counting through the ten breathing repetitions.*

PHOTOCOPIABLE RESOURCE

CLINICIAN INSTRUCTIONS—GROUP DISCUSSIONS

1. **Browse the "information Internet" of the client**

   "Browse" the various topics that the client either alludes to or introduces during his or her verbalizations during the group. Decide which topics or issues may lead to a more expanded or reality-based discussion. From past group discussions, use what is known about a client's knowledge base to stimulate further discussion topics in this area. Clients may be called upon at times to share their knowledge about a topic

   Any mental health or general knowledge topic mentioned, such as "I have been feeling depressed," "I am not doing well with my medication adjustment," "I had a treatment team meeting last week," or other interests mentioned such as sports, travel, religious practice, and hobbies can lead to an expanded discussion of the topic in the context of mental health education, general knowledge, or personal history recapitulation.

2. **Click onto "reality-based links" (RBLs) from the client's verbalizations**

   RBLs are the more logical thoughts or utterances that are imbedded in a client's verbalizations and linked to "intact" and logical thought processes. These links, when "clicked on," will more likely lead to information that can be consensually validated and agreed upon by other group members. RBLs will also be clues to the client's knowledge base and reflect potential discussion topics.

   "Clicking" onto these links will elicit more intact thoughts and memories which the client can more easily expand upon. Deliberately "clicking" onto these links will also help clients to focus and shape their thoughts into a more reality-based discussion.

3. **Operate out of a "reality-based framework"**

   Recognizing the difficulties that many people with schizophrenia have in communicating with each other through a "reality-based framework" and their tendency to bring in tangential associations or "intrusive" thoughts, the therapist focuses discussions on the "here and now" and concrete events that clients are participating in. Group members are encouraged to talk about activities and events from the past week so that the discussion of issues and events are specific and reality-bound.

   The therapist makes an ongoing effort to shape and facilitate conversations through a "reality-based" framework, helping clients to stay focused on information and issues that can be "consensually validated" and understood by all group members. Efforts are made to identify universal themes that all clients can relate to and for which all clients can share relevant experiences that contribute meaningfully to the group discussion.

PHOTOCOPIABLE RESOURCE

4. **Actively use redirection strategies**

   If "delusional material" is brought into the reporting process, only relevant associations are extracted that could lead to reality-based discussion, while acknowledging group members' desire and intention to share information with others (provide *Handout 5: Venn Diagram of Communication Rules* as needed for clients in the group).

   Throughout the discussion phase of the group, the group leader actively *redirects* the conversation to themes and issues that are logical and that lend themselves to a shared discussion (see Figure 4.2: redirection strategies).

5. **Involve all group members at their level**

   Clients' participation levels vary according to their ability level and interest. Some group members may need more active prodding. The group leader can use co-therapists as needed to work individually with those clients who may need more prompting or support to participate in discussions. Throughout the discussion phase, group members are encouraged to ask each other questions or respond to comments, which helps provide social skills training through modeling how to initiate social conversations, listen to others, and sustain conversations.

Appendix F

Sample Paper–Pencil Exercises

- Analogies
- Categorizing, Classifying, or Grouping Objects
- Composition
- Comprehension
- Facts versus Opinions
- General Knowledge
- Grammar Usage
- Matching of Pairs of Words or Concepts
- Mathematics/Measurement
- Sequencing Events and the Concept of Time
- Similarities and Differences
- Synonyms and Antonyms
- Visual Matching Exercises
- Word Meanings and Verbal Comprehension
- Word Search
- Self-reflection
- Miscellaneous Exercises

PHOTOCOPIABLE RESOURCE

Name: ________________________________ Date: ______________

ANALOGIES

Circle the correct answer from the choices given and write the answer on the line.

1. Tall is to Short as Night is to: ____________________

   a) Day b) Right c) Long d) Dark

2. Happy is to Glad as Angry is to: ________________

   a) Smirk b) Scared c) Mad d) Curious

3. Fish is to Water as Bird is to: ____________________

   a) Air b) Feather c) Sea d) Wing

4. Hand is to Glove as Head is to: __________________

   a) Foot b) Face c) Hat d) Neck

5. Few is to Many as Less is to: ____________________

   a) Several b) More c) Big d) Fewer

6. Height is to Tall as Width is to: __________________

   a) Wide b) Fat c) Round d) Thin

7. Ship is to Water as Airplane is to __________________

   a) Waves b) Air c) Flight d) Cloud

8. House is to Roof as Head is to ____________________

   a) Top b) Tile c) Hair d) Neck

9. Seldom is to Often as Scared is to __________________

   a) Nervous b) Brave c) Lost d) Free

10. Bulb is to Light as Furnace is to: __________________

    a) Cold b) Summer c) Fire d) Heat

PHOTOCOPIABLE RESOURCE

Name: ______________________________ Date: ______________

ANALOGIES

Circle the correct answer from the choices given and write the answer on the line.

1. 1 is to 2 as A is to: ____________________

   a) Z b) B c) Letter d) Alphabet

2. Book is to Bookstore as Bread is to: ______________

   a) Loaf b) Table c) Butter d) Bakery

3. Swim is to Pool as Skate is to: ____________________

   a) Water b) Skater c) Rink d) Ice

4. Sleep is to Pillow as Drive is to: ____________________

   a) Car b) Fast c) Night d) Tired

5. Water is to Mop as Snow is to: ___________________

   a) Cold b) Winter c) Boots d) Shovel

6. Clay is to Sculpture as Paint is to: ___________________

   a) Brush b) Portrait c) Artist d) Canvas

7. Skin is to Body as Glove is to: _____________________

   a) Boot b) Mitten c) Hand d) Hat

8. Paint is to Brush as Write is to: ____________________

   a) Paper b) Letter c) Ink d) Pen

9. Quick is to Fast as Scared is to: _________________

   a) Timid b) Slow c) Brave d) More

10. Sunrise is to East as Sunset is to: ____________________

    a) Cold b) West c) Fire d) Summer

PHOTOCOPIABLE RESOURCE

Name: ______________________________ Date: ____________

CATEGORIZING INFORMATION

The following words belong to something or are a part of something. Think about the word and place it under the best category. An example is provided.

<u>Word List</u>

steering wheel, stove, microwave oven, soap, cash register, dishes, tires, money, toilet, engine, dishwasher, toothbrush, passenger, manager, cook, driver, powder, windshield, refrigerator, customers, toaster

Car	Kitchen	Bathroom	Store
Muffler	Dish towel	Scale	Price tag

PHOTOCOPIABLE RESOURCE

Name: ______________________ Date: ____________

CATEGORIZING INFORMATION

List five things you would find in the following places

Bathroom	Garage	Grocery Store
1.	1.	1.
2.	2.	2.
3.	3.	3.
4.	4.	4.
5.	5.	5.

Hardware Store	Bedroom	School
1.	1.	1.
2.	2.	2.
3.	3.	3.
4.	4.	4.
5.	5.	5.

Church	Attic	Hospital
1.	1.	1.
2.	2.	2.
3.	3.	3.
4.	4.	4.
5.	5.	5.

PHOTOCOPIABLE RESOURCE

Name: ______________________________ Date: ____________

CLASSIFYING THINGS

THINK OF HOW YOU WOULD CLASSIFY THE FOLLOWING WORDS AND WRITE NEXT TO EACH WORD YOUR BEST ANSWER. IT MIGHT BE HELPFUL TO THINK OF THE WORD AS A "TYPE OF SOMETHING." FOR EXAMPLE, IF THE WORD WAS HAMMER, YOUR ANSWER WOULD BE TOOL. "A HAMMER IS A TYPE OF TOOL." THE FIRST ONE HAS BEEN DONE FOR YOU.

BEAGLE	**DOG**	FORD	________
LOBSTER	________	NEWSWEEK	________
EARTH	________	SCHWINN	________
LEVIS	________	TIMEX	________
PEPSI	________	MARLBORO	________
TYLENOL	________	OREGANO	________
BASEBALL	________	TOMATO	________
WINTER	________	WRENCH	________
EAGLE	________	MAPLE	________
YELLOW	________	JULY 4TH	________
RAIN	________	NICKEL	________
PYTHON	________	JEOPARDY	________
APPLE	________	EUROPE	________
SIAMESE	________	SONY	________
SWISS	________	RANCH	________
PODIATRIST	________	PECAN	________

PHOTOCOPIABLE RESOURCE

Name: ______________________________ Date: ______________

GROUPING & CLASSIFICATION

Circle the member that does not belong to the group:

1.	Water	Liquid	Juice	Soda
2.	Laugh	Smile	Chuckle	Talk
3.	Spinach	Corn	Peas	Lettuce
4.	Principal	Teacher	Student	Doctor
5.	Microwave	Radio	Stereo	TV
6.	Touch	Taste	Eat	Smell
7.	Plan	Complete	Outline	Develop
8.	Watch	Observe	Notice	Participate
9.	Polar Bear	Seal	Lion	Walrus
10.	North	South	West	Far
11.	Lily	Tulip	Maple	Rose
12.	Moth	Ant	Bat	Mosquito
13.	Rock	Coal	Oil	Gas
14.	Desire	Wish	Dream	Gift
15.	Congratulate	Save	Assist	Rescue
16.	End	Commence	Terminate	Finish
17.	Tomato	Squash	Melon	Pepper
18.	Bicycle	Motorcycle	Scooter	Unicycle
19.	Tree	Leaf	Trunk	Branch
20.	Cotton	Snow	Clouds	Sky
21.	Yell	Scream	Speak	Shout
22.	Sneeze	Cough	Ache	Sniffle
23.	Remember	Recall	Think	Retrieve
24.	Rock	Ice	Brick	Concrete
25.	Oregon	California	Washington	Nevada

PHOTOCOPIABLE RESOURCE

Name: ______________________ Date: ____________

GROUPING

LIST TWO MEMBERS OF EACH GROUP. AN EXAMPLE IS PROVIDED.

FRUITS	APPLE	BANANA
DOGS	________	________
PRESIDENTS	________	________
COUNTRIES	________	________
CARS	________	________
CITIES	________	________
ATHLETES	________	________
POLITICIANS	________	________
RELIGIONS	________	________
TOOLS	________	________
MEDICATIONS	________	________
TREES	________	________
TV SHOWS	________	________
STATES	________	________
STORES	________	________
FLOWERS	________	________
FISH	________	________
SPORTS	________	________
DRINKS	________	________

PHOTOCOPIABLE RESOURCE

Name: ______________________________ Date: ____________

COMPOSITION

Write about a recent activity you participated in that you enjoyed. Describe what you did, where you were, and who you were with. Give your brief essay a title.

Title: ______________________________

PHOTOCOPIABLE RESOURCE

Name: ______________________________ Date: ______________

COMPREHENSION

TIGERS

The tiger is a member of the cat family and is considered to be one of the five "big cats." The other cats in this group are the jaguar, leopard, lion, and snow leopard. Members of this cat group all have a special bone in their throat that allows them to roar. Except for its distinctive roar, tigers have very similar characteristics as house cats. They have the same muzzle and the same canine teeth as a cat. They also have the same body shoulders and curved claws. Tigers live in a variety of climates such as dry forests, tropical rain forests, or in colder climates such as in the polar ice cap region. Tigers eventually peaked in population in the colder parts of Asia. There are five kinds of tigers, the Sumatran, Indochinese, Bengal, South China, and Siberian. Tigers have been in a struggle to survive. Humans have been trying to preserve their habitats and even feed them when food is scarce. However, some tigers do not want help and end up attacking humans. Some people from various cultures are so afraid of tigers that they wear masks on the back of their heads to scare them away. Tigers have survived because of their ability to adapt to the environment and because of their amazing agility and hunting skills. The tiger can look graceful, but it can also look fearsome with its razor-sharp teeth. Tigers manage their land by making a hunting range, which is where they will decide to hunt for their food. Tigers usually live alone and hunt by themselves rather than in groups. Since they are carnivores, tigers only eat meat. To help them find food, the tiger has been given adaptation features such as keen hearing and eyesight and the ability to see both during the day and at night. Answer the following:

1. What are some characteristics of tigers?

   ____

   ____

2. Name four types of tigers.

   ____

   ____

3. Where did tigers peak in population?

   ____

   ____

4. What features help tigers hunt?

   ____

   ____

(Adapted from: Stone, L.M. (2005). *Tigers*. Minneapolis, MN: Carolrhoda Books)

PHOTOCOPIABLE RESOURCE

Name: ______________________________ Date: ____________

FACTS VERSUS OPINIONS

It is important to know the difference between a fact and an opinion in order to understand each other. A fact is something that we all must agree on, such as: The sky is blue.

An opinion is something that we may not all agree on, such as: The best season is summer.

Think about each statement below and write an F next to it if it is a Fact or an O next to it if it is an Opinion.

_____ We all should have a best friend.

_____ We all need food to survive.

_____ All people are friendly.

_____ People should always be happy.

_____ The coldest season is winter.

_____ To be healthy, I should eat a balanced diet.

_____ All people should go to church.

_____ Plants need water and light to survive.

_____ Pizza tastes good.

_____ It is okay to ask someone for help.

_____ Saturday is the best day of the week.

_____ Sports are fun to watch on TV.

_____ Mark Twain is the best author.

_____ Men have landed on the moon.

_____ Everyone should go to college.

PHOTOCOPIABLE RESOURCE

Name: ________________________________ Date: ______________

FACTS VERSUS OPINIONS

A fact is a true statement, something that can be proven.

Here is a fact: A poodle is a breed of dog.

An opinion is what someone thinks or believes.

Here is an opinion: Poodles make the best pets.

We can use both in our communication, but we need to recognize which is which.

Directions: Write "F" beside facts and "O" beside opinions.

_____ 1. Many cleaning products are poisonous if swallowed.

_____ 2. Fruits and vegetables are healthy foods.

_____ 3. Only adults can use cell phones responsibly.

_____ 4. Amusements parks are fun.

_____ 5. The newspaper is informative and useful to read.

_____ 6. Schools provide adequate education for students.

_____ 7. If we could learn more about our hobbies, we'd be more active.

Now, write one fact and one opinion below.

Fact:

____

____

Opinion:

____

____

PHOTOCOPIABLE RESOURCE

Name: ______________________ Date: ____________

GENERAL KNOWLEDGE

Provide the answers to the questions below by writing your response on the line next to the question.

1. How many sides does an octagon have? ____________
2. Who is the vice-president? ____________
3. Name a famous singer. ____________
4. How many continents are there? ____________
5. What is another name for England? ____________
6. In what month is Valentine's Day? ____________
7. Who was FDR? ____________
8. What is an ameba? ____________
9. On what continent is the country Zaire? ____________
10. Name a sports team from Boston. ____________
11. Name two branches of the military. ____________
12. Name two books in the Bible. ____________
13. Name a famous baseball player. ____________
14. Name two types of bread. ____________
15. Name two of the five Great Lakes. ____________
16. What is anesthesia used for? ____________
17. Name a food high in calcium. ____________
18. Name two types of reptiles. ____________
19. Who wrote the Gettysburg Address? ____________
20. Name two types of caffeinated beverages. ____________

PHOTOCOPIABLE RESOURCE

Name: ______________________________ Date: ______________

GENERAL KNOWLEDGE

Provide the answers to the questions below by writing your response on the line next to the question.

1. List two cities in the United States. ____________________
2. Who is the President of the U.S.? ____________________
3. Name a famous football player. ____________________
4. Name two Southern states. ____________________
5. In what month is Labor Day? ____________________
6. Name two types of cars. ____________________
7. In what state is the Bronx zoo located? ____________________
8. He painted the Sistine Chapel. ____________________
9. Where was Abraham Lincoln shot? ____________________
10. Who wrote *The Adventures of Tom Sawyer*? ____________________
11. What does the word CONTENT mean? ____________________
12. What does a locksmith do? ____________________
13. Zoology is the study of what? ____________________
14. He was the first astronaut to land on the moon. ____________________
15. He discovered the light bulb. ____________________
16. Name two past presidents. ____________________
17. What is Martha's Vineyard? ____________________
18. What is yeast used for? ____________________
19. In what sport do you use a putter? ____________________
20. Name a famous movie star. ____________________

PHOTOCOPIABLE RESOURCE

Name: ______________________________ Date: ____________

GRAMMAR USAGE

A. In the sentences below, circle the verbs.

1. Jim washed and waxed his new bike today.
2. Mary took pictures with her new camera.
3. My friend needs help with his math homework.
4. I lost my winter jacket at the concert.
5. We sanded the shed and then painted it green and brown.
6. The chef baked four pumpkin pies.
7. The car drove around the neighborhood and then accidentally hit a tree.
8. My family visited Mexico this summer.

B. Underline the adjective(s) in each sentence and circle the noun(s).

1. Billy likes chocolate milk but hates vanilla ice cream.
2. Mr. Smith ran in four races last summer.
3. The apple pie got burned.
4. We opened three cans of green vegetables for the family dinner.
5. Tina and Mary have blue eyes and brown hair.
6. They ate cold pizza and granola bars on the camping trip to the national park.
7. Billy and his cousin painted their room with blue paint.
8. The president gave a long speech.

PHOTOCOPIABLE RESOURCE

Name: ______________________________ Date: ______________

MATCHING PERSON WITH PLACE

If we want to find someone, we need to know where to look. On the line next to each person in the left-hand column, write in the place from the right-hand column where you would find that person. The first one has been done for you.

PERSON		PLACE
TEACHER	SCHOOL	COURTROOM
MINISTER	______________________	GYM
MECHANIC	______________________	OFFICE
RANGER	______________________	PARK
JUDGE	______________________	SCHOOL
PILOT	______________________	RESTAURANT
CLOWN	______________________	WHITE HOUSE
COOK	______________________	RESTAURANT
PRESIDENT	______________________	CHURCH
DOCTOR	______________________	CIRCUS
ATHLETE	______________________	HOSPITAL
SECRETARY	______________________	PLANE

PHOTOCOPIABLE RESOURCE

Name: ______________________ Date: ____________

MATCHING PROFESSION WITH TOOL

Find the tool or device in the right-hand column that the person listed in the left-hand column would need to perform his/her job. Write the correct answer next to the person. An example is provided.

PERSON		TOOL/DEVICE
CARPENTER	HAMMER	WHISTLE
JUDGE	____________	SHOVEL
NAVIGATOR	____________	RECIPE
CHEF	____________	WRENCH
ELECTRICIAN	____________	GAVEL
PLUMBER	____________	STETHOSCOPE
ASTRONOMER	____________	SCISSORS
GARDENER	____________	AXE
REFEREE	____________	DRILL
POLICE OFFICER	____________	WIRES
MUSICIAN	____________	MAP
DOCTOR	____________	HAMMER
LUMBERJACK	____________	GUITAR
DENTIST	____________	GUN
BARBER	____________	TELESCOPE

PHOTOCOPIABLE RESOURCE

Name: ______________________ Date: ______________

MATHEMATICS

Word Problems:

If Harry drove 120 miles in two hours, how many miles per hour did he average on his trip?
____

John took an exam that had 200 questions. He answered 80% of the questions correctly. How many answers did he get correct? _________

If you give the cashier $1.00 for a cup of coffee that costs 80¢, how much change will you get back? _________

If an orange costs 25¢, how much will seven oranges cost? _________

Money:

2 quarters + 3 dimes + 1 nickel = ______________________

1 half-dollar + 1 quarter + 1 dime = ______________________

3 quarters + 1 nickel + 4 pennies = ______________________

6 quarters + 2 dimes + 2 nickels + 3 pennies = ______________________

4 dollars + 6 dimes + 2 nickels + 3 pennies = ______________________

1 dollar + 6 dimes + 3 nickels + 5 pennies = ______________________

Measurement:

12 in. = ____ ft.	2 ft. = ____ in.	2 lbs. = ____ oz.
1 yd. = ____ in.	120 in. = ____ ft.	1 cup = ____ oz.
18 ft. = ____ yds.	4 yds. = ____ ft.	64 oz. = ____ quarts

PHOTOCOPIABLE RESOURCE

Name: ______________________________ Date: ______________

MATHEMATICS

Multiplication:

3	6	4	7	7	5
× 4	× 6	× 6	× 8	× 9	× 8

12	18	11	24	15	9
× 12	× 3	× 6	× 3	× 7	× 9

Addition:

6	5	12	36	23	156
+ 3	+ 7	+ 15	+ 36	+ 59	+ 237

346	515	120	3436	237	7156
+ 335	+ 734	+ 150	+ 4636	+ 598	+ 6231

Subtraction:

8	7	15	36	123	357
−3	−5	−12	−17	− 59	−167

824	247	155	360	3123	4321
−311	−165	−125	−359	− 1359	−1234

PHOTOCOPIABLE RESOURCE

Name: ________________________________ Date: ____________

SEQUENCING EVENTS

Place the words in correct order by numbering the events from 1–4. Try to identify the event.

Example: Event is: Calling a Friend Dialing – 2 Talking – 3 Hanging up – 4 Remembering phone number – 1	**Event is:** Childhood Old age Birth Adulthood
Event is: Find a pot Watering Getting soil Planting	**Event is:** Showering Eating breakfast Waking up Getting dressed
Event is: Eating Mixing ingredients Baking Heating oven	**Event is:** Paying for items Making a list Going to the store Choosing items
Event is: Stepping on gas pedal Opening door Starting engine Putting key in ignition	**Event is:** Crawling Rolling Over Running Walking

PHOTOCOPIABLE RESOURCE

Name: ____________________ Date: ____________

SIMILARITIES

THINK OF HOW THE FOLLOWING PAIRS OF WORDS ARE SIMILAR. NEXT TO EACH PAIR INDICATE HOW THE TWO WORDS ARE ALIKE. AN EXAMPLE HAS BEEN PROVIDED.

1. MILK–SODA **DRINKS**
2. CRAB–CLAM ____________
3. FORD–DODGE ____________
4. SHOE–SNEAKER ____________
5. PEN–PENCIL ____________
6. SPRING–FALL ____________
7. CLOCK–WATCH ____________
8. MIAMI–ORLANDO ____________
9. PLUM–PEACH ____________
10. OVEN–TOASTER ____________
11. RAKE–SHOVEL ____________
12. NIXON–CARTER ____________
13. DIME–QUARTER ____________
14. TALKING–LISTENING ____________
15. BOOK–MAGAZINE ____________
16. SMILE–LAUGH ____________
17. START–END ____________
18. BROTHER–SISTER ____________
19. STUDENT–TEACHER ____________
20. EGGS–MILK ____________

PHOTOCOPIABLE RESOURCE

Name: ______________________________ Date: ______________

SIMILARITIES AND DIFFERENCES

The following groups of words are similar in some ways and different in some ways.

Think of how the words are similar and how the words are different and write your response in the space.

Words	Similar	Different
Dog–Cat	**Animals**	**Cats can climb trees**
Car–Bike		
House–Tent		
Apple–Banana		
Table–Chair		
Coat–Shirt		
Magazine–Book		
Coffee–Soda		
Joy–Anger		
School–Church		
Girl–Boy		
Snake–Turtle		
First–Last		
Earth–Moon		
Lamp–Flashlight		
Listen–Talk		

PHOTOCOPIABLE RESOURCE

Name: ______________________ Date: ____________

SYNONYMS AND ANTONYMS

Next to each word in the list, write down a word that means the same (synonym) and a word that means the opposite (antonym). An example is provided.

	SYNONYM	ANTONYM
Example: Happy	CONTENT	SAD
1. Sleepy	________	________
2. Handy	________	________
3. Quick	________	________
4. Assist	________	________
5. Dull	________	________
6. Large	________	________
7. Flexible	________	________
8. Organized	________	________
9. Unsure	________	________
10. Bold	________	________
11. Noisy	________	________
12. Destroy	________	________
13. Start	________	________
14. Ignore	________	________
15. Find	________	________
16. Attempt	________	________
17. Fix	________	________
18. Free	________	________
19. Tranquil	________	________
20. Bored	________	________

PHOTOCOPIABLE RESOURCE

Name: ______________________________ Date: ______________

VISUAL MATCHING

Find two of the same figures and label inside of the pair the same number. The first one has been done for you.

PHOTOCOPIABLE RESOURCE

Name: ______________________________ Date: ______________

VISUAL MATCHING

Find the shape that matches. Circle your answer.

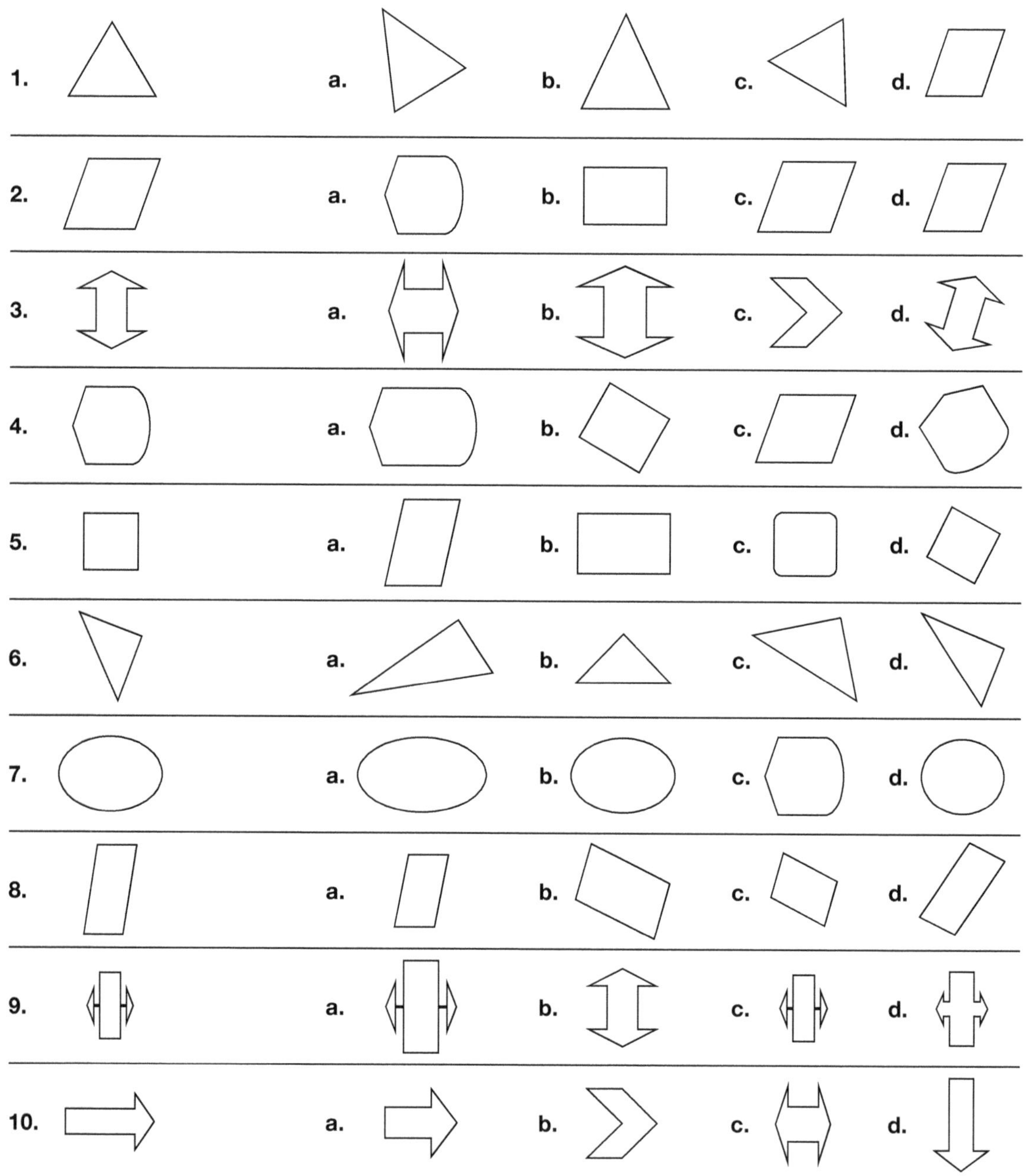

PHOTOCOPIABLE RESOURCE

Name: ______________________________ Date: ____________

WORD MEANINGS

Match the word in the left-hand column with its definition in the right-hand column. Write the letter from the definition in the right-hand column next to the word it matches in the left-hand column.

_____	Satellite	a.	to read or inspect
_____	Compare	b.	an extra amount
_____	Generate	c.	lasting only a moment
_____	Resume	d.	to adjust or adapt
_____	Peruse	e.	to find or uncover
_____	Locate	f.	an orbiting object in the solar system
_____	Ferocious	g.	to bring up or introduce a topic
_____	Tactile	h.	to measure or figure out
_____	Momentary	i.	to look for similarities and differences
_____	Surplus	j.	mean or vicious
_____	Accommodate	k.	pertaining to our sense of touch
_____	Calculate	l.	to start up again
_____	Broach	m.	to make bigger or larger
_____	Exaggerate	n.	to show to be right or reasonable
_____	Justify	o.	to start or develop something
_____	Collaborate	p.	to work together

PHOTOCOPIABLE RESOURCE

Name: ______________________ Date: ____________

WORD MEANINGS

Circle the best definition for the following words:

1. *Genesis*

a. Last

b. Strong

c. Beginning

d. Brave

2. *Support*

a. Ignore

b. Assist

c. Locate

d. Bargain

3. *Illuminate*

a. Take away

b. Remove

c. Arrest

d. Lighten

4. *Versatile*

a. Rigid

b. Adaptable

c. Open

d. Dishonest

5. *Fortitude*

a. Strength

b. Loud

c. Quiet

d. Quick

6. *Genuine*

a. Hopeful

b. Timid

c. Sincere

d. Shy

7. *Accelerate*

a. Handle

b. Throw

c. Hurry

d. Rest

8. *Browse*

a. Clean

b. Sing

c. Glance

d. Send

9. *Optimistic*

a. Tireless

b. Mystical

c. Fatigued

d. Hopeful

10. *Peculiar*

a. New

b. Strange

c. Unique

d. Common

11. *Persistence*

a. Curiosity

b. Efficient

c. Solitude

d. Determination

12. *Diligent*

a. Quick

b. Thorough

c. Frugal

d. Jovial

PHOTOCOPIABLE RESOURCE

Name: ______________________________ Date: ______________

WORD SEARCH—MENTAL HEALTH

FIND THE WORDS IN THE RIGHT-HAND COLUMN HIDDEN IN THE WORD BOX. CIRCLE THE WORDS AS YOU FIND THEM.

E	N	E	I	G	Y	H	P	I	R	I	N	W	A	C
P	V	O	C	S	R	R	A	R	T	A	I	A	A	C
O	E	L	I	S	E	L	E	N	O	E	O	W	C	Y
H	B	M	A	T	L	L	E	C	R	M	A	E	T	H
P	E	E	N	I	A	M	F	V	O	R	A	I	I	T
R	H	T	S	O	T	V	E	C	E	V	L	O	V	A
A	A	N	A	I	I	N	I	N	O	A	E	D	I	P
C	V	E	M	S	O	T	E	T	U	N	L	R	T	M
T	I	M	O	G	N	S	A	T	O	O	T	E	Y	E
I	O	T	O	D	S	O	I	C	O	M	E	R	A	N
C	R	A	I	H	H	R	G	A	I	P	E	R	O	I
E	L	E	R	V	I	K	C	A	B	D	E	E	F	L
S	T	R	P	P	P	E	S	I	C	R	E	X	E	A
N	H	T	S	O	S	U	P	P	O	R	T	M	M	C
F	R	I	E	N	D	S	F	A	M	I	L	Y	I	H

BEHAVIOR
SPIRITUALITY
FEEDBACK
TREATMENT
EXERCISE
SELF CONTROL
MEDICATION
DIET
MOTIVATION
HOPE
ACTIVITY
EMPATHY
TEAM
AWARENESS
PRACTICE
SUPPORT
POTENTIAL
COMMITMENT
HYGIENE
FAMILY
GOALS
RECOVERY
RELATIONSHIPS
FRIENDS

Adapted from: http://www.armoredpenguin.com/wordsearch/

PHOTOCOPIABLE RESOURCE

Name: ______________________________ Date: ______________

WORD SEARCH—ACTIVITIES

FIND THE WORDS IN THE RIGHT-HAND COLUMN HIDDEN IN THE WORD BOX. CIRCLE THE WORDS AS YOU FIND THEM. PUT A STAR NEXT TO THE ONES THAT ARE YOUR FAVORITE ACTIVITIES.

C	I	C	N	I	A	C	V	D	M	I	E	W	E	G	D	O
S	I	G	G	N	I	D	A	E	R	S	G	G	N	N	C	N
N	I	I	G	S	S	E	D	G	E	G	N	I	L	W	O	B
D	A	E	U	G	N	I	Z	I	L	A	I	C	O	S	M	E
R	P	M	M	G	T	N	V	A	R	E	L	R	C	U	N	G
A	S	E	M	A	G	O	E	D	I	V	E	F	G	T	I	I
W	N	L	T	M	M	D	C	M	T	S	V	A	S	P	E	I
I	A	I	E	S	I	I	O	G	O	A	A	M	T	A	C	S
N	N	L	V	O	L	U	N	T	E	E	R	I	N	G	H	D
G	B	V	K	A	I	I	C	X	I	B	T	L	A	N	U	I
S	N	I	Y	I	H	I	E	N	G	B	I	Y	R	I	R	D
R	L	I	K	C	N	R	R	G	S	N	S	V	U	V	C	H
M	N	C	T	I	C	G	T	Y	U	R	P	I	A	I	H	M
P	L	A	Y	I	N	G	S	P	O	R	T	S	T	R	M	E
I	W	N	S	A	R	G	E	G	O	N	I	I	S	D	E	A
C	P	E	T	I	F	W	C	O	M	P	U	T	E	R	S	E
C	P	L	A	Y	I	N	G	C	A	R	D	S	R	S	G	E

WATCHING TV
FAMILY VISITS
DRAWING
READING
TRAVELING
VOLUNTEERING
DRIVING
PLAYING CARDS
EXERCISE
MOVIES
BOWLING
PETS
CONCERTS
BIKING
COMPUTERS
RESTAURANTS
WRITING
VIDEO GAMES
SOCIALIZING
PLAYING SPORTS
MUSIC
CHURCH
WALKING
MEDITATING

Adapted from: http://www.armoredpenguin.com/wordsearch/

PHOTOCOPIABLE RESOURCE

Name: ______________________ Date: __________

SELF-REFLECTION

My favorite food: ______________________

My favorite TV show: ______________________

My favorite time of day: ______________________

My favorite season: ______________________

My favorite place to go: ______________________

My favorite weekend activity: ______________________

My favorite subject in school: ______________________

My favorite animal: ______________________

My favorite dessert: ______________________

My favorite summer activity: ______________________

My favorite sport: ______________________

My favorite way to relax: ______________________

My favorite thing about myself: ______________________

The city and state where I was born: ______________________

How many brothers and sisters I have: Brothers: _____ Sisters: _____

My favorite job: ______________________

States I have visited: ______________________

PHOTOCOPIABLE RESOURCE

Name: ______________________________ Date: ____________

SELF-REFLECTION: GOAL SETTING

I am doing well in the following area:

Things I need to keep doing so I continue to do well in this area:

1. ______________________

2. ______________________

3. ______________________

I need to do better in the following area:

Things I need to do so I can do better in this area:

1. ______________________

2. ______________________

3. ______________________

People and things who/that can help me reach my goals:

1. ______________________

2. ______________________

3. ______________________

Miscellaneous Exercises

PHOTOCOPIABLE RESOURCE

Name: ______________________________ Date: ______________

KNOWING WHAT WE WILL NEED

In order to do things, we must know what we will need. Think of what you would need to do the following activities. Circle the answer that does not belong.

Baking a cake	Planting a garden	Playing cards
1. Ingredients	1. Rocks	1. Name of the game
2. Toaster	2. Water	2. Cards
3. Oven	3. Soil	3. Table
4. Recipe	4. Seeds	4. Rules of the game
Driving a car	**Going to a movie**	**Watching a TV show**
1. Gas	1. Money	1. A drink
2. Car	2. Name of the movie	2. TV
3. Money	3. Popcorn	3. Name of the program
4. Keys	4. Directions to theater	4. Time of the program
Going out to eat	**Calling a friend**	**Washing the dishes**
1. Money	1. Friend's address	1. Water
2. Name of restaurant	2. Phone	2. Dish detergent
3. Hours open	3. Phone number	3. Dish towel
4. A friend	4. Conversation	4. Dishes

PHOTOCOPIABLE RESOURCE

Name: ______________________________ Date: ______________

STATE CAPITALS

List the state or the state's capital for the following:

	State		Capital
1.	______________	1.	ALBANY
2.	______________	2.	DOVER
3.	FLORIDA	3.	______________
4.	______________	4.	BOSTON
5.	OHIO	5.	______________
6.	ARIZONA	6.	______________
7.	______________	7.	SEATTLE
8.	TEXAS	8.	______________
9.	______________	9.	CONCORD
10.	______________	10.	LANSING
11.	GEORGIA	11.	______________
12.	______________	12.	ST. PAUL
13.	MAINE	13.	______________
14.	______________	14.	BOISE
15.	______________	15.	DENVER
16.	ALASKA	16.	______________
17.	VIRGINIA	17.	______________
18.	______________	18.	SANTA FE
19.	HAWAII	19.	______________
20.	INDIANA	20.	______________

PHOTOCOPIABLE RESOURCE

Name: ________________________ Date: ____________

LETTER–WORD ASSOCIATIONS

Think of as many words as you can that start with the following letters:

Words beginning with "S"

1. ____________
2. ____________
3. ____________
4. ____________
5. ____________
6. ____________
7. ____________
8. ____________
9. ____________
10. ____________

Words beginning with "B"

1. ____________
2. ____________
3. ____________
4. ____________
5. ____________
6. ____________
7. ____________
8. ____________
9. ____________
10. ____________

Words beginning with "M"

1. ____________
2. ____________
3. ____________
4. ____________
5. ____________
6. ____________
7. ____________
8. ____________
9. ____________
10. ____________

Words beginning with "P"

1. ____________
2. ____________
3. ____________
4. ____________
5. ____________
6. ____________
7. ____________
8. ____________
9. ____________
10. ____________

PHOTOCOPIABLE RESOURCE

Name: ______________________________ Date: ______________

LOOKING IN THE RIGHT PLACE

Match the PLACES below with the states where they are located:

1.	White House:	____________	WYOMING
2.	San Diego:	____________	NEW JERSEY
3.	Fenway Park:	____________	FLORIDA
4.	Niagara Falls:	____________	NEW HAMPSHIRE
5.	Grand Canyon:	____________	PENNSYLVANIA
6.	Disney World:	____________	NORTH CAROLINA
7.	White Mountains:	____________	RHODE ISLAND
8.	Lake George:	____________	VERMONT
9.	Football Hall of Fame:	____________	CALIFORNIA
10.	Tennis Hall of Fame:	____________	LOUISIANA
11.	Freedom Trail:	____________	UTAH
12.	Atlantic City:	____________	INDIANA
13.	Ben & Jerry's Factory:	____________	SOUTH DAKOTA
14.	Liberty Bell:	____________	MASSACHUSETTS
15.	Indianapolis 500:	____________	WASHINGTON, DC
16.	Mardi Gras:	____________	OHIO
17.	Mt. McKinley:	____________	COLORADO
18.	Cape Hatteras:	____________	MASSACHUSETTS
19.	Yellowstone Park:	____________	NEW YORK
20.	Salt Lake City:	____________	ALASKA
21.	Mount Rushmore:	____________	NEW YORK

References

Abba, N., Chadwick, P., & Stevenson, C. (2008). Responding mindfully to distressing psychosis: A grounded theory analysis. *Psychotherapy Research, 18*, 77–87.

Addington, J. & Addington, D. (2008). Social and cognitive functioning in psychosis. *Schizophrenia Research, 99*, 176–181.

Addington, J., Saeedi, H., & Addington, D. (2006). Influence of social perception and social knowledge on cognitive and social functioning in early psychosis. *British Journal of Psychiatry, 189*, 373–378.

Ahmed, M. (1998). Computer-facilitated therapy: Reality-based dialogue with people with schizophrenia. *Journal of Contemporary Psychotherapy, 28*, 397–403.

Ahmed, M. (2002). Computer-facilitated dialogue with patients who have schizophrenia. *Psychiatric Services, 53*, 99–100.

Ahmed, M., Bayog, F., & Boisvert, C. M. (1997). Computer-facilitated therapy for inpatients with schizophrenia. *Psychiatric Services, 48*, 1334–1335.

Ahmed, M. & Boisvert, C. M. (2002). Cognitive skills group treatment in schizophrenia. *Psychiatric Services, 53*, 1476–1477.

Ahmed, M. & Boisvert, C. M. (2003a). Enhancing communication through visual aids in clinical practice. *American Psychologist, 58*, 815–817.

Ahmed, M. & Boisvert, C. M. (2003b). Multimodal integrative cognitive stimulating group therapy (MICST): Moving beyond the reduction of psychopathology in schizophrenia. *Professional Psychology: Research and Practice, 32*, 644–651.

Ahmed, M. & Boisvert, C. M. (2006a). Using computers as visual aids to enhance communication in therapy. *Computers in Human Behavior, 22*, 847–855.

Ahmed, M. & Boisvert, C. M. (2006b). Using positive psychology with special mental health populations. *American Psychologist, 61*, 333–335.

Ahmed, M. & Boisvert, C. M. (2010, September). Cognitive stimulation, mindfulness strategies, and existential perspectives in group counseling for substance abuse. Presentation conducted at the 23rd Cape Cod Symposium on Addictive Disorders, Hyannis, MA.

Ahmed, M. & Goldman, J. A. (1994). Cognitive rehabilitation of adults with severe and persistent mental illness: A group model. *Community Mental Health Journal, 30*, 385–394.

Ahmed, M., Osser, D., Boisvert, C. M., Albert, L., & Aslam, M. (2007). Rationale for emphasis on management over treatment of schizophrenia in clinical practice. *Annals of Pharmacotherapy, 41*, 693–695.

Alanen, Y. O., de Chavez, M. G., Silver, A. S., & Martindale, B. (Eds.). (2009). *Psychotherapeutic approaches to schizophrenic psychosis: Past, present and future.* New York, NY: Routledge.

American Psychiatric Association. (2013). *Diagnostic and statistical manual of mental disorders* (5th ed.). Washington, DC: American Psychiatric Association Press.

Andreasen, N. C. (1999). A unitary model of schizophrenia. *Archives of General Psychiatry, 56*, 781–787.

Andreason, N. C. & Pierson, R. (2008). The role of the cerebellum in schizophrenia. *Biological Psychiatry, 64*, 81–88.

Anthony, W. A. & Liberman, R. P. (1986). The practice of psychiatric rehabilitation: Historical, conceptual, and research base. *Schizophrenia Bulletin, 12*, 542–559.

Arieti, S. A. (1955). *Interpretation of schizophrenia*. New York, NY: Brunner.

Arnsten, A. (2011). Prefrontal cortical connection: Key site of vulnerability in stress and schizophrenia. *International Journal of Developmental Neuroscience, 29*, 215–223.

Arnsten, A., Mazure, C. M., & Sinha, R. (2012, April). This is your brain in meltdown. *Scientific American, 306*, 48–53.

Baddeley, A. D. (2007). *Working memory, thought and action*. Oxford: Oxford University Press.

Baer, R. A. (2003). Mindfulness training as a clinical intervention: A conceptual and empirical review. *Clinical Psychology: Science and Practice, 10*, 125–143.

Bartenieff, I. & Lewis, D. (2002). *Body movement: Coping with the environment*. New York, NY: Routledge.

Baumeister, A. A. & Francis, J. L. (2002). Historical development of the dopamine hypothesis of schizophrenia. *Journal of the History of the Neurosciences, 11*, 265–277.

Beck, A. T., Rector, N. A., Stolar, N., & Paul, G. (2009). *Schizophrenia: Cognitive theory, research, and therapy*. New York, NY: Guilford Press.

Berrios, G. E. (1985). Positive and negative symptoms and Jackson. *Archives of General Psychiatry, 42*, 95–97.

Bleuler, E. (1908). Die Prognose der Dementia praecox (Schizophreniegruppe). *Allgemeine Zeitschrift für Psychiatrie und psychischgerichtliche Medizin, 65*, 436–464.

Bleuler, E. (1950). *Dementia praecox or the group of schizophrenias*. Transl. by J. Zinkin. New York, NY: International Universities Press. (Original work published 1911).

Boisvert, C. M. & Faust, D. (2002). Iatrogenic symptoms in psychotherapy: A theoretical exploration of the potential impact of labels, language, and belief systems. *American Journal of Psychotherapy, 56*, 244–259.

Braff, D. L. (1993). Information processing and attention dysfunctions in schizophrenia. *Schizophrenia Bulletin, 19*, 233–259.

Brenner, H. D., Roder, V., Hodel, B., & Corrigan, P. (1994). *Integrated psychological therapy for schizophrenic clients*. Seattle, WA: Hogrefe & Huber Publishers.

Brenner, H. D., Roder, V., & Tschacher, W. (2006). Editorial: The significance of psychotherapy in the age of neuroscience. *Schizophrenia Bulletin, 32* (Supplement Issue S1), S10–S11.

Brown, K. W. & Ryan, R. M. (2003). The benefits of being present: Mindfulness and its role in psychological well-being. *Journal of Personality and Social Psychology, 84*, 822–848.

Buss, A. H. & Lang, P. J. (1965). Psychological deficits in schizophrenia: I. Affect reinforcement and concept attainment. *Journal of Abnormal Psychology, 70*, 2–24.

Casey, J. F., Bennet, I. F., Lindley, C. J., Hollister, L. E., Gordon, M. H., & Springer, N. N. (1960). Drug therapy in schizophrenia. A controlled study of the relative effectiveness of chlorpromazine, promazine, phenobarbital, and placebo. *Archives of General Psychiatry, 2*, 210–220.

Censits, D. M., Ragland, J. D., Gur, R. C., & Gur, R. E. (1997). Neuropsychological evidence supporting a neurodevelopmental model of schizophrenia: A longitudinal study. *Schizophrenia Research, 24*, 289–298.

Chadwick, P., Taylor, K. N., & Abba, N. (2005). Mindfulness groups for people with psychosis. *Behavioural and Cognitive Psychotherapy, 33*, 351–359.

Coffey, K. A. & Hartman, M. (2008). Mechanisms of action in the inverse relationship between mindfulness and psychological distress. *Complementary Health Practice Review, 13*, 79–91.

Cowan, N. (2001). The magical number 4 in short-term memory: A reconsideration of mental storage capacity. *Behavioral and Brain Sciences, 24*, 87–114.

Davis, J., Schaffer, B., Killina, G. A., Kinard, C., & Chan, C. (1980). Important issues in the drug treatment of schizophrenia. *Schizophrenia Bulletin, 6*, 70–87.

Davis, K. L., Kahn, R. S., Ko, G., & Davidson, M. (1991). Dopamine in schizophrenia: A review and reconceptualization. *American Journal of Psychiatry, 148*, 1474–1486.

Davis, L., Strasburger, A., & Brown, L. (2007). Mindfulness: An intervention for anxiety in schizophrenia. *Journal of Psychosocial Nursing and Mental Health Services, 45*, 23–29.

Didonna, F. (Ed.). (2009). *Clinical handbook of mindfulness*. New York, NY: Springer.

Drake, R. E. & Sederer, L. I. (1986). The adverse effects of intensive treatment of chronic schizophrenia. *Comprehensive Psychiatry, 27*, 313–326.

Eack, S. M. (2012). Cognitive remediation: A new generation of psychosocial interventions for people with schizophrenia. *Social Work, 57*, 235–246.

Freeman, T. (1977). On Freud's theory of schizophrenia. *International Journal of Psychoanalysis, 58*, 383–388.

Freud, S. (1962). The neuro-psychoses of defence. In J. Strachy (Ed. and Trans.). *The standard edition of the complete works of Sigmund Freud* (Vol. 3, pp. 41–61). London: Hogarth Press. (Original work published 1894)

Fusar-Ploi, P. & Politi, P. (2008). Paul Eugen Bleuler and the birth of schizophrenia. *American Journal of Psychiatry, 165*, 1407.

Gallese, V. & Lakoff, G. (2005). The brain concepts: The role of sensory-motor systems in conceptual knowledge. *Cognitive Neuropsychology, 22*, 455–479.

Garrett, B. L. (2010). *Brain & behavior: An introduction to biological psychology* (3rd ed.). Los Angeles: Sage Publications, Inc.

Geyer, M. A. (2010). New opportunities in the treatment of cognitive impairments associated with schizophrenia. *Current Directions in Psychological Science, 19*, 264–269.

Goldman, R. S., Axelrod, B. N., & Taylor, S. F. (1996). Neurological aspects of schizophrenia. In I. Grant & K. M. Adams (Eds.), *Neuropsychological assessment of neuropsychiatric disorders* (2nd ed., pp. 504–525). New York, NY: Oxford University Press.

Goldman-Rakic, P. S. (1994). Working memory dysfunction in schizophrenia. *Journal of Neuropsychiatry, 6*, 348–357.

Gottdiener, W. & Haslam, N. (2002). The benefits of individual psychotherapy for people diagnosed with schizophrenia: A meta-analytic review. *Ethical Human Sciences and Services, 43*, 163–187.

Grace, A. A. (1991). Phasic versus tonic dopamine release and the modulation of dopamine system responsivity: A hypothesis for the etiology of schizophrenia. *Neuroscience, 41*, 1–24.

Green, M. F. & Nuechterlein, K. H. (1999). Should schizophrenia be treated as a neurocognitive disorder? *Schizophrenia Bulletin, 25*, 309–319.

Green, M. R. (1996). What are the functional consequences of neurocognitive deficits in schizophrenia? *American Journal of Psychiatry, 153*, 321–330.

Green, M. R. (2007). Cognition, drug treatment, and functional outcome in schizophrenia: A tale of two transitions. *American Journal of Psychiatry, 164*, 992–994.

Green, M. R., Kern, R. S., Braff, D. L., & Mintz, J. (2000). Neurocognitive deficits and functional outcome in schizophrenia: Are we measuring the "right stuff"? *Schizophrenia Bulletin, 26*, 119–136.

Haddock, G., Tarrier, N., Spaulding, W., Yusupoff, L., Kinney, C., & McCarthy, E. (1998). Individual cognitive-behavior therapy in the treatment of hallucinations and delusions: A review. *Clinical Psychology Review, 18*, 821–838.

Halford, W. K. & Hayes, R. (1991). Psychological rehabilitation of chronic schizophrenia clients: Recent findings on social skills training and family psychoeducation. *Clinical Psychology Review, 11*, 23–44.

Hatfield, D. R. & Ogles, B. M. (2004). The use of outcome measures by psychologists in clinical practice. *Professional Psychology: Research and Practice, 35*, 485–491.

Heinrichs, R. W. (1993). Schizophrenia and the brain: Conditions for a neuropsychology of madness. *American Psychologist, 48*, 221–233.

Heinrichs, R. W. & Zakzanis, K. K. (1998). Neurocognitive deficit in schizophrenia: A quantitative review of the evidence. *Neuropsychology, 12*, 426–445.

Herz, M. I. & Lamberti, J. S. (1996). Psychotherapy, relapse prevention, and management of relapse in schizophrenia. In M. Moscarelli, A. Rupp, & N. Sartorius (Eds.), *Handbook of mental health economics and health policy: Vol.1: Schizophrenia* (pp. 150–165). New York, NY: John Wiley & Sons.

Hoff, A. L. & Kremen, W. S. (2003). Neuropsychology in schizophrenia: An update. *Current Opinion in Psychiatry, 16*, 149–155.

Hoff, A. L., Sakuma, M., Wieneke, M., Horon, R., Kushner, M., & DeLisi, L. E. (1999). Longitudinal neuropsychological follow-up study of patients with first-episode schizophrenia. *American Journal of Psychiatry, 156*, 1336–1341.

Hoffman, R. E., Pittman, B., Constable, R. T., Bhagwagar, Z., & Hampson, M. (2011). Time course of regional brain activity accompanying auditory verbal hallucinations in schizophrenia. *British Journal of Psychiatry, 198*, 277–283.

Hogarty, G. E., Kornblith, S. J., Greenwald, D., DiBarry, A. L., Cooley, S., Flesher, S. . . . Ulrich, R. (1995). Personal therapy: A disorder-relevant psychotherapy for schizophrenia. *Schizophrenia Bulletin, 21*, 379–393.

Horan, W. P., Harvey, P., Kern, R. S., & Green, M. (2011). Neurocognition, social cognition, and functional outcome in schizophrenia. In G. Wolfgang (Ed.), *Schizophrenia: Current science and clinical practice* (pp. 77–107). New York, NY: Wiley-Blackwell.

Horan, W. P., Kern, R. S., Tripp, C., Hellemann, G., Jonathan, K., Wynn, J. K. . . . Green, M. F. (2012). Efficacy and specificity of social cognitive skills training for outpatients with psychotic disorders. *Journal of Psychiatric Research*, 45, 1113–1122.

Howes, O. D. & Kapur, S. (2009). The dopamine hypothesis of schizophrenia: Version III—the final common pathway. *Schizophrenia Bulletin, 35*, 549–562.

Hurford, I. M., Kalkstein, S., & Hurford, M. O. (2011). Cognitive rehabilitation in schizophrenia: Strategies to improve cognition. *Psychiatric Times, 28*, 43–47.

Huxley, N. A., Rendall, M., & Sederer, L. (2000). Psychosocial treatments in schizophrenia: A review of the past 20 years. *Journal of Nervous and Mental Disease, 188*, 187–201.

Javitt, D. C. & Coyle, J. T. (2004, January). Decoding schizophrenia. *Scientific American, 209*, 48–51.

Kabat-Zinn, J. (1994). *Wherever you go, there you are: Mindfulness meditation in everyday life*. New York, NY: Hyperion.

Kalkstein, S., Hurford, I., & Gur, R. C. (2010). Neurocognition in schizophrenia. In N. R. Swerdlow (Ed.), *Behavioral neurobiology of schizophrenia and its treatment* (pp. 373–390). Berlin and Heidelberg: Springer-Verlag.

Kanas, N. (1996). *Group therapy for schizophrenic clients*. Washington, DC: American Psychiatric Press.

Karon, B. P. (1989). Psychotherapy versus medication for schizophrenia: Empirical comparisons. In S. Fisher & R. P. Greenberg (Eds.), *The limits of biological treatments for psychological distress: Comparisons with psychotherapy and placebo* (pp. 105–150). Hillsdale, NJ: Erlbaum.

Karon, B. P. & VandenBos, G. R. (1981). *Psychotherapy of schizophrenia: The treatment of choice*. New York, NY: J. Aronson.

Katz, H. M. & Gunderson, J. G. (1990). Individual psychodynamically-oriented psychotherapy for schizophrenia clients. In M. I. Herz, S. J. Keith & J. P. Docherty (Eds.), *Handbook of schizophrenia: Psychosocial treatments of schizophrenia* (Vol. 4, pp. 69–90). Amsterdam, the Netherlands: Elsevier Science.

Keefe, R. S., Bilder, R. M., Davis, S. M., Harvey, P. D., Palmer, B. W., Gold, J. M. . . . Lieberman, J. A.; CATIE Investigators; Neuropsychology Work Group. (2007). Neurocognitive effects of antipsychotic medications in patients with chronic schizophrenia in the CATIE trial. *Archives of General Psychiatry, 64*, 633–647.

Kern, R. S., Glynn, S. M., Horan, W. P., & Marder, S. R. (2009). Psychosocial treatments to promote functional recovery in schizophrenia. *Schizophrenia Bulletin, 35*, 347–361.

Keshavan, M. S., Tandon, R., Boutros, N. N., & Nasrallah, H. A. (2008). Schizophrenia, "just the facts": What we know in 2008—Part 3: Neurobiology. *Schizophrenia Research, 106*, 89–107.

Kingdon, D. G. & Turkington, D. (2005). *Cognitive therapy of schizophrenia*. New York, NY: Guilford Press.

Kopelowicz, A. & Liberman, R. P. (1995). Biobehavioral treatment and rehabilitation of schizophrenia. *Harvard Review of Psychiatry, July–August, 3*, 55–64.

Kraepelin, E. (1883). *Compendium der Psychiatrie*. Leipzig: Earth.

Kumar, S. (2010). *The mindful path through worry and rumination: Letting go of anxious and depressive thoughts*. Oakland, CA: New Harbinger Publications.

Kurtz, M. (2013). A social salve for schizophrenia. *Scientific American Mind*, March-April, 63–68.

Laing, R. D. & Esterson, A. (1964). *Sanity, madness and the family*. London: Penguin Books.

Lakhan, S. E. & Vieira, K. F. (2009). Schizophrenia pathophysiology: Are we any closer to a complete model? *Annals of General Psychiatry, 8*, 12–19.

Lang, P. J. & Buss, A. H. (1965). Psychological deficits in schizophrenia: II. Interference and activation. *Journal of Abnormal Psychology, 70*, 77–106.

Laruelle, M., Abi-Dargham, A., Van Dyck, C. H., Gil, R., D'Souza, C. D., Erdos, J. . . . Innis, R. B. (1996). Single photon emission computerized tomography imaging of amphetamine-induced dopamine release in drug-free schizophrenic subjects. *Proceedings of the National Academy of Sciences of the United States of America, 93*, 9235–9240.

Laviolette, S. R. (2007). Dopamine modulation of emotional processing in cortical and subcortical neural circuits: Evidence for a final common pathway in schizophrenia. *Schizophrenia Bulletin, 33*, 971–981.

Lehman, A. F., Carpenter, W. T., Goldman, H. H., & Steinwachs, D. M. (1995). Treatment outcomes in schizophrenia: Implications for practice, policy, and research. *Schizophrenia Bulletin, 21*, 621–630.

Liberman, R. P., Kopelowicz, A., & Young, A. S. (1994). Biobehavioral treatment and rehabilitation of schizophrenia. *Behavior Therapy, 25*, 89–107.

Lieberman, J. A., Stroup, T. S., McEvoy, J. P., Swartz, M. S., Rosenheck, R. A., Perkins, D. O. . . . Hsiao, J. K. (2005). Clinical antipsychotic trails of intervention effectiveness (CATIE) investigators. Effectiveness of antipsychotic drugs in patients with schizophrenia. *New England Journal of Medicine, 353*, 1209–1223.

Lyons, J. (1958). The psychology of angels. *Forum, 2*, 28–30.

Lysaker, P. H., Wilkniss, S. M., Glynn, S. M., & Silverstein, S. M. (2010). Psychotherapy and recovery from schizophrenia: A review of potential applications and need for future research study. *Psychological Services, 7*, 75–91.

MacDonald, A. W. & Schulz, S. C. (2009). What we know: Findings that every theory of schizophrenia should explain. *Schizophrenia Bulletin, 35*, 493–508.

Mace, C. (2008). *Mindfulness and mental health: Therapy, theory and science*. New York, NY: Routledge.

McGrath, J., Sukanta, S., Chant, D., & Welham, J. (2008). Schizophrenia: A concise overview of incidence, prevalence, and mortality. *Epidemiological Reviews, 30*, 67–76.

McGuire, P. K., Shah, G. M., & Murray, R. M. (1993). Increased blood flow in Broca's area during auditory hallucinations in schizophrenia. *The Lancet, 342*, 703–706.

Marder, S. R. & Fenton, W. (2004). Measurement and treatment research to improve cognition in schizophrenia: NIMH MATRICS initiative to support the development of agents for improving cognition in schizophrenia. *Schizophrenia Research, 72*, 5–9.

Mason, S. E. (2000). Group work with schizophrenia: Clinical aspects. *Groupwork, 12*, 27–44.

Mathalon, D. H. & Ford, J. M. (2012). Neurobiology of schizophrenia: Search for the elusive correlation with symptoms. *Frontiers in Human Neuroscience, 6*(136), e270896. doi:10.3389/fnhum.2012.00136

Matsuda, O. (2007). Cognitive stimulation therapy for Alzheimer's disease: The effect of cognitive stimulation therapy on the progression of mild Alzheimer's disease in patients treated with donepezil. *International Psychogeriatrics, 19*, 241–252.

May, R., Angel, E., & Ellenberger, H. F. (Eds.). (1958). *Existence: A new dimension in psychiatry and psychology*. New York, NY: Basic Books.

Mednick, S. A. (1958). A learning theory approach to research in schizophrenia. *Psychological Bulletin, 55*, 316–327.

Miran, M. D. & Miran, E. R. (1999). Neuropsychological therapeutic community treatment for individuals with schizophrenia. *Psychiatric Rehabilitation Journal, 22*, 277–282.

Mohamed, S., Paulsen, J. S., O'Leary, D., Arndt, S., & Andreason, N. (1999). Generalized cognitive deficits in schizophrenia: A study of first-episode patients. *Archives of General Psychiatry, 56*, 749–754.

Mojtabai, R., Nicholson, R. A., & Carpenter, B. N. (1998). Role of psychosocial treatments in management of schizophrenia: A meta-analytic review of controlled outcome studies. *Schizophrenia Bulletin, 24*, 569–587.

Moore, O. K. & Anderson, A. R. (1969). Some principles for the design of clarifying education environments. In D. A. Goslin (Ed.), *Handbook of socialization theory and research* (pp. 571–613). Chicago: Rand McNally.

Morice, R. & Delahunty, A. (1996). Frontal/executive impairments in schizophrenia. *Schizophrenia Bulletin, 22*, 125–137.

Moritz, S. & Woodward, T. S. (2007). Metacognitive training in schizophrenia: From basic research to knowledge translation and intervention. *Current Opinions in Psychiatry, 20*, 619–625.

Mosher, L. R., Vallone, R., & Menn, A. (1995). The treatment of acute psychosis with neuroleptics: Six-week psychopathology outcome data from the Soteria project. *International Journal of Social Psychiatry, 41*, 157–173.

Mueser, K. T. & Berenbaum, H. (1990). Psychodynamic treatment of schizophrenia: Is there a future? *Psychological Medicine, 20*, 253–262.

Mueser, K. T., Bond, G. R., Drake, R. E., & Resnick, J. G. (1998). Models of community care for severe and persistent mental illness: A review of research in case management. *Schizophrenia Bulletin, 24*, 37–74.

Nightingale, L. C. & McQueeney, D. A. (1996). Group therapy for schizophrenia: Combining and expanding the psychoeducational model with supportive therapy. *International Journal of Group Psychotherapy, 4*, 517–533.

Pekala, R. J., Siegal, J. M., & Farrar, D. M. (1985). The problem-solving support group: Structured group therapy with psychiatric inpatients. *International Journal of Group Psychotherapy, 35*, 391–409.

Penn, D. L. & Mueser, K. T. (1996). Research update on the psychosocial treatment in schizophrenia. *American Journal of Psychiatry, 153*, 607–617.

Pfammatter, M., Junghan, U. M., & Brenner, H. D. (2006). Efficacy of psychological therapy in schizophrenia: Conclusions from meta-analyses. *Schizophrenia Bulletin, 32*, S64–S80.

Pinninti, N. R., Rissmiller, D. J., & Steer, R. A. (2010). Cognitive-behavioral therapy as an adjunct to second-generation antipsychotics in the treatment of schizophrenia. *Psychiatric Services, 61*, 940–943.

Rapp, C. A. & Wintersteen, R. (1989). The strengths model of case management: Results from 12 demonstrations. *Psychosocial Rehabilitation Journal, 13*, 23–32.

Razali, S. M., Khan, U. A., & Hasanah, C. I. (1996). Belief in supernatural causes of mental illness among Malay patients: Impact on treatment. *Acta Psychiatrica Scandinavica, 94*, 229–233.

Reichenbach, H. (1961). *The rise of scientific philosophy*. Berkeley, CA: University of California Press.

Rhode Island Department of Mental Health, Retardation and Hospitals, Division of Mental Health. (1986). *Multi-Function Needs Assessment (MFNA)*. L. Jones & M. Dwyer (Eds.). Unpublished inventory.

Riley, E. M., McGovern, D., Mockler, D., Doku, V. C., O'Ceallaigh, S., Fannon, D. G. . . . Sharma, T. (2000). Neuropsychological functioning in first-episode psychosis—evidence of specific deficits. *Schizophrenia Research, 43*, 47–55.

Roder, V., Müller, D. R., Brenner, H. D., & Spaulding, W. D. (2011). *Integrated psychological therapy (IPT) for the treatment of neurocognition, social cognition, and social competency in schizophrenia patients*. Cambridge, MA: Hogrefe.

Rogers, C. (1951). *Client-centered therapy: Its current practice, implications and theory*. Boston, MA: Houghton Mifflin.

Roth, A. & Fonagy, P. (2005). Schizophrenia. In A. Roth & P. Fonagy (Eds.), *What works for whom? A critical review of psychotherapy research* (2nd ed., pp. 265–296). New York, NY: Guilford Press.

Russell, A. J., Munro, J. C., Jones, P. B., Hemsley, D. R., & Murray, R. M. (1997). Schizophrenia and the myth of intellectual decline. *American Journal of Psychiatry, 154*, 635–639.

Saykin, A. J., Shtasel, D. L., Gur, R. E., Kester, B., Mozley, L. H., Stafiniak, P . . . Gur, R. C. (1994). Neuropsychological deficits in neuroleptic naive patients with first-episode schizophrenia. *Archives of General Psychiatry, 51*, 124–131.

Schaub, A., Andreas, K., Brenner, H. D., & Donzel, G. (1997). Developing a group format coping-oriented treatment programme for schizophrenic patients. In H. D. Brenner, W. Boker & R. Genner (Eds.), *Towards a comprehensive therapy for schizophrenia* (pp. 228–251). Seattle, WA: Hogrefe & Huber Publishers.

Schiffman, J., Sorensen, H. J., Maeda, J., Mortensen, E. L., Victoroff, V. J., Hayashi, K. . . . Mednick, S. (2009). Childhood motor coordination and adult schizophrenia spectrum disorders. *American Journal of Psychiatry, 16*, 1041–1047.

Schmahmann, J. (2000). The role of the cerebellum in affect and psychosis. *Journal of Neurolinguistics,* 13, 189–214.

Scott, J. E. & Dixon, L. B. (1995). Psychological interventions for schizophrenia. *Schizophrenia Bulletin, 21*, 621–630.

Seligman, M. E. P. (1995). The effectiveness of psychotherapy. The Consumer Reports study. *American Psychologist, 50*, 965–974.

Seligman, M. E. P. & Csikszentmihalyi, M. (2000). Positive psychology: An introduction. *American Psychologist, 55*, 5–14.

Shapiro, L. (2011). *Embodied cognition*. New York, NY: Routledge.

Sitnikova, T., Goff, D., & Kuperberg, G. R. (2009). Neurocognitive abnormalities during comprehension of real-world goal-directed behaviors in schizophrenia. *Journal of Abnormal Psychology, 118*, 256–277.

Sorensen, H. J., Mortensen, E. L., Schiffman, J., Reinisch, J. M., Maeda, J., & Mednick, S. A. (2010). Early developmental milestones and risk of schizophrenia: A 45-year follow-up of the Copenhagen Perinatal Cohort. *Schizophrenia Research, 118*, 41–47.

Spaulding, W. D., Fleming, S. K., & Reed, D. (1999). Cognitive functioning in schizophrenia: Implications for psychiatric rehabilitation. *Schizophrenia Bulletin, 25*, 275–289.

Spector, A. & Orrell, M. (2006). A review of the use of cognitive stimulation therapy in dementia management. *British Journal of Neuroscience Nursing, 2*, 381–385.

Spector, A., Orrell, M., & Woods, B. (2010). Cognitive stimulation therapy (CST): Effects on different areas of cognitive function for people with dementia. *International Journal of Geriatric Psychiatry, 25*, 1253–1258.

Spindler, K. A., Sullivan, E., Menon, V., Lim, K. O., & Pfefferbaum, A. (1997). Deficits in multiple systems of working memory in schizophrenia. *Schizophrenia Research, 17*, 1–10.

Stone, M., Gabrieli, J. D., Stebbins, G. T., & Sullivan, E. V. (1998). Working and strategic memory deficits in schizophrenia. *Neuropsychology, 12*, 278–288.

Subramanium, K., Luks, T. L., Fisher, M., Simpson, G. V., Nagarajan, S., & Vinogradov, S. (2012). Computerized cognitive training restores neural activity within the reality monitoring network in schizophrenia, *Neuron*, 73, 842–853.

Sullivan, H. S. (1962). *Schizophrenia as a human process*. New York, NY: W. W. Norton & Company.

Susskind, J. E. (2005). PowerPoint's power in the classroom: Enhancing students' self-efficacy and attitudes. *Computers & Education, 45*, 203–215.

Szasz, T. (1961). *The myth of mental illness: Foundations for a theory of personal conduct*. New York, NY: Harper & Row.

Thakkar, K. N., Nichols, H. S., McIntosh, L. G., & Park, S. (2011). Disturbances in body ownership in schizophrenia: Evidence from the rubber hand illusion and case study of a spontaneous out-of-body experience. *PLoS ONE, 6*(10), e27089. doi: 10.1371/journal.pone.0027089

Torrey, E. F. (1983). *Surviving schizophrenia: A family manual*. New York, NY: Harper & Row.

Truax, C. B. & Carkhuff, R. R. (1967). *Toward effective counseling and psychotherapy*. New York, NY: Aldine.

Varlet, M., Marin, L., Raffard, S., Schmidt, R. C., Capdevielle, D., Boulenger, J. P. . . . Bardy, B. G. (2012). Impairments of social motor coordination in schizophrenia. *PLoS ONE, 7*(1), e29772. doi:10.1371/journal.pone.0029772

Whitaker, R. (2005). Anatomy of an epidemic. *Ethical Human Psychology and Psychiatry, 7*, 23–35.

Whitaker, R. (2008). Deinstitutionalization and neuroleptics: The myth and reality. In Y. O. Alanen, M. G. de Chavez, A. S. Silver & B. Martindale (Eds.), *Psychotherapeutic approaches to schizophrenic psychosis: Past, present and future* (pp. 346–356). New York, NY: Routledge.

Woods, B., Thorgrimsen, L., Spector, A., Royan, A., & Orrell, M. (2006). Improved quality of life and cognitive stimulation therapy in dementia. *Aging & Mental Health, 10*, 219–226.

Wykes, T. & Reeder, C. (2005). *Cognitive remediation therapy for schizophrenia*. New York, NY: Routledge.

Wykes, T., Reeder, C., Landau, S., Everitt, B., Knapp, M., Patel, A., & Romeo, R. (2007). Cognitive remediation therapy in schizophrenia. *British Journal of Psychiatry, 190*, 421–427.

Yalom, I. D. (1983). *Inpatient group therapy*. New York, NY: Basic Books, Inc.

Index

The word order is letter by letter; locators to plans and tables are in *italics*; locators in **bold** refers to handouts, questionnaires and worksheets; numbers in headings have been listed as if they are written.

C

D

E

I

J

K

L

M

N

T

For Product Safety Concerns and Information please contact our EU
representative GPSR@taylorandfrancis.com
Taylor & Francis Verlag GmbH, Kaufingerstraße 24, 80331 München, Germany

www.ingramcontent.com/pod-product-compliance
Ingram Content Group UK Ltd.
Pitfield, Milton Keynes, MK11 3LW, UK
UKHW050757180926
475701UK00007B/1105

* 9 7 8 0 4 1 5 6 3 2 1 5 7 *